STRENGTHS GYM

Build and exercise your strengths!

Carmel Proctor and Jenny Fox Eades

Positive Psychology Research Centre, Guernsey

Published by
Positive Psychology Research Centre
PO Box 544
St. Peter Port, Guernsey
Channel Islands, GY1 6HL
Email: info@pprc.gg
Website: http://www.pprc.gg

First published in Guernsey in 2009

© PPRC 2009

® Strengths Gym is a registered trademark of Carmel Proctor and Jenny Fox Eades

ISBN: 978-0-9562282-3-9

British Library Cataloguing-in-Publication Data
A catalogue record for this book is available from the British Library

All rights reserved. No part of this publication may be reproduced, stored in a retrieval system, or transmitted in any form by any means (electronic, mechanical, photocopying, recording or otherwise), without either the prior written permission of the publisher, or a license permitting restricted copying in the United Kingdom issued by the Copyright Licensing Agency Ltd, Saffron House, 6-10 Kirby Street, London, EC1N 8TS. This book may not be lent, resold, hired out or otherwise disposed of by way or trade in any form of binding or cover other than that in which it is published, without the prior consent of the Publisher. Requests for permissions should be directed to the Publisher.

Cover design by John White Design Partnership, Guernsey

Printed in Guernsey

CONTENTS

An Introduction to Strengths Gym

Why *Strengths Gym*?	1
What is a Strength?	1
Some Principles Behind *Strengths Gym*	1
Using *Strengths Gym*	3
The Student Booklet	5
Students and Teachers as Co-Learners	5
Philosophy for Communities/Children	5
Solitary Work, Paired Work, Teamwork	6
Strengths Builders	6
Strengths Challenge	6
Year 7 Strengths Builders	7
Year 8 Strengths Builders	7
Year 9 Strengths Builders	7
Songs, Films, Quiet Moments and Funny Moments	7

The Strengths Sessions

1.	Love of Beauty	8
2.	Courage	11
3.	Love	14
4.	Prudence	18
5.	Teamwork	22
6.	Creativity	26
7.	Curiosity	30
8.	Fairness	34
9.	Forgiveness	38
10.	Gratitude	42
11.	Honesty	45
12.	Hope	49
13.	Humour	53
14.	Persistence	56
15.	Open-Mindedness	60
16.	Kindness	63
17.	Leadership	66
18.	Love of Learning	70
19.	Modesty	74
20.	Wisdom	78
21.	Self-Control	82
22.	Social Skills	86
23.	Spirituality	90
24.	Enthusiasm	94

Appendix

Sources for Stories Included	97

Bibliography

100

STRENGTHS GYM

An Introduction to *Strengths Gym*

Welcome to the teacher's handbook for *Strengths Gym*. This manual is designed to for use with the Year 7, Year 8, and Year 9 *Strengths Gym* programme.

This programme draws on the latest research from the field known as **Positive Psychology**, that is the psychology of being happy, successful, and living life to the full. Whereas clinical psychology focuses on repairing what is wrong, positive psychology helps people who feel fine to feel even better.

In the school environment, positive psychology facilitates effective teaching and learning. Individuals learn how to be effective and successful and make the most of their lives. One key subject of positive psychology is **strengths** and it is this subject that lies at the heart of the *Strengths Gym* programme.

Why *Strengths Gym*?

A traditional approach to Personal, Social, and Health Education (PSHE) focuses on subjects such as drug and alcohol misuse, avoiding teenage pregnancy and sexually transmitted diseases, bullying, and depression. Students can find such lessons relentlessly negative and even rather depressing.

One of the key insights of positive psychology is that we get more of what we focus on. This course looks at personal well-being from a positive perspective, providing opportunities to consider prudent and considerate behaviour, a healthy lifestyle, and good relationships. It does this through a focus on the behaviour we *do* want rather than on the behaviour we don't want. In particular it allows behaviour to be looked at in the light of the strengths we already possess – and would benefit from using more.

What is a Strength?

Strengths are evident in each of us from a young age. A strength is a way of thinking, feeling, or behaving that is either innate or which has developed early in life.

Strengths can be used in different areas of our lives.

We all have multiple strengths, some that we use often, some that we are not currently using very much, and some we don't yet know about. When we use our strengths we feel energised, absorbed, authentic, and that 'this is the real me'.

Our strengths are our areas of greatest potential growth, the areas where we will excel. While it is possible for us to become very good at something that is not a strength, we are unlikely to excel in that area. That is why helping students explore and develop their own strengths is such an important part of education. We want to help them find the areas in which they will excel.

Working on our strengths is always more effective and rewarding than fixing our weaknesses, and in order to fix our weaknesses effectively we need to be using our strengths.

The strengths in *Strengths Gym* are based on the Values In Action (VIA) strengths classification (Peterson & Seligman, 2004). However, these strengths are only a starting place – there may be hundreds of strengths. The more you look for strengths, the more you find them.

Some Principles Behind *Strengths Gym*

Strengths-spotting is a skill that can be learned

One of the key aims of *Strengths Gym* is for students to become more aware of strengths – in themselves, in other people, and in the world around them. This can lead to increased self-esteem, academic achievement, and 'prosocial' behaviour (e.g., better teamwork, improved social skills). Students learn that it is ok to be different; indeed that it is good to be different, because a team needs people with different strengths in order to succeed.

Becoming more aware of our strengths can also improve mental health since noticing strengths encourages a positive, rather than a negative, outlook on life.

Strengths can be improved

The activities for students are called **Strengths Builders** and **Strengths Challenges** because they are designed to exercise and grow strengths. All the strengths in this course may be considered 'character strengths' – i.e., they are usually considered to contribute to good character. All of them are valuable characteristics and worth working on. Strengths are not fixed – the more we practise and use a strength the more we have of it.

We get more of what we focus on

The act of paying attention to a subject primes us to notice that subject and, if it is an action, to perform it more. For example, thinking about courage and seeing ourselves as courageous makes us more likely to perform courageous acts; thinking about kindness and seeing ourselves as kind makes us more likely to do kind things.

Just introducing the concept of strengths to students will have a positive effect on them.

Intrinsic motivation is more effective than extrinsic motivation

Intrinsic motivation – *doing something because we want to do it* – is more effective, research tells us, than extrinsic motivation – *doing something because somebody else tells us to do it or for a reward*. We are intrinsically motivated to use our strengths. Although there are extrinsic rewards in the course, they are awarded by the students to themselves.

Autonomy, or choice, encourages intrinsic motivation

Choice is important in encouraging a sense of well-being and intrinsic motivation – each session has a choice of Strengths Builders for the student to work on. The Strengths Challenge is presented as a possible homework exercise and is *always* freely chosen. Teacher autonomy is also important. There are a range of options for opening activities and closing activities so that you can chose those *you* will most enjoy working with.

Priming the environment is effective

Research has shown that the images and words we see and hear around us *do* affect our behaviour at an unconscious level. Therefore each session contains a suggestion for incorporating the strength into a display for the classroom.

Story-telling is one of the most powerful of teaching techniques

Teachers have used story-telling throughout history because it is a very effective teaching method that engages the imagination, emotion, and reason of students. A story is provided for each session that demonstrates the strength being used in either a fictional or a real-life situation. Both students and teachers are encouraged to find and tell their own Strengths in Action stories.

Kieran Egan's (2005) work on imaginative teaching makes the point that all teaching should be more like story-telling. Teachers need to ask, 'What is the story of the lesson?' as a journalist might ask, 'Where is the story here?' Students need to find personal meaning in the content of what they learn, and to engage with it on an emotional as well as a cognitive level. Stories are a wonderful way to engage the emotions and the imagination as well as the reason. Finding their own strengths within the stories they hear will help students make a personal link to the lesson content and increase their motivation to learn.

Strengths can be found across the curriculum

Taking *Strengths Gym* out of the PSHE lesson and finding opportunities to focus on strengths across the curriculum will also help students make a meaningful connection with the subject matter they are studying. To take maths as an example, students might find out about the passion for order that motivated Pythagoras and his followers, their **persistent** belief that numbers held the key to understanding the cosmos. Then students use their own **persistence**, their own capacity to be ordered and methodical, in exploring aspects of Pythagoras's theories. The students find their own human qualities, their own strengths, reflected in the content and the process of the lesson and in the people behind those lessons.

Subject specialists will be better placed than we are to realise which strengths their particular subject lends itself to exploring. However, suggestions have been included for how each strength could be thought about in one or more traditional curriculum areas. Taking a broad approach to using *Strengths Gym* by embedding it into the curriculum as a whole will help schools develop a coherent approach to strengths and well-being across the school.

Students are natural leaders in their particular strengths

Students will possess many of the strengths explored in this programme. As a starting point, each student will choose five strengths from the list of twenty-four strengths that make up the programme that they feel are their top strengths. Teachers are encouraged to let those students high in a particular strength take the lead in discussions and in generating ideas for further activities. At the end of the programme, each student is invited to re-evaluate their choice of their top five strengths and consider how and why their chosen strengths may have changed.

Setting goals is an important part of achieving success

Understanding the importance of goals and being able to set them is a key feature in achieving success in any field. Throughout the course many of the Strengths Builders and Strengths Challenges will involve the students setting goals and working hard to achieve them. Each time a student reaches a goal or completes the Strengths Challenge for an individual session they can reward themselves by placing a sticker on the Strengths Cartoon.

A student work-booklet is a starting place

As part of the *Strengths Gym* course, students should be provided with a separate work-booklet in which to record their work on the Strengths Builders and Strengths Challenges. Once the students begin to realise how to spot their own strengths through the Strengths Builders and Strengths Challenge exercises, they may wish to continue finding other examples. They can keep their own files of material that reflects strengths or you may begin a class set of strengths files.

Enjoyment matters

When we enjoy what we do, we do it better. The lessons should be engaging and enjoyable for you and for your students. If they are, they will also be effective.

Using *Strengths Gym*

A flexible programme

Strengths Gym is intended to be a flexible programme. Strengths Builders vary in how long they take to do and some can be done in minutes or even seconds while others may take hours, depending on the motivation and interest of the students.

Schools can use *Strengths Gym* as a constructive way to start each day and devote some time to it during registration or tutorial sessions.

Alternatively the ideas and activities listed for each strength may be used to construct PSHE lessons that focus on one or more strengths. Some schools devote full days to PSHE or Citizenship and these could be devoted in full or in part to one or more strengths. Schools might consider replacing Anti-Bullying Day with Random Acts of Kindness Day, for example, and measure the difference in behaviour.

The material in the handbook and on the web page is also suitable for assemblies. Assemblies offer great potential for establishing and communicating the shared values of a school and for providing time to reflect on what is best about a community and about individuals. Using assemblies to focus on strengths, to tell inspiring stories, and to have a quiet, positive, reflective start to a day will support learning and set the tone for the day.

A menu format has been adopted for the sessions so you can choose activities that you feel will suit your class or group and ensure they have a variety of activities over the weeks. At the same time, all the activities will contribute towards a focus on the strength presented in a given session. **Enjoyment matters.**

An important insight from positive psychology is that our mood affects our ability to learn effectively. When we are cheerful we think more creatively and openly and our memories and vocabularies function better. How you open a lesson, a session or an assembly will therefore set the tone for how receptive students are.

Whether *Strengths Gym* is used to provide the basis for an assembly or a PSHE lesson, the opening and closing moments are particularly important. Collecting games, video clips, and meditations that can be used to focus on a strength at the start of a session and which either *cheer students up* or *calm students down* is recommended. Serenity and amusement are both positive emotions that have a broadening effect on our thinking, a positive impact on how open we are to other people and make us more creative and more able to learn (Frederickson, 2009). You might explore a mixture of **Funny Moments** and **Quiet Moments** to start your lessons and find those that suit your class best, or alternatively you may wish to use others that you develop yourself.

Endings are also important – a positive end to an event stays with us more than any possible low points that occurred during it and colours how we remember it.

Suggestions of Songs, Films, Quiet Moments and Funny moments, additional student activities, and links to YouTube clips have been provided on the *Strengths Gym* web site: http://www.strengthsgym.co.uk.

Reflection and dialogue are at the heart of *Strengths Gym*.

For each session, reflective **Thinking Questions** are included in order to open up discussions and to explore the uses and applications of particular strengths across the curriculum and beyond school. These may form a short introduction to a lesson, with the rest of the time spent on the Strengths Builders, or alternatively discussion can form the whole of the lesson. A lesson spent thinking and talking about strengths is a lesson well spent even if nobody picks up a pen the whole time.

The model used for discussion and reflective Thinking Questions is sometimes known as **Philosophy for Communities** or **Philosophy for Children**. This form of discussion can certainly be used effectively with children, but it is equally effective with teenagers and adults. It is more formally known as dialogic teaching. Since it forms an important part of this approach there is more information on how to use it effectively at the end of this section.

Autonomy matters

Each lesson needs to contain a choice of activities for the student – this is important since choice encourages intrinsic motivation. However, students do not need lots of options – two is usually enough. If you decide to spend the lesson in discussion, as suggested above, then choice is inherent in any group discussion – you choose whether to participate, what to say, or whether to agree or disagree with what others say.

Strengths in Action Stories

Each week there is a story that shows the strength in action. You can tell the story as an opening activity – engaging with stories, especially well-told stories, is a very satisfying Quiet Moment. You might:

- Read the story aloud or ask the students to read it silently
- Tell the story to the class
- Ask students to prepare and tell the story to the class

If you begin to *tell* stories and encourage your students to do the same you can work on your story-telling skills with the students over the duration of the programme.

Ideas for follow-up activities that students may choose to do at home are also provided as Strengths Challenges. The opening and closing sessions have a rather different format but the same principles of choosing an opening activity, focussing on strengths, and then choosing a satisfying and reflective closing activity apply.

The Student Booklet

The student booklet is intended as a record of their personal exploration of strengths. In it they can collect comments, thoughts, and the stickers they award themselves. Each week there is a definition of the strength you are focussing on. There is also a choice of Strengths Builders for students to do and the optional follow-up activity, the Strengths Challenge. If you decide to watch a film that shows the Strength in Action and discuss it, instead of doing the Strengths Builders for that section, the students can still read about the strength for themselves and see how to use it more and/or complete the Strengths Builders and Strengths Challenge in their own time.

Students and Teachers as Co-Learners

Teachers are not 'experts' in the area of strengths, but co-learners. The teacher facilitating the Strengths Session has just as much to learn about strengths as the students themselves. Indeed, where the strength of the session is not high on a teacher's personal list, it is an opportunity to learn from students even more than usual. Some of the students in the class may have much more of a particular strength than their teacher.

For this reason, teachers are encouraged to join *Strengths Gym* for themselves and to work alongside their students very explicitly. Teachers should have a Student Booklet of their own, join in with discussions or with Strengths Builders wherever possible (without dominating either the discussion or the activity) and attempt Strengths Challenges when time permits. They should also award themselves, or fail to award themselves, stickers for the Strengths Challenges they attempt. Students will love the fact that they may get more stickers than their teachers!

Philosophy for Communities/Children

Philosophy for Children, also called 'dialogic teaching', is an open-ended approach to discussion around a question chosen by the students themselves. The goal of philosophy is for the students to develop a line of reasoning, to listen to one another, to engage with other ideas, and to learn to discuss issues calmly and thoughtfully. The stimulus for discussion can be a story, a poem, a piece of art, or something they have heard on the news. In the context of this course the stimulus may be the Strengths in Action story, an associated film, or the definition and benefits of the strength you are going to focus on.

Adults should refrain from correction or presenting information, which is surprisingly difficult, especially for teachers! Instead students are encouraged to explore and extend their own thinking. Adults may challenge ideas but the aim is not to impose ideas but to ask students to stretch their own powers of logic and reasoning and to challenge one another. Practised regularly, philosophy helps students to grow in confidence and in respect for themselves and one another and is a very practical and effective way of building social and emotional skills as well as the ability to listen, to consider other viewpoints, to disagree with others politely, and to experience others disagreeing with you.

A philosophy session as part of *Strengths Gym*

If you are going to include philosophical discussion as part of your *Strengths Gym* sessions then both the physical and emotional environment need to be considered. Ideally, students and any adults present should face each other by sitting in a circle so that everyone can see everyone else.

Of course the physical environment of many schools is not ideal, but you must remember that these physical factors have a real impact both on the emotional experience of the session and on the intellectual content.

Following the opening of your choice (whether it is a Story, a Quiet Moment or a Funny Moment, a previously viewed film showing the Strength in Action, or just quiet reading of the definition of the strength in question), ensure that there is some quiet *thinking time* during which the students can come up with questions to discuss. It works well to ask them to do this in pairs. This encourages less confident students to express their views because they have a partner to back them up. Then their questions are written up carefully and grouped or connections between them noticed. The students choose which question to start with. Drawing a distinction between 'factual' questions and 'thinking' questions will help. The latter are open-ended questions that will lead to a more wide-ranging discussion from which the students can choose, while acknowledging the importance of all their questions.

Each session contains suggested reflective Thinking Questions that you can use to start a discussion, but it is valuable to work towards the students generating questions of their own. When this does happen, you might save a reflective question for a closing activity, asking them to sit and just think about their own responses to a question for the last minute of the lesson.

The aim is for the teacher to facilitate the discussion, but not to impose their views. Try to get the students to justify and develop their ideas. Teachers should also encourage the students to listen to each other and, at the end, summarise the different ideas that have been expressed. If there is another adult present they could be asked to produce a mind map of the discussion as it develops, but the teacher facilitating the discussion should not do this as it will distract the students.

Encourage reflection on the process that focusses on the strength being discussed by asking further questions. For example: Did we listen to each other? Were we fair in allowing each other turns to speak? Did we work together to build a discussion? Did we reach any conclusions (this may not happen)? Were we generous in paying attention to each other and in how we agreed or disagreed or changed our minds?

Used well, philosophical discussion can both focus attention *upon* strengths and provide opportunities to *use* strengths in the classroom.

Solitary Work, Paired Work, Teamwork

There has been a shift in education over the past twenty years. Twenty years ago school was an introvert's dream. It was possible to work alone at a desk and not communicate with anyone for hours. Today students are expected to be far more sociable, and collaborative working is very common. This may improve students' social skills but, for some, teamwork will always remain an area of weakness. It needs to be recognised that for students who find groups difficult, group-work activities provide them with a double task. They must do both the task in hand *and* work hard just at being in the group. More sociable students, to whom a group is a natural and easy situation, have, by contrast, only one task to perform.

Just as the new emphasis on social and emotional skills in schools allows extrovert and sociable students to flourish, it is important that more solitary students receive similar opportunities. There are careers where the ability to motivate oneself and to work alone for long periods are important. Dickens did not write his novels in a team! Such students need some time to follow their own strengths – the strengths of independent, solitary working.

Strengths Builders

Each week the student booklet contains a choice of Strengths Builders. The Strengths Builders may, if students wish, be done in pairs or small groups. Equally they may be done alone if the student prefers. The exception to this is during the week when the focus is on 'teamwork'. Then, all students *do* need to have a go at working in a team – even those for whom this is not a strength. For such students, this week constitutes a Strengths Challenge and due respect needs to be paid to their efforts.

Strengths Challenge

Each week the student booklet contains a Strengths Challenge. The Strengths Challenge serves two purposes. For students with a lot of the strength in question it provides ideas for using that strength more and for increasing enjoyment and energy levels. For students with less of that strength it offers a chance to build it. For these students, completing the Strengths Challenge is a major achievement. The Strengths Challenge should always be optional. Students (and teachers) who complete the challenge can reward themselves by placing a sticker on the Strengths Cartoon of that strength.

Year 7 Strengths Builders

The first option each week is to Design a Superhero for the strength. Encourage students to use their humour, their design skills, and their creativity to come up with a Superhero for each strength. They might consider:

- A name
- A secret identity
- The kind of 'mission' the superhero will undertake
- A story to illustrate the hero's character
- The hero's appearance

This is an ideal group activity though, once more, if students prefer to work alone it is important to respect this. Large pieces of paper (lining paper is good for this) are ideal and can encourage students to draw their hero and map out his or her essential features. Drawing round an actual student so it is literally 'life-sized' can be fun. Over the weeks a gallery of 'Strengths Superheroes' can be created. The second Strengths Builder will be an activity or game, usually for pairs or groups, though students can work alone if they prefer.

To facilitate student choice it will help if a range of materials is made available for each lesson. Paper, scissors, magazines for a collage approach, and pens, pastels or chalks should, if possible, be at hand if students wish to use them.

Year 8 Strengths Builders

The first option each week is the Strength in Action story. Students are encouraged to remember a time when they or somebody they know used the strength in a situation. Students must come up with a real situation in which they feel that the strength being explored was used. In order to be applicable to all ability levels, students may write or draw or tell the story of the Strength in Action.

The second option each week is designed to get the students to use the strength or to find out more about it. The activities can be completed individually, in pairs, or in groups. Teachers are invited to get students to share their findings with the rest of the class or with their partner(s).

Year 9 Strengths Builders

The first option each week is the Create Your Own Strength in Action Story. Students are encouraged to make up a story that contains a character or characters who use the strength in a situation. Students are invited to be very creative and imagine detailed scenarios of the strength being used in action. Again, in order to be applicable to all ability levels, students may write or draw or tell their story of the strength in action.

The second option each week is designed to further develop students' use of the strength and their knowledge of it. Once more, the activities can be completed individually, in pairs, or in groups. Teachers are invited to get students to share their findings with the rest of the class or with their partner(s).

Songs, Films, Quiet Moments and Funny Moments

For each strength, suggestions of Songs, Films, Quiet Moments and Funny Moments, additional student activities, and links to YouTube clips have been provided on the *Strengths Gym* web site: http://www.strengthsgym.co.uk.

The Strengths Sessions

<u>**ONE**</u>

Love of Beauty

Love of beauty is the ability to find, recognise, and take pleasure in beauty and goodness. A person with this strength feels wonder while walking in the woods or reading a story about kindness. A lack of this strength leads to a blinkered approach to all that is beautiful and moving, or to cynicism. It is a strength that leads to joy, to finding meaning in life, and to deep connections with other people.

It is characterised not by an intellectual exercise but by emotional responsiveness, a tendency to feel awe, admiration, wonder, and a sense of being elated by what you see or hear about. It may be closely linked to other strengths such as curiosity and love of learning – as people seek out new areas these can trigger awe, gratitude, and spirituality.

It is a subtle response, not apparent in clear actions like other emotions, but rather in stillness, open mouth, wide eyes, goose bumps, tears, or a lump in the throat. In drama, an ancient Hindu theory held that the presentation of emotions on a stage (or in a story) elicits a parallel emotional response in the audience – an echo of the real emotion. The audience may be 'carried away' into the world of the story and this was seen as a spiritual state that transcended self.

Awe seems to make people less materialistic and more loving. Awe may be a religious response to the divine but also to nature, to art, or to people of great insight or to moral goodness. William James, a psychologist who studied religion in the last century, contrasted the healthy-minded versus the sick soul. The healthy-minded see everything in life as beautiful or good; filled with grateful admiration they are open to the world and to experience, seeing the world as a manifestation of divinity. The sick soul, by contrast, sees evil, decay, and temptation everywhere; heaven and salvation lie elsewhere, so such people are emotionally unresponsive to the world around them, to beauty, or to excellence.

Key features of Love of Beauty:

- Is a 'transcendent' strength; i.e., it 'takes us out of ourselves'
- Can be a response to physical beauty, to a skill or talent, or to moral goodness
- Is an emotional not an intellectual response

Definition: You notice and love beautiful things, in art, nature, or in people.

Benefits: Love of beauty invokes positive emotions like awe and wonder. Positive emotions are linked to well-being, mental health, resilience, and creativity.

Quotes:

'Beauty is unbearable, drives us to despair, offering us for a minute the glimpse of an eternity that we should like to stretch out over the whole of time.' – **A. Albert Camus**

'The ideals which have lighted me on my way and time after time given me new courage to face life cheerfully, have been Truth, Goodness, and Beauty…The ordinary objects of human endeavour -- property, outward success, luxury -- have always seemed to me contemptible.' – **Albert Einstein**

'The most beautiful experience we can have is the mysterious – the fundamental emotion which stands at the cradle of true art and true science.' – **Albert Einstein**

'Everything has beauty, but not everyone sees it.' – **Confucius**

Thinking Questions:

- Does beauty have a purpose – does it 'do' anything?
- What would the world be like without beauty?
- Is there a disadvantage or problem with loving beauty?

Strengths Builders and Strengths Challenges:

Year 7

Strengths Builders:

1. Design a Love of Beauty Superhero.
2. Write or draw some beautiful things you have seen.

Strengths Challenge:

What do you think is the most beautiful thing in the world? Why?

Year 8

Strengths Builders:

1. Strength in Action Story – Can you remember a time when you or somebody you know truly showed their Love of Beauty? Write or draw or tell a story of Love of Beauty in action.
2. Animal Beauty Contest – Which animals do you consider beautiful? Why? Work with some friends to collect different examples of beautiful animals and then see if you can put them in order of beauty. Which is the most beautiful, which one comes next? Compare your list with another group.

Strengths Challenge:

Look for beauty on your way to school. Tell a friend or family member what you noticed.

Year 9

Strengths Builders:

1. Create your own Strength in Action Story – Make up a story that contains a character or characters that display a Love of Beauty in a situation. Write or draw or tell your story of Love of Beauty in action.
2. Beauty Map Of The World – Make a map of the most beautiful places in the world or within a country of your choice. Team up with some friends to draw a map that points the way to beauty spots across the world or within the country of your choice. Compare your map with another group.

Strengths Challenge:

Find out about two different types of artwork. For example:

- Pottery and Papier Mache
- Watercolour and Oil Painting
- Knitting and Cross-Stitch

Try and make a piece of artwork using one of the methods listed above or one you discovered on your own. Or find an example of something you consider to be beautiful or an example of excellence, such as a scientific invention, car design, or architecture.

Closing Activity:

1. Re-show one of the beauty video clips but in silence
2. Reflect for one minute on something you find beautiful

Display Suggestion: Ask students to look in magazines for images they consider beautiful and bring them in to create a collage.

PSHE: Programme of Study for Key Stage 3 Links

Personal well-being

Key Processes:

2.1 Critical reflection

Love of beauty is a strong and positive emotion. Choosing to focus on what is beautiful, what is uplifting and valuable can boost positive emotion, our immune system and increase our sense of meaning and well-being.

2.3 Developing relationships and working with others

The ability to see the good in others can help us build positive relationships. Responding positively to the strengths of others will predispose us to get on with them and predispose other people to like us.

Story: The Moon Can't Be Stolen

An old monk sat outside his hut gazing at the full moon, which flooded his mountainside with light. He noticed a man creeping up the path towards the hut. The man went into the monk's hut planning to steal all he could but the hut was empty – the old man had no possessions.

As the thief turned and crept away the monk called, 'You have come a long way, my friend. I cannot let you go away empty-handed.' And the monk took off his clothes and gave them to the thief. The puzzled thief walked back down the mountainside, clutching the clothes in his arms. The monk sat down once more and smiled as he gazed, shivering, at the moon. 'Poor man,' he said. 'I wish I could have given him the gift of this beautiful moon.'

Opportunities to build Love of Beauty across the curriculum:

Art: *Encourage students to notice beauty in art and to strive to produce beautiful work.*

Science: *Science is full of wonder at both the micro and macro levels. The natural world is a source of wonder and beauty.*

PE: *Sport and exercise have an aesthetic element to them that students can learn to appreciate.*

Technology: *Students can learn that something can be beautiful as well as functional.*

TWO

Courage

Courage, or bravery, is only required in the presence of fear; unless one experiences the sensation of fear, no bravery is required to overcome this sensation. Bravery is often seen in terms of physical valour and has associations with war and great deeds (often male associations). Younger children will tend to see bravery in these physical terms. However, courage can also be seen in more everyday terms, in traits like endurance or in overcoming common fears like public speaking. Courage may also be part of what sustains successful intimate relationships since honesty and vulnerability require risk.

While it may not be clear how to encourage bravery in battle, it is clear that we can encourage students to face up to everyday challenges and to take appropriate actions in the face of their fears.

For teenagers there are additional fears to face up to – the fear of being laughed at by their peers, the fear of not fitting in, the fear of not being 'up to' the challenges of adulthood, the fear of their unknown future. Learning also requires us to overcome fear – the fear of failure, the fear of not understanding. For some students, just being in a group is an anxiety-provoking situation.

To be brave, an act must be voluntary, it must involve the mastery of fear rather than be fearless, and it must be worthwhile. Taking stupid risks is rashness, not bravery.

Teachers can set useful examples for students by doing things that might make them feel nervous, learning a new skill or doing something else that is outside their 'comfort zone'. Bravery is encouraged by building self-confidence and by a sense of group loyalty – we may dare things for our group that we would not dare for ourselves. The root of the word courage is 'heart' (Latin cor) and 'encouragement' means, literally, 'giving heart to'. Encouragement is vital for developing a positive self-concept, higher motivation, the ability to learn from our mistakes and perseverance. In contrast, psychologists have linked discouragement to mental illness and the breakdown of interpersonal relationships. Bravery can also, it is suggested, be fostered by relationships that involve what psychologists call 'psychological presence' – i.e., mutual respect, admiration, validation, and acts of kindness. It can be seen as holding fast to virtues such as kindness, duty, truthfulness, and a delight in what is good.

Key features of Courage:

- Implies the presence not the absence of fear
- Is an important feature of learning
- Is fostered by positive relationships
- CAN be physical but also has mental and emotional aspects

Definition: You do the right thing even if you are scared. You stand up for what is right.

Benefits: Courage enables a person to exercise many other strengths (e.g., kindness, friendship). Courage allows us to move outside our comfort zones, to take risks, to develop close relationships. Courage enables us to practise self-awareness and to challenge prejudice and discrimination.

Quotes:

'The essence of human bravery is refusing to give up on anyone or anything.' – **Trungpa**

'Moral excellence comes about as a result of habit. We become just by doing just acts, temperate by doing temperate acts, brave by doing brave acts.' – **Aristotle**

'You gain strength, courage and confidence by every experience in which you look fear in the face. You must do the thing which you think you cannot do.' – **Eleanor Roosevelt**

Thinking Questions:

- What does courage mean to you?
- Can you be brave if you're not afraid?
- What different kinds of courage are there?
- Can you be too brave?
- How might you use courage at school?

Strengths Builders and Strengths Challenges:

Year 7

Strengths Builders:

1. Design a Courage Superhero.
2. Write or draw or tell a story of a time when you have shown courage.

Strengths Challenge:

Think of somebody you know, or somebody famous, who you think showed a lot of courage. What did this person do for you to think of them as courageous or brave?

Year 8

Strengths Builders:

1. Strength in Action Story – Can you remember a time when you or somebody you know chose not to do something wrong, even though their friends were doing it and might have teased them for not going along with it? Write or draw or tell a story of Courage in action.
2. Think of two people from history who were famous for being courageous. In what way were they courageous? Compare your own ideas with a friend. Decide which of the people on your lists was the most courageous. Why?

Strengths Challenge:

Watch the news this week or read the papers and try to find a story where somebody showed courage. Share the story with a friend or family member.

Year 9

Strengths Builders:

1. Create your own Strength in Action Story – Make up a story that contains a character or characters who choose not to do something wrong, even though their friends are doing it and might tease them for not going along with it. Write or draw or tell your story of Courage in action.
2. Think of something that is outside your comfort zone, something that will need courage for you to do. Tell one person you trust what that is – then do it!

Strengths Challenge:

Speak to someone today that you have wanted to speak to for a long time, but have not had the courage to speak to before. Think about how it made you feel to overcome your fear of speaking to them.

Closing Activity:

1. Think for one minute, in silence, about something that scares you, something that you have to show courage to do.

2. Tell a Courage in Action story.

Display Suggestion: Create a display based on professions that students feel require courage, e.g., fireman, nurse, soldier, or teacher.

PSHE: Programme of Study for Key Stage 3 Links

Personal well-being

Key Concepts:

1.1 Personal identities

Courage is required to look at ourselves honestly, to develop awareness of both strengths and weaknesses.

1.2 Risk

A degree of courage is required to form intimate relationships. For students for whom social and emotional skills are NOT a strength, a considerable degree of courage may be required to acquire competence in these areas.

Story: The Rescue of the Danish Jews

Denmark was invaded by Germany in 1940 but the Danish government remained in power and refused to pass laws against the Danish Jews. People in other countries sometimes disparagingly referred to Denmark as 'Hitler's Canary'. However, despite this, there was an active Danish resistance, of whom about 3,000 were killed during WWII.

In 1943 a German told a Danish politician that Germany planned to overthrow the Danish government and deport all the Jews in Denmark to concentration camps. In a unique and spontaneous act of courage, the Danish people concealed their Jewish neighbours and smuggled them out on fishing boats to Sweden. The rescue lasted ten days. As a result of many individual acts of courage, less than 2% of Denmark's 7,000 Jews died.

There is a Jewish saying: 'Whoever saves a single life saves the entire world.'

Opportunities to build Courage across the curriculum:

Drama: *Considerable courage is required to perform in front of others, and even professional actors get very scared before a performance.*

PE: *Endurance is a quiet kind of courage that can be developed and highlighted in PE.*

History: *History is full of extraordinary individuals who showed courage, and students can research these for themselves.*

THREE

Love

Love is one of the strengths of the heart. Considered an innate evolutionary trait, love encompasses thought, feeling, and behaviour. The ability to love and to be loved has a powerful effect on psychological and physical health throughout our lives. Babies whose needs are reliably met develop what is referred to as 'secure attachment' to their caregiver and this secure base allows them to feel safe when close to the loved one, to turn to them for comfort, to get upset when the loved one leaves and to explore confidently when they are available. Secure attachment leads to confident exploration – both as a baby and later in life. We learn best when we feel safe and we learn, ultimately, within trusted relationships.

Secure attachment as a baby leads to positive relationships in later life – including with teachers. Securely attached children are better liked by teachers, and are less attention-seeking and impulsive. Secure attachment – or the capacity to love and feel loved – allows adolescents and adults to cope better with the normal stresses of life and to become more skilful at forming enduring, intimate bonds.

Though early relationships are highly influential, people have relationships with different individuals throughout their lives and every relationship has the potential to modify attachment patterns. A teenager who is insecurely attached can and will benefit from a relationship with a trustworthy teacher who likes them and sees their potential. Sensitivity on the part of others fosters our own ability to love and to be loved. Students can also learn to show sensitivity themselves in their relationships with others.

Four basic elements of love are care, responsibility, respect, and knowledge (Niemiec & Wedding, 2008). In a loving relationship individuals trust each other, listen to each other, express vulnerability, and provide benefits to one another in a way that increases the enjoyment of both parties. A teacher who trusts, likes, is honest with, and enjoys the company of young people can have a profound and lasting influence.

Key features of Love:

- The capacity to love and be loved is innate, but requires trustworthy relationships to develop fully
- Can be developed and built by trusting relationships throughout our lives
- Has different forms and different elements – like care, responsibility, respect, and knowledge

Definition: You love the people who are important to you and you show that love by what you say and do.

Benefits: Love is essential to well-being and to physical and psychological health. Securely loved young people learn more effectively.

Quotes:

'The Grand essentials of happiness are: something to do, something to love, and something to hope for.' – **Allan K. Chalmers**

'Love and kindness are never wasted. They always make a difference. They bless the one who receives them and they bless you, the giver.' – **Barbara de Angelis**

Ecclesiastes 3:1–8:

To every thing there is a season, and a time to every purpose under the heaven:

A time to be born, and a time to die; a time to plant, and a time to pluck up that which is planted;

A time to kill, and a time to heal; a time to break down, and a time to build up;

A time to weep, and a time to laugh; a time to mourn, and a time to dance;

A time to cast away stones, and a time to gather stones together; a time to embrace, and a time to refrain from embracing;

A time to get, and a time to lose; a time to keep, and a time to cast away;

A time to rend, and a time to sew; a time to keep silence, and a time to speak;

A time to love, and a time to hate; a time of war, and a time of peace

Thinking Questions:

- What is love?
- Why does love matter?
- Is love ever wrong?
- We love our friends and our family a little differently; how many other types of love can you think of?

Strengths Builders and Strengths Challenges:

Year 7

Strengths Builders:

1. Design a Love Superhero.
2. Make a card for someone you love.

Strengths Challenge:

Do something nice for someone you love. You could:

- Give them a flower
- Make them a card or picture
- Do a favour or good deed for them

Year 8

Strengths Builders:

1. Strength in Action Story – Can you remember a time when you or somebody you know did something out of Love for someone else? Write or draw or tell a story of Love in action.
2. Write a love poem or draw a love card. Give it to someone you love.

Strengths Challenge:

Tell a family member or friend that you love them.

Year 9

Strengths Builders:

1. Create your own Strength in Action Story – Make up a story that contains a character or characters who did something out of Love for someone else. Write or draw or tell your story of Love in action.
2. Send someone you love a poem or love quote. Need help? Go to: http://lovepoemsandquotes.com for ideas or for existing love poems and quotes.

Strengths Challenge:

Send your friends or family an e-card from: http://www.lovecards.com or send a text and tell them you love them.

Closing Activity: 'The Life That I Have'

Read the poem (below) aloud to the class and then invite them to sit quietly and bring to mind somebody they love or somebody who loves them.

Display Suggestion: 'Love is like a butterfly, as soft and gentle as a sigh, the multi-coloured moods of love are like its satin wings' (from the theme tune by Dolly Parton to the television series *Butterflies* written by Carla Lane).

The Multicoloured Moods of Love: A collage of images, perhaps in the shape of a butterfly, of the many kinds of love – romantic love (between old and young); family love; friendship; the love of comrades – soldiers are willing to die for their friends; altruistic love.

PSHE: Programme of Study for Key Stage 3 Links

Personal well-being

Key Concepts:

1.4 Relationships

Key Processes:

2.1 Critical reflection

2.3 Developing relationships and working with others

Story: The Story of Violette Szabo

As a young woman, the daughter of an English father and a French mother, Violette lived in London during the early years of WWII. She met a young French soldier and they fell in love, married, and had a baby. Then Violette heard that her husband had been killed during fighting in North Africa.

She was approached by officials who wanted her to work undercover with the French resistance, a group called SOE, or Special Operations Executive. Violette took the painful decision to leave her daughter for her parents to care for while she went to serve her country.

She was invited to select a poem which would become the code for the secret messages she carried. She would need to learn the poem by heart and then to conceal it, at any cost, if she were captured. If she revealed it, many people would lose their lives. In memory of her beloved husband, she selected the poem 'The Life That I Have' by Leo Marks:

The life that I have
Is all that I have
And the life that I have
Is yours

The love that I have
Of the life that I have
Is yours and yours and yours

A sleep I shall have
A rest I shall have
Yet death will be but a pause

> For the peace of my years
> In the long green grass
> Will be yours and yours
> And yours
>
> Violette was eventually captured by the Nazis, tortured, and killed. She never revealed the poem.

Opportunities to build Love across the curriculum:

English and Drama: *Most stories, finally, revolve around love. Poetry and literature are full of examples of love, some happy and others 'who loved not wisely but too well' (Othello).*

FOUR

Prudence

Prudence is an unglamorous, but highly valuable, strength. It can be thought of as wisdom in practice, a far-sighted, flexible, and moderate approach to living the good life. The word has its origins in the Latin word *provideo*, meaning 'far-sightedness'. Prudence protects us from excess and leads us to make good choices, for ourselves and those around us. Its opposites are thoughtlessness, recklessness, or foolishness.

Prudence has negative associations for many people, having come to be associated with a narrow, financially cautious, and rather rigid approach to life. However, this is to miss the essential aspects of prudence, which are that it is about the whole of life, not just our use of money, and that it protects us as much from rigidity and obsession as it does from heedless extravagance. It is characterised by what Buddhists would call the 'middle way' between excess and denial, and is a strength that lends balance and harmony to life.

Prudence implies reflection and a deliberate and considered approach to thinking and problem-solving. Imagination is a key element in prudence; we have to be able to identify imaginatively with a future self in order to postpone immediate pleasures in pursuit of that self.

Setting good goals for the future and drawing up our own flexible but effective guidelines for achieving those goals are part of prudence. Selecting achievable goals that fit in with our own strengths, values, and circumstances also contributes to a prudent approach to life.

Prudent people tend to be happier and more popular. Conscientious, dependable people make better friends than those who are impulsive and who let us down. Prudence is positively associated with psychological well-being, with success at school and at work and even with longer life, possibly because prudent people eat sensibly, exercise and follow the advice of their doctors.

Key features of Prudence:

- Is about a balanced approach to the whole of life, not just money
- Is concerned with the choice, planning and pursuit of good long-term goals
- Involves seeking one's own self-interest but not at the expense of others

Definition: You make good choices. You think before you act or speak.

Benefits:

- Prudent people reach their desired goals
- Prudent people make good life decisions
- Being prudent will help you achieve the future you desire

Quotes:

'Look before you leap.' – **Samuel Butler**

'It is by the goodness of God that in our country we have those three unspeakably precious things: freedom of speech, freedom of conscience, and the prudence never to practice either of them.' – **Mark Twain**

'Ours is a world of nuclear giants and ethical infants. If we continue to develop our technology without wisdom or prudence, our servant may prove to be our executioner.' – **Omar Bradley, General**

'I believe that we are solely responsible for our choices, and we have to accept the consequences of every deed, word, and thought throughout our lifetime.' – **Elizabeth Kubler-Ross**

'Science is organized knowledge. Wisdom is organized life.' – **Immanuel Kant**

Thinking Questions

- What is prudence?
- What does it mean to act prudently?
- How can being prudent make a positive difference in your life?
- What are the disadvantages of prudence?

Strengths Builders and Strengths Challenges:

Year 7

Strengths Builders:

1. Design a Prudence Superhero.
2. Prudent people know how to look after themselves well. Think of healthy ways you can cheer yourself up when you feel low. Make a list and write them down.

Strengths Challenge:

Make a goal for the future and decide how you are going to reach it.

Year 8

Strengths Builders:

1. Strength in Action Story – Can you remember a time when you or somebody you know set a goal and was able to reach it because they planned along the way how to achieve it? Write or draw or tell a story of Prudence in action.
2. Make a list of five examples of prudent behaviour (for example, a prudent person would look after their health by eating right and exercising so they can live a long life). Compare your list with a friend and try and determine together whether your examples are good ones and true examples of prudence.

Strengths Challenge:

Think of two people you know, or from history, that you think have displayed the strength of prudence. What is it that makes them a good example of a prudent person?

Year 9

Strengths Builders:

1. Create your own Strength in Action Story – Make up a story that contains a character or characters who set a goal and are able to reach it because they planned along the way how they were going to achieve it. Write or draw or tell your story of Prudence in action.
2. Think of an important decision that you must make now, or at some point in the future, such as whether or not to go to college or university. Make a 'pros' and 'cons' list for each of your choices. Could you do this for other things in your life in order to help you make good choices and plan for the future?

Strengths Challenge:

For the whole day, think before you speak and remember to say 'please' and 'thank you'.

Closing activity: Spend one minute quietly thinking of one wise, prudent choice you might make in the week ahead. Write it down in a notebook planner if you wish.

Display suggestion: The Future

Prudent behaviour in the present very much depends on our being able to imagine real benefits in the future. Create a collage of what the students hope their futures will look like.

PSHE: Programme of Study for Key Stage 3 Links

Personal well-being

Key Concepts:

1.2 Healthy lifestyles

1.3 Risk

1.4 Relationships

Good choices and prudent behaviour extend to all areas of life – physical, mental and emotional. Knowing how to choose a healthy lifestyle, manage risk appropriately, and invest time in relationships contributes to our overall well-being and happiness.

Key Processes:

2.1 Critical reflection

2.2 Decision-making and managing risk

2.3 Developing relationships and working with others

Students from homes where planning for the future, reflective decision-making and balanced goals are not the norm will need additional support in developing prudence at school. First they will need to see others modelling this behaviour, and then they will need to experience an environment in which they are encouraged to develop it for themselves.

Story: The Biblical Story of Joseph and Pharaoh

A story of prudence that is thousands of years old is told in the scriptures of the Jewish and Christian faiths. It is the story of Joseph.

Joseph was one of 12 sons of Jacob. Now Jacob loved Joseph more than his other sons and unwisely spoiled him in front of his brothers, showering him with gifts. The brothers grew to hate Joseph and one day they decided to get rid of him. They beat him up but couldn't bring themselves to kill him, so instead they sold him to slave traders, telling their father that he was dead.

Joseph was taken to Egypt and was bought by a high-ranking Egyptian called Potiphar and at first he did well, because of his obvious honesty and wisdom. But the Egyptian's wife saw how handsome Joseph was and tried to persuade him to make love to her. When Joseph refused she accused him of attacking her. Potiphar had Joseph thrown into jail.

There Joseph met two men – Pharaoh's cup-bearer, the man who poured wine for the King of Egypt, and Pharaoh's baker. Both of them were troubled by strange dreams which they told to Joseph.

The cup bearer had dreamed he saw three vines covered with grapes. He squeezed the grapes into a cup and gave it to Pharaoh who drank from the cup. Joseph believed, as did many ancient people, that dreams were sent by God to teach us about the future. So Joseph said, 'The dream is God's way of telling you that in three days you will be free and will serve Pharaoh as you did before.'

> The baker then told Joseph his dream. He had dreamed he was carrying three baskets of bread for Pharaoh on his head but birds flew down and ate all of the food. Joseph said, 'The dream is God's way of telling you than in three days you will be executed by the king.
>
> Three days later the cup-bearer was released, the baker was hanged.
>
> Two years later, Joseph was still in jail when Pharaoh himself was troubled by strange dreams. His cup-bearer remembered the wise Hebrew, Joseph, who had interpreted his dream and so Pharaoh sent for Joseph and told him his dreams.
>
> Pharaoh had dreamed he was standing on the banks of the River Nile when he saw seven fat cows climb out of the water and begin to feed on rich grass. They were followed by seven thin, weak, ugly cows. The thin cows ate the fat ones and remained as thin as ever. Then he dreamed he saw seven golden, fat ears of corn. Next to them grew seven thin, shrivelled ears of corn which swallowed the fat plants up.
>
> Joseph said, 'The dream is God's way of telling you that seven years of good harvest are on their way which will fill your barns with corn and your land with food. But after that there will be seven years of poor harvests and, unless you prepare for these lean years, your people will starve. You must act wisely and appoint someone to save the food you grow in the seven good years so that it lasts you through the famine.'
>
> So Pharaoh appointed Joseph to be that man. Joseph became, after Pharaoh, the most powerful person in Egypt and saved the lives, not just of the Egyptian people, but of his own brothers as well.

Opportunities to build Prudence across the curriculum:

PE: *Setting personal fitness goals and working towards them.*

Food technology: *Making healthy choices in terms of diet and nutrition.*

PSHE: *Economic well-being and financial capability.*

Any subject: *Setting goals, working to achieve those goals, maintaining an appropriate balance between work and social life. Very academic students can do too much work and that is not prudent.*

FIVE

Teamwork

Teamwork is related to other concepts like citizenship, social responsibility, and loyalty. All involve putting the common good above our own interests, and a concern for others, a co-operative approach to life. They are strengths that influence how we respond to groups beyond our immediate circle.

Psychologists argue that citizenship, social responsibility, and teamwork can be learned and movements like the Boy and Girl Scouts have aimed to teach good citizenship for many years. There is also evidence that working for the common good is good for us. Community participation, co-operation, and social cohesion all contribute to physical and mental health.

In schools, students who participate in extra-curricular activities, especially those with a community orientation, are more positive towards their fellow students and towards society as a whole. Schools can promote good citizenship in their students by modelling respect for all and equality, and by helping students feel valued and listened to. Citizenship and teamwork are reciprocal – when young people feel valued and consulted they are more likely to value the community and identify with its goals.

Employers who consider employee mood and who work to enhance it through goal achievement, employee recognition and involving employees in challenging tasks also encourage loyalty to the organisation and better teamwork.

Evidence is growing that participation in community service increases tolerance, trust, concern for equal opportunities and, for offenders, a decreased risk of reoffending.

Key features of Teamwork:

- Is learnable
- Is good for us
- Is encouraged by example and is reciprocal; young people are more likely to co-operate when they feel valued

Definition: You work well with others, you always do your fair share – and sometimes more!

Benefits: Community involvement and co-operative behaviour is linked to better physical and mental health, while voluntary work is associated with longer life and better health among the elderly.

Quotes

'I suppose leadership at one time meant muscles; but today it means getting along with people.' – **Gandhi**

'We don't accomplish anything in this world alone ... and whatever happens is the result of the whole tapestry of one's life and all the weavings of individual threads from one to another that creates something.'
– **Sandra Day O'Connor**

Thinking Questions

- What is teamwork?
- What are the advantages of teamwork?
- When is teamwork NOT a good thing?
- Should we always be loyal to a team?

Strengths Builders and Strengths Challenges:

Year 7

Strengths Builders:

1. Create a Teamwork Superhero.

2. Play a game of Giant Pick-Up Sticks – Play in teams of three. One person spots the stick to pick up and the other two have to do exactly what they say. The referee can award points for:

    - The number of sticks you pick up
    - Good teamwork

Strengths Challenge:

Volunteer to help with something around the house or garden.

Year 8

Strengths Builders:

1. Strengths in Action Story – Can you remember a time when you or somebody you know was a really good Team player? Write or draw or tell a story of Teamwork in action.

2. Work with a friend or a group of friends to come up with a list of activities that you do at school that involve teamwork.

Strengths Challenge:

Stay after school for an activity that involves teamwork – it might be a sport, music, or the debate club.

Year 9

Strengths Builders:

1. Create your own Strength in Action Story – Make up a story that contains a character or characters who use Teamwork to accomplish a task. Write or draw or tell your story of Teamwork in action.

2. Strengths-Spotting – Building good teams means spotting and using the strengths of each team member. In small groups, identify each other's strengths and think about how you might use those different strengths to:

    - Play a game
    - Organise a party
    - Solve a maths problem

Strengths Challenge:

If you see litter on the ground pick it up and put it in the bin. It takes teamwork to keep the areas around us clean.

Closing activity: I wouldn't be here without...

Spend one minute thinking about people you need or who help you in some way – parents, friends, teachers, the milkman, the people who empty your dustbins, your grandparents. How do you help them?

Display suggestion: Our Teams

We are all members of many teams – our family, our class, our work group, our town, our country, the Scouts, the swimming club, the church or Mosque. Create a display that shows the breadth of 'teams' that students are part of.

PSHE: Programme of Study for Key Stage 3 Links

Personal well-being

Key Concepts:

1.1 Personal identities

1.4 Relationships

1.5 Diversity

Connections to groups are fundamental to our sense of personal identity and help to provide a sense of purpose and meaning. Working for something beyond ourself or even our family contributes to our well-being. Learning to work with others and build positive relationships is crucial for long-term happiness. Empathy is biased towards those who are similar to us but young people can be taught to look beyond their immediate circle and to consider the needs of others.

Key Processes:

2.1 Critical reflection

2.3 Developing relationships and working with others

Students who have a growing awareness of their own strengths will realise that they have things to offer to any team and, similarly, that students who are very different to themselves have different strengths to offer. Good teams contain very different members with a broad cross-section of strengths.

Story: Working All Night

An army engineer, we'll call him Jack, was stationed near Basra during the Iraq war. Jack was an 'armourer' with the Royal Electrical and Mechanical Engineers, the 'Kwik Fit' of the British Army. A broken gun? Jack would fix it. A gun-stand that was missing a leg? Jack would find a new leg to replace the one that was missing. A tank that wouldn't move? Jack would have it on the road again in no time. Not a glamorous job for a solider, but an important one.

As the war came to an end, the city of Basra was in chaos. There was no food, no electricity and no clean water. The population desperately needed food and medicines but the local port had been heavily mined and no aid ships could get in or out. Things were looking grim.

One afternoon, there was a knock at Jack's workshop door and a soldier stood there. He had a diagram of a tool he needed and he gave it to Jack. Jack looked at the diagram and told the soldier it would take him about a week to make. 'I need it by 6 am tomorrow,' the soldier replied. 'It's urgent.'

So Jack called some mates and they worked all afternoon, all evening, and then all night making the tool the soldier needed. By 6 am it was ready and the soldier turned up and took it away.

That night Jack heard on the news that the port had been cleared of mines and the first aid ships had been able to sail in, to the relief of the civilian population.

The next day the soldier came back with a crate of beer for Jack and his mates. The soldier, Jack then found out, was a warrant officer in the Special Boat Service or SBS. He had needed the tool to disarm the mines. The warrant officer had swum out into the harbour and had gone from mine to mine with the tool Jack had made. He had disarmed every single bomb by hand so that the aid ships could come in.

The amazing courage of that SBS warrant officer meant that the people of Basra got the food they needed – but they wouldn't have got it without Jack, either.

Opportunities to build Teamwork across the curriculum:

PE: *Focus on good teamwork and fair play rather than winning at any cost.*

History: *Teamwork is an essential aspect of much successful human endeavour – collaboration brought about the abolition of slavery, the emancipation of women, the reform of prisons and hospitals.*

Science: *Marie Curie and her husband were the team who discovered radioactivity; many scientific advances came from teams rather than individuals.*

Any subject: *Co-operative working in the classroom is a way of putting teamwork into action but it should be used alongside other teaching methods. For some students, teamwork is very challenging and they work better alone – such students need opportunities to work in the way that is best for them while also needing to be able to work in a team when necessary.*

SIX

Creativity

Creativity is the ability to think a little differently, to have original thoughts and ideas that have value, to find novel solutions to problems. It is often thought of as synonymous with being artistic, but this is much too narrow. Scientists are creative, mathematicians are creative, and people can find creative solutions to interpersonal problems – all without the ability to draw or paint! There are many different kinds of creativity. It is sometimes divided into 'Big C' creativity – the creativity of great poets, artists, and scientists – and 'Small c' creativity – people who find creative solutions to everyday problems, who think differently, and who challenge conformity.

Creative people tend to be independent thinkers, to be non-conformist and unconventional – they are also more likely to be introverts. They may have wide interests and are generally curious. Artistically creative people tend to be emotionally sensitive, though this is not true of scientific creators. In general, creativity is encouraged in young people by open, flexible teachers who support free exploration and by environments that are informal and supportive. The instruction *'Be creative'* has a marked effect on creativity! Creativity is inhibited by time pressure, constant scrutiny or frequent examination, and by constraints being placed on the possible range of solutions.

It is possible that encouraging creativity in itself is less effective than encouraging the strengths that are linked to it – curiosity, intrinsic motivation, risk-taking, and self-management. It is worth noting, however, that no matter how creative a student, it is estimated that it still takes ten years of hard work to produce a high level of creative work.

To be truly creative, students need to be willing and able to risk failure – to achieve excellence one must be willing to risk chaos. This is also true of creative teaching.

Key features of Creativity:

- Can occur in all subjects of the curriculum – and beyond the curriculum
- Is often accompanied by non-conformity and independent thinking
- Is encouraged by flexible, creative teaching

Definition: You think a bit differently. You find new ways to do things and have good ideas

Benefits: Creativity is intrinsically satisfying – it feels good. When we create we enter the state of 'flow', we are absorbed in what we are doing, we are fully focussed and functioning at our optimal level.

Quotes:

'Twenty years from now you will be more disappointed by the things that you didn't do than by the ones you did do. So throw off the bowlines. Sail away from the safe harbour. Catch the trade winds in your sails. Explore. Dream. Discover.' – **Mark Twain**

'The key question isn't: "What fosters creativity?" But why in God's name isn't everyone creative? Where was the human potential lost? How was it crippled? I think therefore a good question might be not why do people create? But why do people not create or innovate? We have got to abandon that sense of amazement in the face of creativity, as if it were a miracle if anybody created anything.' – **Abraham Maslow**

'It is better to have enough ideas for some of them to be wrong, than to be always right by having no ideas at all.' – **Edward de Bono**

'Creativity requires the courage to let go of certainties.' – **Erich Fromm**

Thinking Questions:

- What is creativity?
- Is everyone creative in some way?
- Can creativity be bad?

Strengths Builders and Strengths Challenges:

Year 7

Strengths Builders:

1. Design a Creativity Superhero.
2. Make a card or poem or piece of artwork for a friend or family member.

Strengths Challenge:

Make a list of creative people or things.

Year 8

Strengths Builders:

1. Strength in Action Story – Can you remember a time when you or somebody you know used their Creativity? Write or draw or tell a story of Creativity in action.
2. Creativity is doing things differently. If you were in charge of designing the school day, what would you do that was different but still helped everybody to learn?

Strengths Challenge:

Watch a TV programme about something creative. It might be about:

- House design
- Gardening
- Music or art

Share what you learn with a friend or family member.

Year 9

Strengths Builders:

1. Create your own Strength in Action Story – Make up a story that contains a character or characters who used Creativity in a situation. Write or draw or tell your story of Creativity in action.
2. Inventors are creative people. Team up with a friend and design and draw plans for a new invention that will help you do something that you do every day a little bit easier. If you are brave share your invention idea with the class.

Strengths Challenge:

Design a collage of pictures, fabric, or photographs of your choice, or create a collage of pictures from the Internet on a computer. Give your collage to a friend or family member when you are finished.

Closing Activity: Spend a minute thinking about this question – 'If you were a god who could create a world of your own, what would it be like?' You can make notes if you like or sketch the 'world' you'd make.

Display Suggestion: The Spectrum of Creativity

Perhaps using a rainbow as a template, encourage students to create or collect images that show creativity in action within all the different subjects they study at school

PSHE: Programme of Study for Key Stage 3 Links

Personal well-being

Key Concepts:

1.1 Personal identities

Students who are not 'artistic' in the accepted sense may not see themselves as creative, but everyone has the ability to think creatively and to develop that ability further.

1.2 Risk

The ability to be creative requires individuals to take risks – risk is a vital part of the creative process.

A supportive group facilitates the development of creativity.

Key Processes:

2.1 Critical reflection

All students can develop their strengths in creative ways.

Drawing creatively on strengths when target-setting increases the likelihood of meeting those targets. Research shows that where targets are congruent (i.e., they fit with existing strengths and values), we are more likely to achieve them.

The more creative students can be in learning to enhance their positive emotions and manage their negative emotions, the happier and more successful they are likely to become.

Creativity is an approach that can be brought to any aspect of social or emotional intelligence. Students can think creatively about how to build friendships, work together in teams, and motivate themselves to learn or to manage their own feelings.

Story: The Yoruba Creation Myth

There are different versions of this myth, as is common with stories that come from essentially oral cultures. Our version combines elements from several retellings.

In the beginning there were the gods, the sky, and a baobab tree. Most of the gods were happy to sit around their baobab tree in the sky doing nothing all day, but Obatala was an artist who loved exploring and making and finding out – and he soon got bored. So Obatala wandered away from the baobab tree looking for something to do and, as he wandered, he peered down into the mists below. There he caught a glimpse of something moving, something shining and shimmering in the light and he realised that there were waters far, far beneath him. So Obatala went to the supreme god, Olorun, and asked if he might go down and explore and make things and find out what was there.

Olorun agreed and they went to the god who could see the future, Orunmila, and asked him what to do. And Orunmila told Obatala that he would need a gold chain – a very long one – a snail shell full of sand, a white hen, a pine nut and a black cat. So Obatala went to the other gods and begged them for their gold jewellery – their bangles and their bracelets, their necklaces and their rings and he took all that gold to the goldsmith who melted it down and forged the longest chain the world has ever seen. Then Obatala took a snail shell full of sand, a white hen, a pine nut and a black cat and he hung the chain from a corner of the sky and began to climb down. He climbed and he climbed. He climbed and he climbed. He climbed and he climbed for seven days and seven nights until he reached the waters far below.

Then, as Orunmila had told him, he sprinkled the sand out of the snail shell and dropped the white hen on top of it. The hen pecked and scrabbled at the sand, which spread out to make land – mountains and hills and valleys. And Obatala climbed off the chain and began to explore. He planted the pine nut, which grew into a tree – and then into an entire forest. And he lived among the trees with his black cat for company.

But soon, Obatala grew bored once more – he wanted to explore and make things and find out what was there. So he left the forest and began to walk around the new land. Coming to a pond and feeling thirsty he bent down to drink and saw his own reflection gazing back at him, and that gave Obatala an idea for something else he could make. He took some wet clay from the side of the pond and began to shape it into figures, clay people who looked just like him. But the figures just stood there, lifeless, and once more Obatala felt frustrated and lonely and – bored.

Olorun looked down at Obatala and took pity on him. So Olorun breathed life into the figures so that soon the earth was filled with human beings, exploring, making things, and finding out for themselves. And with humans to look after and help, Obatala found he was never bored again.

Opportunities to build Creativity across the curriculum:

It is easy to see the possibilities for using creativity in the expressive arts or in English. However, we can be creative in any subject.

Science: *Focus on the creative innovations we need to solve global warming, the creative discoveries of Einstein or Edison.*

Maths: *Any problem can be solved in different ways. How many ways can students find to solve a single problem?*

PE: *Team sports can involve creative strategies; we find creative ways to train and exercise.*

SEVEN

Curiosity

Curiosity is universal. We all experience becoming involved in the plot of a book or film, wondering why somebody behaves in a certain way, or what the answer to this crossword clue is. People vary, however, in the depth and breadth of their curiosity and in their willingness and capacity to experience it.

Curiosity feels good, it is a positive emotional state and it is associated with positive outcomes, with enhanced performance, greater life satisfaction, increased motivation, feelings of competence and control. In academic settings greater curiosity is associated with greater learning, engagement and performance. It has a positive impact on relationships, on subjectivity and, it is suggested, on longevity.

Any new experience engenders a mixture of pleasurable excitement and anxiety. Where there is too little anxiety or challenge, boredom results. Where there is too much anxiety, and an individual does not feel safe enough to explore, mental or physical withdrawal results.

Psychologists argue that the conditions for increasing or supporting curiosity are autonomy, competence, and relatedness. Positive relationships with teachers, feelings of comfort and safety, a sense of choice, knowledge of one's own strengths and abilities, will all help fuel a willingness and ability to experience curiosity and positively affect learning. When students feel safe enough to fail they will be able to take risks, and real learning is a risky business.

Curiosity is fuelled by increased knowledge and awareness of gaps in that knowledge. It is inhibited by an excessive preoccupation with self, by fear of criticism or excessive surveillance, by a failure to appreciate what you don't know, by overconfidence or high anxiety. External rewards can also diminish curiosity about certain tasks.

Key features of Curiosity:

- Is universal but some people experience it more than others
- Is encouraged by feelings of autonomy, competence and relatedness
- Feels good, and has a very positive effect on learning and performance

Definition: You ask lots of questions. You want to find out, try new things, explore new places, and meet new people.

Benefits: Curiosity is related to higher performance at work and higher academic performance. It is also related to subjective well-being, positive relationships, and longevity.

Quotes:

'It is a miracle that curiosity survives formal education.' – **Albert Einstein**

'The cure for boredom is curiosity. There is no cure for curiosity.' – **Ellen Parr**

'I could not, at any age, be content to take my place by the fireside and simply look on. Life was meant to be lived. Curiosity must be kept alive. One must never, for whatever reason, turn their back on life.' – **Eleanor Roosevelt**

Thinking Questions:

- Why are humans curious?
- Is there good curiosity and bad curiosity?
- What would it be like to have NO curiosity?

Strengths Builders and Strengths Challenges:

Year 7

Strengths Builders:

1. Design a Curiosity Superhero.

2. Try to find out something new. You could:

   - Look in a book
   - Look on the internet
   - Ask an 'expert'

Strengths Challenge:

Eat a food you have never tried before or cook a new recipe.

Year 8

Strengths Builders:

1. Strength in Action Story – Can you remember a time when you or somebody you know was so Curious about something that they had to find out more about it? Write or draw or tell a story of Curiosity in action.

2. Look up something or someone that you have always been curious about, but never investigated.

Strengths Challenge:

Find out more about the neighbourhood or area that you live in. What was it like a long time ago? See if you can find somebody who has lived there long enough to know and ask them to tell you all about it.

Year 9

Strengths Builders:

1. Create your own Strength in Action Story – Make up a story that contains a character or characters who were so Curious about something that they had to find out more about it. Write or draw or tell your story of Curiosity in action.

2. Start a Travel Book – Look up places that interest you and that you would like to visit some day. Collect clippings from magazines and newspapers or the Internet that do articles on these places and paste them into your book.

Strengths Challenge:

Listen to music that you have never listened to before, such as Classical, Country, Jazz, or your parent's favourite music. Listen for long enough (more than one song!) to decide whether or not you like it. Think about what you like and do not like about the new type of music.

Closing activity: If you could go back in time and ask one person one question, what would it be?

Display suggestion: The Unknown

Ask students for their suggestions for images suggested by the phrase Unknown. Help them create their own unique artwork.

PSHE: Programme of Study for Key Stage 3 Links

Personal well-being

Key Concepts:

1.1 Personal identity

1.3 Risk

1.4 Relationships

1.5 Diversity

Key Processes:

2.1 Critical reflection

2.2 Decision-making and managing risk

2.3 Developing relationships and working with others *Too much focus on ourselves can inhibit curiosity, but students do need to know that they have strengths and to feel competent before they can take the necessary risks to learn. Students with more curiosity form better relationships, being more open to others and to differences.*

Story: John Rae

The Northwest Passage is a route through the Arctic Ocean, along Canada's northern coast, connecting the Atlantic and Pacific Oceans. The route was sought for hundreds of years as it shortens sea journeys around the globe and helps trade. Many explorers braved the snow and the ice of the arctic to find it. Many of them died.

One man who was determined to find the Northwest Passage was a man from Orkney, from the far north of Scotland, a doctor by the name of John Rae.

Most Victorian explorers went out on expeditions dressed in clothes they'd bought in London or New York, with modern equipment and modern ideas of how to survive in the snow and the ice. They were full of contempt for the clothes, the equipment, and the customs of the people who lived in the Arctic all year round, the Inuit people. But not John Rae. John was curious about how the Inuit survived their long, harsh, cold winters; about how they travelled and about how they hunted. So he studied the Inuit, he watched them, he asked them questions, he learned from them.

When the time came for John to search for the Northwest Passage he dressed in Inuit clothes, he survived by hunting and travelling like the Inuit and, as a result, he could travel further and faster than any other Western explorer. Where other Victorian explorers died, John survived. Where other Victorian explorers failed to find the Northwest Passage, John succeeded.

John was still exploring in his seventies, still finding new routes through the Arctic wastes, still learning from his friends the Inuit, still curious about the world around him.

He is buried in St Magnus Cathedral, on the Islands of Orkney where he was born.

Opportunities to build Curiosity across the curriculum:

It is hard to limit curiosity to particular subjects since all learning involves finding out about what we don't know. Consider the following:

Languages: *A focus on other cultures, on differences.*

Maths, Technology, and Science: *A focus on the great discoveries of the past – and what is still waiting to be discovered. What **don't** we know in maths, technology and science?*

RE: *The debate about whether God exists and whether miracles happen might stimulate curiosity.*

PE: *There is challenge in learning any new sport and in learning about the capabilities of our own bodies.*

Humanities: *A focus on differences, on other cultures.*

EIGHT

Fairness

Fairness is concerned with moral judgement, with a sense of right and wrong, and a concern for equality and justice. A sense of justice can be seen as passing through different stages:

1. keeping to the rules to avoid punishment or out of self-interest
2. a concern for conforming to the rules of the group and the laws of society
3. an awareness of the rights and obligations of all members of society and a concern for justice

There is also a caring aspect to fairness, a concern for the needs and well-being of the other person and a sense of the importance of maintaining relationships.

When we consider ourselves a 'fair' person we are more likely to behave fairly, and behaving fairly encourages us to consider ourselves a 'fair' person. Living up to our evaluation of ourselves in this way builds confidence and self-esteem.

A sense of fairness is associated with more social and less antisocial behaviour, increased morality and liberal attitudes, more career fulfilment and community involvement.

Research indicates that classroom discussion between students of ethical issues and a caring school community promote the development of a sense of fairness in young people. Teachers who demonstrate reflection on ethical issues and an appreciation for diversity can help students develop their own capacity for reflection and fairness.

Key features of Fairness:

- Has aspects of justice and care for others
- Is encouraged by ethical debate and discussion

Definition: You treat everyone the same. You give everyone an equal chance. You keep to the rules.

Benefits:

- Development of a moral identity, and better understanding of what is morally right and wrong
- Self-evaluation, self-reflection, and increased self-esteem
- Achievement of living up to your own ideal
- Problem-solving and getting along with other people
- Empathy, placing yourself in another's shoes

Quotes:

'It's not fair to ask of others what you are unwilling to do yourself.' – **Eleanor Roosevelt**

'Since others have to tolerate my weaknesses, it is only fair that I should tolerate theirs.' – **William Allen White**

'Fairness is what justice really is.' – **Potter Stewart**

'Recently a young mother asked for advice. What, she wanted to know, was she to do with a 7-year-old who was obstreperous, outspoken, and inconveniently wilful? 'Keep her' I replied. The suffragettes refused to be polite in demanding what they wanted or grateful for getting what they deserved. Works for me.' – **Anna Quindlen**

'When you meet someone better than yourself, turn your thoughts to becoming his equal. When you meet someone not as good as you are, look within and examine yourself.' – **Confucius**

Thinking Questions:

- What is fairness?
- What does it mean to act fairly?
- How can fairness make a positive difference in your life?
- What are the disadvantages of fairness?

Strengths Builders and Strengths Challenges:

Year 7

Strengths Builders:

1. Design a Fairness Superhero.

2. In a group, try to make up a story about something unfair. You could think about somebody who:

    - Got somebody into trouble
    - Cheated at a game and won
    - Pretended to have done some work
    - Kept something all to themselves

   If you feel brave, share your story with the class.

Strengths Challenge:

Watch or listen to the news this week. Look out for stories that seem to be about fairness or unfairness. Share one with your teacher.

Year 8

Strengths Builders:

1. Strength in Action Story – Can you remember a time when you or somebody you know made a Fair decision or treated someone Fairly? Write or draw or tell a story of Fairness in action.

2. Robin Hood has been a symbol of fairness in England for hundreds of years. Robin Hood fought against the Normans to free poor Saxons. If Robin Hood lived today, who would he struggle against and who would he support? Who does our society not treat fairly?

Strengths Challenge:

Admit to a mistake you have made – or to something you do wrong – and take responsibility for it by putting it right or apologising.

Year 9

Strengths Builders:

1. Create your own Strength in Action Story – Make up a story that contains a character or characters who are in a situation where they make a Fair decision or treat someone Fairly. Write or draw or tell your story of Fairness in action.

2. Fairness at School – Can you think of things that are unfair at school? How would you make them fairer if you were in charge? What is fair at school?

Strengths Challenge:

Find an example of a person, animal, or group that has been treated unfairly, either now or in history.

Closing activity: Spend one minute quietly thinking of someone you know who is fair. Think about how you might copy that person this week.

Display suggestion: Battles for Justice

Consider some of the battles for justice of the past – the abolition of slavery, universal suffrage, civil rights – and create a collage based around them.

PSHE: Programme of Study for Key Stage 3 Links

Personal well-being

Key Concepts:

1.4 Relationships

1.5 Diversity

Caring for others and a concern for their well-being and happiness is an important aspect of fairness. An appreciation of diversity and the importance of equal rights help build moral reasoning.

Key Processes:

2.1 Critical reflection

2.3 Developing relationships and working with others

Self-awareness and reflection help to develop a sense of fairness and a concern for dealing sensitively and fairly with other people.

Story: Rosa Parks

Rosa Parks, a black woman, was born in Alabama in 1913. When Rosa was growing up, blacks and whites were kept apart in Alabama– they went to different schools, they rode on separate parts of buses. Blacks were allowed to vote but it was made as hard as possible for them to do so.

Rosa went to a school for black girls. The school, which was burned down twice, was run by white teachers, teachers who were shunned by the rest of their community.

White children were taken to school by bus. Black children walked.

In 1955, when she was 42, a driver told Rosa to give up her seat on the bus to a white man. Rosa refused. She was not the first black person to do this. Nine months before, 15-year-old Claudette Colvin did exactly the same thing. Rosa's action and her arrest sparked what became known as the Montgomery Bus Boycott, a political and social protest against the unfairness of segregation. The struggle lasted a year and led to a decision by the United States Supreme Court that the laws of Alabama requiring segregated buses were unconstitutional. It was a small but important step towards a fairer society, a society in which a black man might enter the White House.

Opportunities to build Fairness across the curriculum:

History: *Focus on justice and injustice and civil rights struggles.*

RE: *Appreciation of diversity, the struggle for religious freedoms.*

Any subject: *Work on creating a fair school in which diversity is valued and all opinions are respected.*

NINE

Forgiveness

Forgiveness is a strength that reacts to other events, but the willingness to forgive, or 'forgivingness', can be present all the time. It is the ability to move on from hurt feelings and thoughts, to stop feeling hostile towards somebody or something that has wounded us and think and behave towards them positively once more.

There are people, like those in the story below, who forgive great hurts with immense courage. Most of us are not called on to show that degree of forgiveness, but the daily hassles of life – and dealing with other people who are always imperfect – allow for frequent opportunities to forgive – or not.

Forgiveness is not the same as forgetting or saying that something was not wrong. Rather it is a choice not to continue to harbour hostile feelings and thoughts against another person, a shift of mind. It is not the same as reconciliation. We may – or may not – wish to become reconciled with someone after we have forgiven them.

A failure to forgive hurts us rather than the wrongdoer. Ruminating on past hurts keeps the pain of them alive and disturbs our peace of mind. Forgiveness can produce an increase in joy, energy, and creativity. Brooding on past wrongs can consume our thoughts and impede our own personal growth.

Forgiving ourselves is also important. We are human – we make mistakes. It may be that learning to be gentle and forgiving with ourselves is a first step in learning to forgive others. Failure to forgive oneself is linked to depression and guilt (Niemiec & Wedding, 2008).

The ability to listen to others, to show empathy, helps us to forgive. For this reason, activities that encourage students to actively listen to one another – like philosophy – may play an important part in encouraging the development of forgiveness. A willingness to forgive seems to develop with age – perhaps we become more accepting of imperfection as we get older. Older adults are generally more willing to forgive than younger adults or children.

Key features of Forgiveness:

- Is a willingness to shift our thinking from hostility to kindness
- Is not the same as forgetting – or as reconciliation
- Can develop with age

Definition: When people hurt or annoy you, you get over it quickly. You let your anger fade away and are happy to be friends again. You aren't spiteful; you never try to 'get even'.

Benefits: People who find it easier to forgive suffer less depression, anxiety, anger, and hostility. It has been suggested that a willingness to forgive may prevent both mental and physical ill health but more evidence is needed to substantiate this (Peterson & Seligman, 2004).

Quotes:

'Forgiveness is really nothing more than an act of self-healing and self-empowerment. I call it a miracle medicine. It is free, it works and has no side effects.' – **Eva Kor**

'To forgive is to remember we have room in our hearts to begin again – and again, and again.' – **Anon**

'To forgive is really to remember that we are so much more than our mistakes.' – **Anon**

'Only the brave know how to forgive.' – **Laurence Sterne**

'O Lord, remember not only the men and women of good will, but all those of ill will. But do not remember all the suffering they have inflicted upon us. Remember the fruits we have brought thanks to this suffering –

our comradeship, our loyalty, our humility, our courage, our generosity, this greatness of heart which has grown out of all this. And when they come to judgment, let all the fruits we have borne be their forgiveness.'
– Found in Ravensbuck concentration camp, 1945

'An eye for an eye will make the whole world blind.' – **Mahatma Gandhi**

Thinking Questions:

- Is forgiveness important?
- What can a lack of forgiveness lead to?
- Is forgiveness ever wrong?

Strengths Builders and Strengths Challenges:

Year 7

Strengths Builders:

1. Design a Forgiveness Superhero.
2. Think of somebody who has hurt or annoyed you. Imagine the hurt or anger as a balloon. In your imagination, let it fly away, taking your anger with it. Draw the balloon if you want. Tear it up and throw it in a bin.

Strengths Challenge:

It can be hard to forgive ourselves when we get things wrong. This week, practise forgiving yourself when you make mistakes.

Year 8

Strengths Builders:

1. Strength in Action Story – Can you remember a time when you or somebody you know Forgave someone for something that they did wrong? Write or draw or tell a story of Forgiveness in action.
2. Make a list of things you find hard to forgive. Compare your list with a friend. Can you think of one way you might become more forgiving?

Strengths Challenge:

This week, when people annoy you, try to respond with forgiveness not anger. It can be difficult. See how you do.

Year 9

Strengths Builders:

1. Create your own Strength in Action Story – Make up a story that contains a character or characters who were able to Forgive someone for something that they did wrong. Write or draw or tell your story of Forgiveness in action.
2. Write a letter of forgiveness to someone who has done something wrong to you; do not send it, but read it over once each day for a week.

Strengths Challenge:

Send a make your peace e-card from: http://www.makeyourpeace.org.uk to someone that you are in conflict with or who has done something wrong to you as your first step towards forgiveness. Or be a peacemaker at school and help others to forgive each other.

Closing Activity: Play some quiet music and ask students to think quietly to themselves of all the benefits forgiveness can lead to.

Display Suggestion: Bridges

Bridges are often a metaphor for forgiveness. Create a Forgiveness display that has different sizes, shapes and kinds of bridge – either drawn or cut out from magazines or collected from the Internet.

PSHE: Programme of Study for Key Stage 3 Links

Personal well-being

Key Concepts:

1.4 Relationships

Relationships require forgiveness to grow and to flourish. The inability to forgive can seriously impede intimate, trusting relationships.

Accepting that other people are fallible is a vital part of building healthy relationships. Even when we are badly hurt, a failure to forgive wounds us rather than the other person.

Key Processes:

2.1 Critical reflection

The ability to accept our weaknesses and mistakes – in effect, to forgive ourselves – is a key to positive mental health.

Students must have the confidence to fail and to be less than perfect in order to develop true self-awareness.

Being able to accept that other people make mistakes is a crucial social skill.

Guilt and shame can be particularly challenging emotions. They may impel us to action – to remedy what we have done wrong. Alternatively they may require us to forgive ourselves.

Story: The Forgiveness Project

There are many stories on this website: http://www.theforgivenessproject.com. One of the most moving is told by Andrew Rice, whose brother David was killed by terrorists on 11 September 2001 when planes were flown into the World Trade Centre in New York. Andrew was devastated by his brother's death but troubled by his country's response – to cause more innocent deaths.

A man who is alleged to have been one of the bombers, Zacharias Moussaoui, has been held in solitary confinement in the USA since 2001. In 2002 his mother, Madam al-Wafi, asked to meet with the families of some of the victims. She wanted to ask for their forgiveness. Andrew and some other family members agreed to meet her in New York City in November 2002. As they waited in a private university building, a mother whose son was killed in the World Trade Centre went down the hall to meet her. They heard footsteps, then silence. Then they heard the sound of weeping. Finally both women came into the room; both were mothers, both had their arms around each other. By now the whole group was crying. Madame al-Wafi spent three hours with the families and told them how the extremist group had given her mentally ill son a purpose in life.

'One day,' Andrew writes, 'I'd like to meet Zacharias Moussaoui. I'd like to say to him, "You can hate me and my brother as much as you like, but I want you to know that I loved your mother and I comforted her when she was crying".'

Opportunities to build Forgiveness across the curriculum:

History: *Focus on the work of reconciliation in Northern Ireland or South Africa.*

RE: *Forgiveness is an important component of faith. Compare teachings on forgiveness in different faith traditions.*

TEN

Gratitude

Gratitude is one of the strengths that makes us happiest. It implies a focus on the good things that life brings and a value for everything and everyone. It connects us to others and fosters an awareness of our interdependence. Interestingly, children and teenagers with a strong sense of gratitude do well academically.

Gratitude may be defined as a sense of thankfulness in response to a gift – either a concrete gift or the gift of a beautiful sunset, friendship, or smile. It is a sense of having benefited from what has taken place. Its opposites are glaringly negative: ungrateful, entitled, rude, and unappreciative.

Gratitude is also characterised by a sense of wonder at the ordinary things in life. Students may take good things for granted but they can still be encouraged to notice and appreciate the good things around them and to practise the ancient art of saying 'thank you'. In that sense, gratitude is a skill, an attitude that can be learned and practised. In studies, keeping a 'gratitude journal' on a daily or weekly basis has a measurable effect on adults' alertness, enthusiasm, determination, and energy levels. It has even been shown in studies to improve mental health.

Expressing appreciation is one of the cornerstones of successful marriages and this can be extended to other relationships as well. Taking the time to thank people builds good relationships and expresses a sense of their value to us.

Gratitude may be inhibited by stress and by being under pressure – gratitude is a skill of reflection; it takes time to stop and appreciate what is good in life.

There is a wonderful gratefulness website at: http://www.gratefulness.org – a beautiful site to visit and a practical source of great ideas for building gratitude.

Key features of Gratitude:

- Is closely linked to happiness
- Deepens relationships
- Improves well-being
- Can be increased by practice

Definition: You notice and enjoy the good things in your life. You always say 'thank you' and can usually find something to feel good about.

Benefits: Increased happiness, fulfilment, alertness, enthusiasm, determination, and energy levels. Students with a lot of gratitude tend to do well academically. A person who sees the good in others is likely to have good relationships.

Thinking Questions:

- What does gratitude mean to you?
- What is the effect of having no gratitude?
- What are the opposites of gratitude?
- Can you be too grateful?
- What might gratitude mean at school?
- Why is it important to be grateful?
- What are the benefits of being grateful in life?

Strengths Builders and Strengths Challenges:

<u>Year 7</u>

Strengths Builders:

1. Design a Gratitude Superhero.

2. This week write or draw three things each day that you are most grateful for. Start with today.

Strengths Challenge:

Notice the things people do for you. Say thank you.

<u>Year 8</u>

Strengths Builders:

1. Strength in Action Story – Can you remember a time when you or somebody you know was really Grateful about something? Write or draw or tell a story of Gratitude in action.

2. Make a list of things you feel grateful for. Compare your list with a friend. Illustrate this list if you want to with images from magazines or your own drawings and turn it into a work of art.

Strengths Challenge:

Thank You Post-It Notes – Carry a set of post-it notes in your bag. Whenever you can, leave a little 'thank you' note – for a teacher, a cleaner, a friend, or your mum or dad.

<u>Year 9</u>

Strengths Builders:

1. Create your own Strengths in Action Story – Make up a story that contains a character or characters who are really Grateful about something. Write or draw or tell your story of Gratitude in action.

2. Gratitude Letter – Write a letter of gratitude to someone who has done something for you but you never thanked them properly. Send the letter to them.

Strengths Challenge:

What are you grateful for? Record your Top Ten at: http://www.thegratitudelist.com.

Closing Activity:

1. Think for one minute in silence about one thing you are grateful for.

2. Tell a Gratitude in Action story.

Display suggestion: Make a 'things to be grateful for' collage using images from magazines or the Internet.

PSHE: Programme of Study for Key Stage 3 Links

Personal well-being

Key Concepts:

1.4 Relationships

Appreciating what is good in those around us, and expressing appreciation, is a key to healthy relationships.

Expressing appreciation for others is a key to good relationships.

Noticing the positive in our life improves our happiness levels and our mental health. Expressing positive emotion increases our happiness levels even further.

Story: The Spirit of the Corn

In a land far away and long ago, there was a village where the sun always shone and the rain always fell and the soil was rich and fertile and the corn grew and grew and grew and there was lots to eat. There was so much to eat, in fact, that the people grew careless. They forgot to work in the fields, so the weeds grew. They forgot to store their corn carefully, in baskets or holes in the ground so the mice got in and stole it and the rain came in and made the corn rot away. Worst of all, they forgot to say thank you to the spirit of the corn.

In all the village, there was only one man who remembered to weed his fields, who remembered to store his corn carefully in baskets and holes in the ground, who remembered to say thank you to the spirit of the corn. His name was Dayohagwenda.

One day, Dayohagwenda was walking in the forest when he met an old man, sitting by a hut full of holes and surrounded by weeds. The man was dressed in rags and he was weeping.

'Grandfather, why are you weeping?' asked Dayohagwenda.

'I am weeping,' the old man said, 'because your people have forgotten to weed my corn. Because they have forgotten to store my corn carefully in baskets or holes in the ground. Because they have forgotten to say thank you for my corn.'

Dayohagwenda realised that this was not an ordinary old man. This was the spirit of the corn and he was weeping because he thought he had been forgotten.

Dayohagwenda rushed back to his village where the people were on the edge of starvation and close to death. He told them what he had seen. He told them what he had heard. He told them that the spirit would help them if they remembered him again.

Then Dayohagwenda dug up his own corn and found that there was more there than when he stored it away – ten times more. He shared it with his people so that they did not starve.

After that, the sun always shone and the rain always fell and the corn grew and grew and the people of the village remembered to work in the fields and dig up the weeds. They remembered to store the corn carefully in baskets or holes in the ground. And they remembered to say thank you to the spirit of the corn.

Opportunities to build Gratitude across the curriculum:

English: *Thank you letters are a formal 'ritual' for increasing gratitude and are ready for a revival. Thank you notes to former teachers, to kitchen and office and site staff, to visitors and governors from students would help everyone associated with the school to feel appreciated.*

RE: *Giving thanks for food is a common religious practice. Students might research prayers of thanks from different faith traditions.*

ELEVEN

Honesty

Honesty, to younger children, means not telling lies. As we mature we can also appreciate its more subtle aspects – integrity and authenticity. Integrity means being true to our values – whether or not they are popular – and behaving in a straightforward and honest way with everyone. Somebody who is authentic is genuine, trustworthy, and does what they believe to be right. Integrity implies self-awareness – we know ourselves and can look honestly even at the parts of ourselves we don't like. We understand our own feelings and are free to express them – when appropriate.

Ensuring that young people are exposed to environments and engaged in relationships that allow them to be autonomous and make genuine choices enables authenticity to grow and flourish. Where there is an undue amount of external control it becomes harder to behave authentically. Inauthenticity may also result from what psychologists refer to as 'contingent positive regard', i.e., 'I will think well of you IF you... behave... get A*s... are thin... become a doctor...' The young person has to become something they are not in order to retain the good opinion of those they love or admire.

Positive role models can encourage honesty and integrity in young people – studying the lives and sacrifices of individuals such as Martin Luther King, Nelson Mandela, and Aung San Suu Kyi is worthwhile. Closer to home, students sense and respond to integrity in parents and teachers and in their peers.

Prejudice and discrimination may inhibit authenticity – if we are not accepted for who we really are it becomes harder for us to be open about our true nature. An overemphasis on materialism may also impede authenticity – we are worthwhile only if we have the right things, looks, shape, job, etc.

Because authentic people understand themselves, they know what they really need and what they truly enjoy. This means they often make good choices and set appropriate goals for themselves – goals they are also more likely to achieve. A key aim of *Strengths Gym* is to increase self-awareness – a true knowledge of our strengths and weaknesses – and hence to build authenticity.

Integrity yields social benefits – people with integrity tend to be well liked. However, there are exceptions to this as the story below illustrates. Our integrity may lead us to make ourselves unpopular if we stand up for unpopular causes. While manipulators and liars can succeed, on the whole it is co-operators and those who operate in a trustworthy fashion who fare best in life. Again, the story below is one example of this. Being honest is also good for us – it leads to less stress and tension. Integrity is correlated with positive mood, life satisfaction, and good relationships.

Key features of Honesty:

- Includes being truthful but goes beyond not telling lies
- Has mental health benefits – you sleep well with a good conscience
- Can make you popular and successful
- Is encouraged by autonomy – choice – and by good role models

Definition: You are an open and truthful person. You stand up for what you believe in; you say what you think.

Benefits: People tend to like honest individuals; being honest with yourself means you can meet your own needs appropriately, set good goals and feel at peace with yourself.

Quotes:

'If we are not trusted, we have no business.' – **Larry Page**

'Believe nothing just because a so-called wise person said it. Believe nothing just because a belief is generally held. Believe nothing just because it is said in ancient books. Believe nothing just because it is said to be of divine origin. Believe nothing just because someone else believes it. Believe only what you yourself test and judge to be true.' – **The Buddha**

'Thou shalt not be a victim. Thou shalt not be a perpetrator. Above all, thou shalt not be a bystander.' – **Holocaust Museum, Washington DC**

'The ideals which have lighted me on my way and time after time given me new courage to face life cheerfully, have been Truth, Goodness, and Beauty ... The ordinary objects of human endeavour – property, outward success, luxury – have always seemed to me contemptible.' – **Albert Einstein**

'Always tell the truth. That way, you don't have to remember what you said.' – **Mark Twain**

Thinking Questions:

- Is it always right to tell the truth?
- What is integrity?
- What is trust – and how do you earn it?

Strengths Builders and Strengths Challenges:

Year 7

Strengths Builders:

1. Design an Honesty Superhero.
2. Play Is It True? with a friend, or in groups. Take it in turns to say three things about yourself. Two of them must be false, one of them true. Your friends have to guess which statement is true.

Strengths Challenge:

This week, try stopping and thinking before you speak. Try to say only what is true and what you really mean.

Year 8

Strengths Builders:

1. Strength in Action Story – Can you remember a time when you or somebody you know stood up for themselves or somebody else even though it was scary, but they knew they had to because it was the right thing to do? Write or draw or tell a story of Honesty in action.
2. What do you think is really important in life? What are the things you would stand up for? Can you think of something you feel is important enough to stand up for, even against your friends? Design a poster to show how important it is.

Strengths Challenge:

For two days do not say anything about yourself or other people or situations that is not true.

Year 9

Strengths Builders:

1. Create your own Strength in Action Story – Make up a story that contains a character or characters who stood up for themselves, or of a time when they knew they had to face something scary, but did

it anyway because they knew it was the right thing to do. Write or draw or tell your story of Honesty in action.

2. Be Honest – Share something about yourself with your friend that is honest but which they don't know. It could be:

- Some thing you like or dislike
- A past experience
- A skill you haven't told anyone about
- A goal you haven't said anything about

Strengths Challenge:

Try not to tell any lies, even small ones (like giving someone a compliment when you don't mean it). If you do tell one, admit it and apologise right away.

Closing Activity: Spend a minute thinking about a person you trust. Why do you trust them?

Display Suggestion: People we trust

A display of pictures of people we consider trustworthy – friends, parents, famous figures.

PSHE: Programme of Study for Key Stage 3 Links

Personal well-being

Key Concepts:

1.1 Personal identities

We cannot be honest with others until we are honest with and accepting of ourselves.

1.4 Relationships

Honesty is an important principle in any relationship. Without trust it is hard to have positive relationships.

1.5 Diversity

Practising tolerance allows other people to be authentic, to show us their true selves. Therefore, we can help others to be honest and authentic by our own attitudes.

Key Processes:

2.1 Critical reflection

We cannot stand up for values if we do not know what they are.

It requires honesty to develop self-awareness – and also courage.

2.3 Developing relationships and working with others

We have a duty to be trustworthy and to keep promises. This creates the environment for other people to be authentic.

People with a lot of integrity are often well liked. Honesty and integrity lie at the heart of building positive relationships.

Understanding ourselves and looking honestly at how we feel and at what motivates us builds our ability to be honest and authentic with others. We cannot 'manage' our feelings if we do not know what they are.

Story: The Quakers

The Society of Friends, sometimes called the Quakers, is a Christian group founded in the 17th century. Quakers believe that God exists in everyone and that there is no need for priests or complicated religious services. They also believed – at a time when this was seen as almost madness – that the rich and powerful and the poor were really equals AND that men and women were equals. They were among the first to campaign for women's rights and were leaders in the anti-slavery movement. They pioneered humane treatment of the mentally ill and prisoners. Quakers believe strongly in truth and integrity; a person's word, they would say, is their bond or promise. As a result, Quakers refuse to swear oaths in court or of allegiance to the King or Queen – they believe that you should always speak the truth, everywhere.

In the past their willingness to stand up for these values has had mixed results. The early Quakers were hated and persecuted – they were beaten, banned from going to university, sometimes arrested, tortured, and imprisoned, even executed. During the world wars many Quakers refused to fight – they believe violence is always wrong. Again, they were ridiculed, accused of cowardice, laughed at. Some Quakers served as stretcher-bearers and ambulance drivers – they risked their lives but still refused to fight.

However, another result of the Quakers' integrity and honesty was more positive. Quakers were trusted – people knew they were honest so they would choose to do business with them. Quaker businesses became very successful indeed. Quakers founded some highly successful businesses that are still operating 200 years later – Rowntree, Fry, Cadbury, Clarks shoes were all founded by Quakers.

Standing up for your beliefs will not always make you popular but it will make you respected.

Opportunities to build Honesty across the curriculum:

History: *Focus on individuals or groups like the Quakers who stood up for what they believed despite persecution.*

RE: *Like the suggestion above, focus on those who were persecuted for refusing to compromise their beliefs.*

Science: *Galileo suffered for pursuing truth in the face of religious dogma. Find other examples of scientists who were not afraid to be unpopular by questioning orthodoxy.*

PE: *Old fashioned 'fair play' and keeping the rules is one aspect of honesty.*

TWELVE

Hope

Hope and optimism are closely linked concepts. Hope is sometimes seen more as an emotion and optimism as a way of thinking. One outcome of this is that hope, as an emotion, is infectious – we can spread hope by being hopeful ourselves. Hope is also one of the strengths that lie closest to the heart of the teaching profession. We are educators because we have hope for the future and hope for our students. We expect that positive things will happen, that the future is worth educating our students for, that our students are well worth educating. It is our trust in our students that builds their trust in themselves.

A key feature of optimism is 'explanatory style' – particularly how we explain bad events to ourselves. An optimistic explanation for a bad event is specific, 'this particular thing went wrong', and temporary, 'it went wrong *this* time'. By contrast, a pessimistic explanation for a bad event is permanent, 'everything always goes wrong', and pervasive, 'I can't do anything right'. This can also be called 'always and everything thinking' or simply 'Eeyore Thinking' after the gloomy donkey in A. A. Milne's *Winnie the Pooh*.

People may have a more or less optimistic or hopeful temperament from birth; however, optimism is also a skill, a way of thinking that can be learned. Goal-setting is a key aspect of hope and optimism. A goal needs two elements – the determination and desire to achieve it and the belief that actions can be taken that will help to achieve it.

Key features of Hope and Optimism:

- A positive expectation that good things will happen and that actions can be taken to bring about good things
- Hope – an emotion that can be modelled and passed on
- Optimism – a way of thinking about present and future events that can be learned

Definition: You look forward to the future and work hard to make your dreams come true. You trust that good things will happen.

Benefits: Hope and optimism are associated with many positive outcomes (although whether they *cause* them is a more complex question). Hopeful people are healthier, happier, and have good personal relationships.

Quotes:

'The grand essentials of happiness are: something to do, something to love, and something to hope for.' – **Allan K. Chalmers**

'...just as despair can come to one another only from other human beings, hope, too, can be given to one another only by other human beings.' – **Elie Wiesel**

'Listen to the Exhortation of the Dawn!
Look to this Day!
For it is Life, the very Life of Life.
In its brief course lie all the
Verities and Realities of your Existence.
The Bliss of Growth,
The Glory of Action,
The Splendor of Beauty;
For Yesterday is but a Dream,
And To-morrow is only a Vision;
But To-day well lived makes
Every Yesterday a Dream of Happiness,
And every Tomorrow a Vision of Hope.

Look well therefore to this Day!
Such is the Salutation of the Dawn!' – **Kalidasa**

Thinking Questions:

- What are hope and optimism?
- Can we build hope and optimism?
- What are the disadvantages of hope?
- Why do we need hope?
- Are hopes and dreams the same thing?

Strengths Builders and Strengths Challenges:

Year 7

Strengths Builders:

1. Design a Hope Superhero.
2. Think of one goal you are hoping to achieve. Write it down or draw it. Think about what you have to do to make your dream come true.

Strengths Challenge:

Write or draw your important goal again. Put the paper up where you can see it. Try to do something every day to make your dream come true. When you do, make a small tick on the page. When you achieve your goal, make a huge tick and pat yourself on the back.

Year 8

Strengths Builders:

1. Strength in Action Story – Can you remember a time when you or somebody you know believed in something that they wanted to happen, and it happened? What things did they do in order to make what happened more likely? Write or draw or tell a story of Hope in action.
2. Play Eeyore Thoughts with a friend – Imagine something goes wrong (for example, you forget to hand in your homework). Think of the three worst possible things that could result from this. Then think of the ten most things that could result from this (for example, you have to stay behind after school to complete the work and because you are late going home you bump into Johnny Depp or Pamela Anderson on the way).

Strengths Challenge:

Write down one goal you would like to achieve in the next few months or weeks. Mark on a calendar the date when you would like to achieve it by. Make plans for how you will reach the goal by the date you have chosen.

Year 9

Strengths Builders:

1. Create your own Strength in Action Story – Make up a story that contains a character or characters who believed in something that they wanted to happen, and it happened. Include what things they did in order to make what happened more likely. Write or draw or tell your story of Hope in action.
2. Wish List – Write down your goals for the next week, the next month, or the next year on a calendar. Think about how you can reach these goals. Make real plans that will help you reach them.

Strengths Challenge:

Spend some time carefully thinking about your future and what you would like to achieve or who you would like to become. Share your ideas with your teacher, friends, or family.

Closing Activity: Think again about a goal you would like to achieve. Imagine yourself achieving this goal, picture it happening like a film playing in your head.

Display Suggestion: 'Listen to the exhortation of the dawn'

Sunrise is a powerful symbol of hope. Can you collect a collage of sunrise pictures and similar symbols the pupils suggest for themselves?

PSHE: Programme of Study for Key Stage 3 Links

Personal well-being

Key Concepts:

1.1 Personal identities

Optimism is to an extent innate but is also a skill that can be learned.

Key Processes:

2.1 Critical reflection

A knowledge of strengths and an appreciation of achievements can help students believe that they can influence their own future.

Goal-setting is a key aspect of optimism.

2.2 Decision-making and managing risk

Feeling hopeful can help students make positive choices.

Optimistic students find it easier to persist academically because they believe that they will succeed. Increasing optimism may therefore have a positive impact upon academic success.

Story: A Cow Named Tutti

This is a story about a journalist who is also a farmer, about an African village and about a pregnant cow named Tutti.

The journalist, who is also a farmer, is called Paul Heiney and he writes for *The Times* newspaper. In 1994, Paul came across a group of farmers who had decided to do what they do best to make a difference to the world. And what they did best was – cows. So this group started a charity called Send a Cow and they persuaded Paul and the readers of *The Times* to pay for a cow – just one – to be sent to a village in Africa – in Uganda.

The rule was that the family who got the pregnant cow would give away its first calf to another family, and when that cow had a calf they would give that away to another family and so on. A small, simple scheme, paid for by small donations from these farmers and a group of *The Times* readers.

In 2008, Paul went back to see what difference one cow could possibly have made. What he found was that it had made all the difference in the world.

For example, Mrs Luyombyas showed him her house – made of brick – with real windows that shut. Before, she and her children slept on the floor of a mud hut. The milk from the cow had made them all healthier so they could work harder. The surplus milk from the cow had been sold so they had money – where before they had none. Also, the dung from the cow made a huge difference because it nourished the poor soil so there was more food to eat and to sell.

What did they do with the money – after they had a house, with real windows – oh, and real luxury – beds? They spent it on their children's education. Mrs Luyombyas' daughter now has a degree in education and her son has one in engineering – paid for by a cow. As they say, education is their children's freedom, and once their children are educated, then it is their turn, the turn of the mothers, to study and to learn to be better farmers.

What of the cows that are descended from Tutti? Now they are spreading across Uganda to Rwanda, where ten years ago rival Tutsis and Hutus massacred each other. Now there is an additional rule – a Tutsi family must give their calf to a Hutu family and a Hutu family must give theirs to a Tutsi. A small sticking plaster on a terrible wound – but a sticking plaster all the same.

Did those farmers change the world? Yes they did – because little changes add up, little actions matter. What little action can you take today that will make the world a tiny bit better?

Opportunities to build Hope across the curriculum:

Science: *Science is a fundamentally hopeful subject; it is forward-thinking, seeking to understand and to change life for the better.*

RE: *Hope is a fundamental concept in all faiths.*

PE: *Optimism is essential to competitive sports – if there is no hope of winning, why take part? Belief is a huge element in success.*

THIRTEEN

Humour

Humour is the ability to look on the lighter side of life, to find the funny side of a situation and to make others smile or laugh. Humour can lift the spirits, 'take us out' of ourselves and help us to deal with troubles in a positive, if not always pleasurable, way. There is a dark side to humour, where it is expressed as ridicule or sarcasm, which seeks to attack or wound. Positive humour implies a sympathetic heart that sees the shortcomings in a situation but is tolerant of them. Humour can be defensive and arise as a way of dealing with adversity, where it can be most useful in alleviating, suppressing, or even removing negative feelings.

There seems to be a strong link with playfulness since humour is essentially a playful attitude to ideas. It is unclear how to encourage the development of humour but it may be that helping children and young people to maintain a playful attitude to situations will also support humour. Certainly, an adult who models the ability to see humour, particularly in difficult situations, will assist students in continuing to develop a sense of humour of their own.

Humour is closely linked to a cheerful attitude and, while the data on the long-term health benefits of humour are unclear, laughter has a positive physical and emotional impact.

Key features of Humour:

- Useful in situations of adversity
- Linked to playfulness
- May have physical and mental benefits

Definition: You like to laugh and to make others laugh or smile. You can see the funny side of a situation, you can think of a funny remark or joke to cheer others up.

Benefits: Humour helps you through the hard times in life. Laughter improves mood and has physical benefits; it can reduce stress and even boost the immune system.

Quotes:

'Better to remain silent and be thought a fool than to speak out and remove all doubt.' – **Abraham Lincoln**

'If you want a guarantee, buy a toaster.' – **Clint Eastwood**

'If you think that something small cannot make a difference- try going to sleep with a mosquito in the room.' – **Unknown**

Thinking Questions:

- What does humour mean to you?
- Why do you think humans evolved to have a sense of humour?
- Is humour always a good thing?

Strengths Builders and Strengths Challenges:

Year 7

Strengths Builders:

1. Design a Humour Superhero.
2. Learn a simple magic trick or joke and perform it or tell it to your friends.

Strengths Challenge:

Look for the funny side of things that happen at school. When you go home, tell somebody what happened and try to make them laugh.

Year 8

Strengths Builders:

1. Strength in Action Story – Can you remember a time when you or somebody you know used Humour in a situation? Write or draw or tell a story of Humour in action.

2. Start a Joke Book. Find a funny image to put on the cover and ask everyone you know for their funniest joke. Write them down or ask them to write them down.

Strengths Challenge:

Watch a comedy on TV and then tell someone about it and try to make them laugh.

Year 9

Strengths Builders:

1. Create your own Strength in Action Story – Make up a story that contains a character or characters who are involved in a really funny situation or event. Write or draw or tell your story of Humour in action.

2. Work with a friend and draw a comic strip or small comic book, or write your own comedy script. If you are feeling brave perform your comedy script for the class or share your comic strip or book with the other students.

Strengths Challenge:

Ask a teacher if you can organise a lunchtime comedy club. Invite other students to tell jokes, perform funny sketches, etc.

Closing activity: Hold a swift, 'worst joke' competition.

Display suggestion: Cartoon Gallery.

Ask students to collect their favourite and funniest cartoons and display them, or even get students to draw some of their own.

PSHE: Programme of Study for Key Stage 3 Links

Personal well-being

Key Concepts:

1.2 Healthy lifestyles

Key Processes:

1.3 Developing relationships and working with others

For some students, humour is a key tool in building friendships.

Learning how to use humour effectively and appropriately is an important social skill.

Learning how to cheer yourself up and increase your own happiness is a vital personal skill.

Story: The Parrot and the Conjurer

There was once a conjurer who worked on a cruise ship. On each cruise he did the same act and after a while the captain's parrot began to heckle him. 'It's up his sleeve,' the parrot would squawk, or, 'It's the five of clubs.' This annoyed the conjurer but there wasn't much he could do about it so he just tried to ignore the parrot and carry on.

One night there was a terrible storm. The ship sank and everyone was drowned – everyone except the conjurer and the parrot who washed up together on a desert island.

Now the parrot was usually a very talkative bird but the storm seemed to have had a bad effect on him because now he said nothing at all, he just sat and looked at the conjurer. Days passed and the parrot said nothing, he just sat and looked at the conjurer. Weeks passed and the parrot said nothing, he just sat and looked at the conjurer.

Then after months and months of silence the parrot finally spoke. It said, 'Alright, I give up, what have you done with the ship?'

Opportunities to build Humour across the curriculum:

Drama: *Comedy and comic acting or stand-up are obvious ways to foster humour.*

English: *Appreciating the humour in literature and being able to write in an amusing way.*

Languages: *Appreciating the different kinds of humour found in different countries.*

FOURTEEN

Persistence

Finishing what we have started, sticking at something in the face of obstacles or boredom is what is referred to as persistence or industriousness. Persistence does not guarantee success but success is often unobtainable without it. It is not a universal good – sometimes it is right to give up and move on to something else. Success, and indeed wisdom, may depend on knowing when to persist and when it is just not worth it. Persistence may enhance enjoyment – we feel prouder of a task that requires persistence than of one that comes easily to us.

Persistence is related to failure in a positive way. For example, the great military generals of history were not individuals who never failed, but individuals who learned from mistakes and went on to solve problems in innovative ways.

Adults will persist longer at a task if it is labelled 'difficult'. This is because there is less threat to self-esteem in failing a 'difficult' task, than an 'easy' one. Children, however, seem to persist longer if told that a task is 'easy' and 'fun'. An element of choice will also increase the likelihood of persistence since if people feel responsible for choosing a task it makes it more relevant to them.

There may be times when people self-handicap and fail to persist in order to protect or enhance their self-esteem. They may not revise for an exam, for example. If they fail they can then claim this was due to lack of preparation. If they do well without any revision it must mean they are really clever! Such self-handicapping may indicate that self-esteem is fragile.

It is important to attribute failures to things within the student's control, i.e., to low effort not to low ability. A study suggests teachers tend to attribute failure in boys to low effort and failure in girls to low ability so this tendency would be worth keeping in mind. Children improved in persistence when they were trained to take responsibility for their failure and to attribute it to insufficient effort. This encourages the belief that outcomes are under their control and that they should keep going. Setting goals and creating plans to achieve them, making lists of things to do and ticking them off one by one are practical tools for building persistence.

Key features of Persistence:

- Is affected by expectations of success
- Is linked to optimism and self-esteem
- Is supported by positive mood or thoughts
- Is supported by praise for effort NOT ability

Definition: You stick at things until you finish. You like to keep working until you get there.

Benefits: Success very, very rarely comes without persistence. In fact, the secret of success can be said to be persistence plus a dose of optimism and passion. It is the achievements that needed hard work and persistence that we really enjoy.

Quotes:

'Making your mark on the world is hard. If it were easy, everybody would do it. But it's not. It takes patience, it takes commitment, and it comes with plenty of failure along the way. The real test is not whether you avoid this failure because you won't. It's whether you let it harden or shame you into inaction, or whether you learn from it; whether you choose to persevere.' – **Barack Obama**

'Most of the important things in the world have been accomplished by people who kept on trying when there seemed to be no hope at all.' – **Dale Carnegie**

Thinking Questions:

- Can you succeed without persistence?
- Is persistence always a good thing?

Strengths Builders and Strengths Challenges:

Year 7

Strengths Builders:

1. Design a Persistence Superhero.
2. Choose and start a project that will require persistence. Set a goal and keep going until you achieve it. Start a plan for your project now. You could:
   - Read a book
   - Learn a sport
   - Start a small vegetable patch or pot
   - Build a garden pond
   - Knit a garment

Strengths Challenge:

Learn a magic trick and keep going until you perfect it. Once you have mastered it, perform it for the class.

Year 8

Strengths Builders:

1. Strength in Action Story – Can you remember a time when you or somebody you know stuck at something no matter how much they wanted to give up – and finally succeeded? Write or draw or tell a story of Persistence in action.
2. With a friend or in a group learn to play a new card game. Make sure to learn all the rules and keep practising until you can play well. Need help finding a good game? Go to: http://games.yahoo.com/card-games.

Strengths Challenge:

Learn a poem or the lyrics to a song by heart. Tell it to your class if you are feeling brave.

Year 9

Strengths Builders:

1. Create your own Strength in Action Story – Make up a story that contains a character or characters who are Persistent and keep working at something no matter how much they want to give up, until they finally succeed. Write or draw or tell your story of Persistence in action.
2. Make a list of activities or tasks you are required to do at school in which you need to use Persistence in order to complete them. Order your list from the hardest to the easiest. Compare your list with a friend. See if you can start one today.

Strengths Challenge:

What other strengths might a person who is very persistent, such as a famous inventor, have?

Closing Activity:

1. Reflect: is persistence one of your key strengths?
2. Close your eyes and recall a happy memory. Good mood improves the ability to persist.

3. Tell a Persistence in Action story.

Display Suggestion: A Mosaic pattern, embroidery, or weaving all require persistence. Start a display that will, by its nature, take time to finish. Set a goal of the end of term.

PSHE: Programme of Study for Key Stage 3 Links

Personal well-being

Key Concepts:

1.1 Personal identities

Persistence, which leads to achievement, builds what psychologists call 'self-efficacy', a sense that 'I can do things', which is vital to self-esteem.

Story: Thomas Edison

'Genius is 1% inspiration, 99% perspiration.'

Born in 1847, Thomas Edison is known worldwide as a famous inventor – he invented the electric light bulb, and many other things too. He was successful – but success didn't come easily to him and he only succeeded because he didn't give up.

Thomas spent only 12 weeks at school – when he was 7. His poor behaviour and lack of concentration led his teacher to say that he had serious problems and would never amount to anything. So his mother withdrew him from school and, convinced that he was bright, she taught him at home. Thomas could have been devastated by what the teacher said but he didn't give up. He read widely, he began to do his own scientific experiments... and he kept going.

The family was not well off. Thomas had to help to earn a living by selling sweets and newspapers on railway trains and growing vegetables to make ends meet. In early life he developed hearing problems – yes, Thomas had special needs! He said his hearing became much worse when a train conductor hit him round the head and threw him off the train because a case he was carrying caught fire – it was the case in which he kept the chemicals for his experiments – but Thomas wasn't put off – he kept going.

He was given his first proper job as a telegraph operator when he was 19 but he didn't want to give up reading or experimenting so he did night shifts, which were quieter, and spent the rest of the time on his experiments. One night he spilt sulphuric acid on his boss's desk. The next day he was fired. He went to live with a friend who put him up for nothing. He was poor, he was jobless, he was homeless... but Edison didn't give up. He kept going and his first patented invention was recorded when he was 22.

By the time he was 29 Edison had made enough money from his inventions to open a laboratory and to employ workers to help with his experiments. It was the world's first industrial research lab and it went on to produce one of Edison's most famous inventions – the electric light bulb. Edison did not invent the *first* light bulb, but he did invent the first light bulb that worked well enough to sell. He changed first one thing, then another. He and his workers tried endless experiments – some say as many as 499 – all failures. But then the 500th experiment was a success. Why? Because Edison didn't give up – he believed he would succeed, so he worked as hard as he could and he kept going.

Edison wasn't just an inventor. Selling sweets and newspapers on trains when he was a hard up teenager showed him he was also a natural born businessman and he founded 14 different companies in his lifetime, one of which – General Electric – is still trading and is one of the largest companies in the world. Like Edison, it keeps going.

Opportunities to build Persistence across the curriculum:

PE: *Developing skill at any sport requires persistence and the acceptance of failure – some of the time.*

English: *There is a renewed interest in learning poetry by heart – a great opportunity to practice persistence.*

Languages: *Learning other languages requires persistence.*

Music: *Mastering an instrument requires persistence.*

FIFTEEN

Open-Mindedness

Open-mindedness is an uncommon strength, in that most of us possess its opposite – *myside bias* – to a greater or lesser extent. Myside bias is the tendency to look for, and find, evidence that supports what we already think – we read newspapers whose bias we agree with, we mix with people who share our political and cultural prejudices.

Open-mindedness is a way of thinking that examines all sides of an argument, plan or belief equally. It is not an indecisive form of thinking – there is evidence that open-minded thinkers make better decisions because they don't ignore evidence they don't like or jump to conclusions. Open-minded thinkers will change their minds when confronted with evidence that contradicts their opinions.

Open-mindedness sometimes, but not always, increases with age and education. It can be inhibited by time pressure. Other things that inhibit open-mindedness are our tendency to seek out evidence that confirms our existing beliefs, our tendency to believe the first evidence we find more than subsequent evidence, and a tendency to polarise, to be more critical of evidence that contradicts our beliefs than we are of evidence that supports it.

It is possible that the deliberate teaching of enquiry and dialogue and encouragement to look for opposing evidence may encourage the development of open-mindedness. In a study, philosophy students were less prone to myside bias than other graduates.

Key features of Open-Mindedness:

- Corrects the natural human tendency to find evidence to support what we are already thinking
- May be encouraged by philosophical enquiry and dialogic teaching

Definition: You enjoy meeting people with different ideas and backgrounds. You can see different points of view.

Benefits: More complex, balanced thinking is associated with better results in many cognitive tasks. Open-mindedness protects people from being manipulated and can help with stress management.

Quotes:

'Two people can look at the same thing and see something entirely different.' – **Johnny Nesbit**

'I have often said that if science proves facts that conflict with Buddhist understanding, Buddhism must change accordingly.' – **The Dalai Lama**

Thinking Questions:

- What is open-mindedness?
- What are the advantages of being open-minded?
- What are the disadvantages of being open-minded?

Strengths Builders and Strengths Challenges:

<u>Year 7</u>

Strengths Builders:

1. Design an Open-Mindedness Superhero.
2. Play Same or Different. Work with a partner. Can you find three things you agree about and three things you disagree about? Try this with as many people as you can.

Strengths Challenge:

For one week make sure that you listen to people and hear what they are saying before making a decision about how you think or feel about what they are saying.

Year 8

Strengths Builders:

1. Strength in Action Story – Can you remember a time when you or somebody you know was able to be Open-Minded in a situation and see things from someone else's point of view? Write or draw or tell a story of Open-Mindedness in action.

2. Look in a newspaper. Can you find an opinion or idea you agree with? Can you find one you disagree with? Compare your views with a friend.

Strengths Challenge:

Choose a topic that people have strong opinions about, like hunting or abortion. Ask lots of people what they think and try to collect as many different opinions as you can. Make a list!

Year 9

Strengths Builders:

1. Create your own Strength in Action Story – Make up a story that contains a character or characters who use Open-Mindedness in a situation. Write or draw or tell your story of Open-Mindedness in action.

2. With a partner, discuss your opinions about whether you should wear school uniforms. Discuss the issue from your point of view and from that of your school and parents. What is your point of view? What is the point of view of your school, your parents, or the community?

Strengths Challenge:

If you could rename this strength, what name would you choose?

Closing Activity: Try to recall a time you changed your mind and realised you were wrong about something or someone.

Display Suggestion: Things we think.

Use thought bubble templates to create a collage of opinions and ideas, emphasising the fact that we can hold different opinions about many things.

PSHE: Programme of Study for Key Stage 3 Links

Personal well-being

Key Concepts:

1.5 Diversity

Key Processes:

2.1 Critical reflection

2.3 Developing relationships and working with others

Students need to be able to appreciate the value of difference and of different opinions, as well as to critically examine their own.

Story: Oskar Schindler

Oskar Schindler was a German businessman and factory owner. After the German invasion of Poland he employed cheap Jewish labour in his factories. He did well, earning a lot of money and going to parties with SS officers.

Then, in 1942, he watched a raid by the SS on the Krakow Ghetto where Jews were rounded up for the concentration camps. This experience changed Schindler's life. He was appalled by the murder of some of the Jews who had worked for him, and so he began to take steps to protect them. He used his money, not for himself, but to bribe guards; he persuaded officials that women, children, and people with disabilities were 'essential mechanics, helping the war effort'; he smuggled children out of the ghetto and into safety.

By the end of the war he was penniless, having spent his fortune protecting the lives of 1200 Jews. He is known by Jews today as 'One of the Righteous'.

Opportunities to build Open-Mindedness across the curriculum:

Philosophical enquiry: *Used in any lesson, this process for encouraging students to examine both sides of an argument may lead to an increased tendency to be open-minded.*

RE: *The study of other faiths lends itself to considering views you don't agree with and examining your own.*

Collaborative working in any setting will help students appreciate that people think differently, have different opinions and different strengths.

SIXTEEN

Kindness

Kindness, generosity, compassion, altruistic love, and care are all closely related terms that indicate warmth towards others, a willingness to give without expecting anything back and a belief in the value of others. Such attitudes lie at the heart of moral and spiritual life in all major religions, stretching as far back as the Roman goddess Cura, the goddess of care. Helping others, though done for its own sake, has positive benefits for mental and even physical health, particularly as people age. It is therefore a useful strength, and indeed habit, to build when young.

It is possible that a kind disposition is largely inherited, but this is not to say that there is nothing we can do to encourage its development. One interesting fact is that people with a positive mood are more willing to help others than those with a neutral mood. Cheerfulness and a positive outlook encourage kindness.

There is little research to indicate what works in encouraging kindness and altruism. It is probable that kindness is learned mostly by example and is encouraged by a high degree of emphasis on its importance and value. Highlighting and valuing kindness and creating a strong sense that a classroom or a school is a place where kindness is the norm may encourage students to value and express kindness for themselves.

Key features of Kindness:

- Showing kindness to others both results from and leads to positive emotions
- People who help others have been shown to feel happier and to be healthier, especially in old age
- Kindness to others often leads to reciprocal kindness being shown to us so it can be a useful tool for building friendships
- Kindness is the cement that builds and strengthens positive relationships

Definition: You think about how other people feel, you do and say things to make other people happy. You are never too busy to do a favour.

Benefits: Kindness builds positive relationships, feels good to both parties and can improve our mental health.

Quotes:

'Being kind is more important than being right.' – **Johnny Nesbit**

'Be kind, for everyone you meet is fighting a hard battle.' – **Philo**

'The little unremembered acts of kindness and love are the best parts of a person's life.' – **William Wordsworth**

'Kindness has always mattered to our father. He taught us to honour people, and he has encouraged us since before I can remember to empathize with human suffering. When I was a teenager he'd say, "Ann, go and do something that helps people. Do something of service. It will always make you feel good about your life."' – **Ann Curry**

Thinking Questions:

- Is kindness important?
- Is there a difference between kindness and love?
- Is kindness ever wrong?

Strengths Builders and Strengths Challenges:

Year 7

Strengths Builders:

1. Design a Kindness Superhero.

2. Play the game of Stop-n-Go – Get a group of friends to hold hands in a circle. Get a teacher to yell 'Go' and walk in a circle until someone in the chain yells 'Stop'. Whoever yelled 'Stop' must say something nice about the person in the chain on their right side. The teacher must then say 'Go' again and the game has to go on until every person in the chain has had a chance to say something nice to the person next to them.

Strengths Challenge:

Do something today for a friend or family member that is kind. You could:

- Pay a compliment
- Spot and name a strength
- Make a cup of tea or coffee
- Smile at somebody
- Offer to help

Year 8

Strengths Builders:

1. Strength in Action Story – Can you remember at time when you or somebody you know has been Kind enough to do a favour for a friend or help someone who needed it? Write or draw or tell a story of Kindness in action.

2. With a friend, make a list of 'kind acts' you could do at school or at home. Share them out between you, do them and then report back to each other on how you felt.

Strengths Challenge:

Volunteer – when you hear somebody ask for help, put your hand up.

Year 9

Strengths Builders:

1. Create your own Strength in Action Story – Make up a story that contains a character or characters who are Kind to someone else by doing a favour for them or helping them when they needed it. Write or draw or tell your story of Kindness in action.

2. Think of some random acts of kindness you could carry out in the week ahead. Write them in your journal and tick them as you do them. If possible make them anonymous.

Strengths Challenge:

Go to: http://www.wisdomquotes.com/cat_kindness.html and pick a kindness quotation for the week and then write it in your notebook. Why not pick a new one for every week!

Closing Activity: Reflect for one minute on a kind person or a kindness you have shown or received.

Display Suggestion: Take one or more kindness quotes (you can find more at: http://www.actsofkindness.org) and use them as the basis for a display. You might adopt a graffiti style for the lettering and add to it images from magazines or the Internet that show kindness in practice.

PSHE: Programme of Study for Key Stage 3 Links

Personal well-being

Key Concepts:

1.4 Relationships

- Understanding that relationships affect everything we do in our lives and that relationship skills have to be learnt and practised.

Kindness to ourselves and others is one of the most important social skills students can learn.

Key Processes:

2.3 Developing relationships and working with others.

Pupils should be able to:

- Use social skills to build and maintain a range of positive relationships.

Kindness endears us to others and can lead to lasting friendships. Little kindnesses build strong relationships.

Students need to understand that one of the most effective ways of helping ourselves to feel good is to forget about ourselves and focus on other people's happiness.

Story: A Bowl made of Wood (from *The Old Man and his Grandson* by the Brothers Grimm)

An old woman lived with her son and his wife and their little son. This old woman loved her family very much and she helped them all she could, watching the child while his parents were busy working on the farm.

At night the farmer's wife lit the candles, laid a cloth on the table and got out her best china for dinner, but the old woman's hands shook as she ate and often she spilled her food and her drink onto the snowy white tablecloth. The farmer's wife would mop up the mess impatiently and the man would sigh and say nothing.

One evening the old woman was more tired and shaky than usual and as she raised her cup to her lips it fell from her hand and smashed on the floor tiles. The farmer's wife scolded her mother-in-law for her clumsiness and the farmer sighed and said nothing as his wife cleared up the mess. The farmer said nothing when his wife went to the dresser and took down a wooden cup and a wooden bowl and placed them before his mother. He said nothing when a tear rolled down his mother's face.

A few days later the farmer found his son whittling away at a piece of wood with his penknife. 'What you are making, little one?' he asked.

'I'm making two wooden bowls, one for you and one for mummy, ready for when you are old and shaky like Nana,' the boy replied with a smile.

The farmer said nothing, but that night the finest china was placed in front of the old woman, and the farmer and his wife cleared up all her spills with respect and tenderness.

Opportunities to build Kindness across the curriculum:

Drama: *Role play is a good opportunity to explore the different outcomes of kindness and unkindness.*

English: *Kindness and unkindness are frequent themes in literature.*

Consider holding a 'Kindness Day' rather than an Anti-Bullying Day. Research from positive psychology (Bargh, Chen & Burrows, 1996) suggests it may be more effective.

SEVENTEEN

Leadership

Leadership can be thought of as a role or a position that involves directing others, and it can also be thought of as a collection of personal qualities that motivate and enable a person to help, guide, and inspire others.

When somebody occupies a leadership position but lacks the personal qualities to lead they may be said to lack authority. When somebody has personal leadership qualities but does not occupy a leadership position then they may be said to exercise moral authority or influence.

The qualities that contribute to the strength of leadership include intelligence, social and emotional intelligence, empathy, self-awareness, honesty, and determination. Some of the best leaders are not necessarily charismatic, they are humble and persistent.

The teacher becomes a leader when he or she moves from 'delivering the curriculum' or 'managing the classroom' to inspiring students with a love of learning and a sense of their potential and then enabling them to fulfil that potential. Students become leaders not just when they assume a leadership position – head of house or team captain – but when they exercise a positive influence with their peers or with younger students.

We are all responsible for leading ourselves – for our own positive growth and development. Most of us are also in the position of leading others in some capacity – whether as teachers, parents or managers.

Leaders want power – which may be an uncomfortable thought – but they want power for the right reason, which is to help other people. Role models like Ghandi and Martin Luther King clearly demonstrate that, at its best, leadership is a form of service to others and is inspired by a desire to serve others.

Key features of Leadership:

- Can be seen as a strength or personal quality as well as a role
- Can be exercised without a formal leadership role
- Involves a clear motivation to help other people

Definition: You help other people get things done. You set a good example. You like organising activities and making things happen.

Benefits: Leading other people well benefits *them* and benefits *us*. There is huge satisfaction in helping other people to grow and develop. The Dalai Lama calls helping others being 'wisely selfish' since it results in our own happiness.

Quotes:

'Life's persistent and most urgent question is: what you are doing for others?' – **Martin Luther King Jr**

'If your actions inspire others to dream more, learn more, do more and become more, you are a leader.' – **John Quincy Adams**

Thinking Questions:

- What is leadership?
- What makes a good/bad leader?
- Can anybody be a leader?

Strengths Builders and Strengths Challenges:

Year 7

Strengths Builders:

1. Design a Leadership Superhero.

2. Can you think of somebody who is a good leader? With a friend, try to decide what makes them a good leader. Make a list of these things. Can you try to be a little bit like them?

Strengths Challenge:

Volunteer to organise the students of your class to take part in a group activity. You could encourage everyone to:

- Pick up litter
- Tidy the classroom
- Make a 'thank you' card for one of the caretakers or cleaners or teachers

Year 8

Strengths Builders:

1. Strength in Action Story – Can you remember a time when you or somebody you know displayed good Leadership skills? Write or draw or tell a story of Leadership in action.

2. Teachers are leaders. Design your ideal teacher. Make a list of what they would do and what they would be like. You can draw a diagram if it helps!

Strengths Challenge:

The best leaders are often both modest and kind. Can you find kind and encouraging things to say to younger pupils at school, younger friends or siblings, or just to your classmates?

Year 9

Strengths Builders:

1. Create your own Strength in Action Story – Make up a story that contains a character or characters who display good Leadership skills. Write or draw or tell your story of Leadership in action.

2. What makes a good leader? Can you make a list of qualities that make a leader a good leader?

Strengths Challenge:

Volunteer to complete or organise a group to complete an unpleasant task and make sure that it gets done.

Closing Activity: Spend a minute thinking about one leadership quality you can show today.

Display Suggestion: Good Leaders of the World

Create a display that contains words that show the characteristics of good leaders together with pictures of people the students consider to be good leaders today or from history.

PSHE: Programme of Study for Key Stage 3 Links

Personal well-being

Key Concepts:

1.1 Personal identities

1.4 Relationships

Key Processes:

2.1 Critical reflection

2.3 Developing relationships and working with others

> **Story: A Wise Ring and a Good King**
>
> King Solomon was one of ancient Israel's most famous and wisest leaders. This story is told about him.
>
> The captain of King Solomon's guards was a brave and loyal man who loved his king and who did whatever he was asked to do. One day, King Solomon heard the guard talking to his friends, 'Whatever the king asks me to do,' said the captain, 'I can do it. I can do any and everything he asks of me.'
>
> Now King Solomon thought the guard was boasting and decided to teach him a lesson in modesty. 'I shall set him an impossible task,' thought the king, 'to teach him that nobody can do everything.'
>
> King Solomon summoned his captain of the guards and told him that he had heard of a magical ring that would make a happy man sad and a sad man happy. He asked the captain to find the ring and bring it to him before six months had passed.
>
> The captain at once said that he would find the ring and set out to look for it. He asked at all the jewellers' stalls in the market but none of the stall holders had ever heard of such a ring. He asked all the merchants that he knew, but none of them had ever heard of such a ring either. He travelled more widely, to all the cities in Israel, asking everyone he met if they knew of a ring that would make a happy man sad and a sad man happy, but each person he asked shook their head.
>
> The captain visited all the ports and all the bazaars throughout the length and breadth of Israel, but nowhere could he find a trace of the magic ring. The man grew miserable and tired and desperate as the weeks passed and turned into months – he feared that at last he would let down his beloved king. As he turned and travelled sadly back to the palace of King Solomon, when his six months were nearly up, he passed a small boy selling trinkets on the roadside. Determined to keep trying till the very end, he asked the boy if he had a ring that would make a sad man happy and a happy man sad. The boy shook his head puzzled, but the boy's grandfather overheard the captain's request. The old man smiled and said, 'I think I can give you the ring you seek,' and he took a simple gold band and engraved some words upon it and gave it to the captain. The captain's tired face lit up with joy when he read what was written upon the ring and he turned and headed back to the king's palace with a new spring in his step.
>
> King Solomon was feasting with his friends when the captain entered the palace. The king didn't want to embarrass the man and quietly went up to him to reassure him that it was alright to fail sometimes and that nobody could do everything he was asked to do. But the captain handed the king the ring and the king's face fell. On the ring were the Hebrew letters gimmel, zayin and yud and they stood for the saying, 'This too shall pass,' meaning that nothing lasts for ever. As the king looked at his palace and his friends and his wealth he remembered that one day it would all be gone. He also realised that, to anyone who was suffering misfortune, the words would bring comfort, because unhappiness fades with time. This was indeed the magic ring that would make a happy man sad and a sad man happy that he had asked his captain to find for him.
>
> Then King Solomon smiled and asked his captain's pardon for trying to catch him out. He took a great diamond ring from his finger and placed it on the captain's hand and he put the ring the captain had brought for him onto his finger instead. Whenever the king looked at the ring, it reminded him of the value of love and of loyalty and of how soon all things pass, and it helped him to rule wisely and well throughout his long life.

Opportunities to build Leadership across the curriculum:

History: *Studying great leaders, like Napoleon and Churchill, can lead to discussion of what makes good leadership.*

RE: *Great religious leaders provide more opportunities to study what makes a good leader.*

PE: *PE is an obvious subject in which to work on good leadership.*

Any group work can provide opportunities for students to exercise good leadership, to learn to listen, to encourage others, to help others agree and complete a task.

EIGHTEEN

Love of Learning

Love of learning is a desire to acquire new skills or knowledge or to build on existing skills and knowledge. It is closely related to creativity and can lead to more satisfaction and enjoyment of school, better relationships with teachers, and a greater sense of optimism about the future. Continuing to learn new things helps us remain mentally flexible as we age.

Learning contains an element of anxiety – we have to be able to tolerate uncertainty and a degree of failure in order to learn something new. For this reason, students who already feel a high degree of anxiety may find learning more challenging.

Somebody who loves to learn experiences positive feelings as they learn something new, or after a period of study. Such positive feelings help them persist and to bear the frustrations that learning entails. Love of Learning is not dependent on benefits such as exam success or career prospects but is a love of learning new things for their own sake. Even those who do not enjoy learning generally usually enjoy learning about something of particular interest to them and this can be used to build a love of learning more generally.

Love of learning gives students intrinsic motivation – they learn because they want to, not because they have to. It is possible that an overemphasis on grades and exams in schools may actually inhibit a genuine love of learning.

Love of learning is promoted by a focus on 'mastery' goals; i.e., learning skills and gaining competence, rather than on 'performance' goals – getting good marks, scoring 10 out of 10. It is encouraged by praise that focuses on effort rather than achievement. It is also facilitated by a positive view of failure – failure is GOOD – it is how we learn.

To praise a child for intelligence is like praising them for having blue eyes – what counts is how they *use* that intelligence.

Key features of Love of Learning:

- Is an intrinsic motivator
- Is promoted by a focus on mastery not performance
- Is enhanced by praise for effort, not attainment
- Requires a positive view of failure

Definition: You love learning new things. You enjoy finding out how to do things, you like discovering things you didn't know before.

Benefits: Love of learning helps students to enjoy school, to remain flexible as they enter the workplace and to age positively.

Quotes:

'We must learn to reawaken, and keep ourselves awake.' - **Henry David Thoreau**

'The beginning of knowledge is the discovery of something we do not understand.' **Frank Herbert**

'The good life is inspired by love and guided by knowledge.' **Bertrand Russell**

Thinking Questions:

- Is learning important?
- Where do you learn the most?

- Is there a disadvantage to loving to learn?

Strengths Builders and Strengths Challenges:

Year 7

Strengths Builders:

1. Design a Love of Learning Superhero.

2. Make a list of things that interest you. Try to find out one new fact about each of the things on your list and write them down on a new facts list. Swap your new facts with a friend. To find your facts you could:

    - Look in a book
    - Look on the Internet
    - Ask an 'expert'

Strengths Challenge:

Find out even more about something that interests you. You could:

- Watch a documentary
- Look in a book
- Look on the Internet
- Ask an 'expert'

Year 8

Strengths Builders:

1. Strength in Action Story – Do you or somebody you know love to learn new things? Write or draw the story of Love of Learning in action.

2. Look in a dictionary for a word you don't know. Read the definition and make up a sentence with the word in it. Say the sentence to a friend and see if they can guess what the word means. Try to guess what their word means. Here are some uncommon words to start you off:

    - Tremulous
    - Noctilucent
    - Flibbertigibbet
    - Loquacious

Strengths Challenge:

Think of one or more individuals from history who loved learning new things. For example, you could research famous inventors or scientists. Find out what you can about them. Ask your teacher if you can present your findings to the class.

Year 9

Strengths Builders:

1. Create your own Strength in Action Story – Make up a story that contains a character or characters who Love to Learn. Write or draw or tell your story of Love of Learning in action.

2. Investigate the history of a famous monument; find out why it was built, who built it, and who it was built for? Examples include:

    - The Statue of Liberty
    - The Eiffel Tower

- Nelson's Column
- The Taj Mahal

Strengths Challenge:

Find out about a famous inventor. Why was their invention so important? Tell a family member or friend what you find out about this inventor. Examples include:

- Thomas Edison
- Alexander Graham Bell
- Henry Ford

Closing Activity: Share one thing you have learned in this lesson. This may be an idea you hadn't thought of before or an opinion somebody expressed which you didn't know they held.

Display Suggestion: Giant Steps.

Think, with your students, of great steps forward in learning – how to make fire, how to make clothes, how to speak, the wheel, agriculture, how to write, how to make metal, etc. Use these stepping stones to build a pathway from the past to the future. Perhaps they can imagine future steps forward in learning?

PSHE: Programme of Study for Key Stage 3 Links

Personal well-being

Key Concepts:

1.3 Risk

All learning involves risk – we have to risk the discomfort of not understanding in order to push ourselves beyond what we already know.

1.4 Relationships

All learning happens in a relationship, and the quality of our relationships affects the quality of our learning.

Key Processes:

2.1 Critical reflection

2.2 Decision-making and managing risk

Story: Afghanistan

The right to a free education for all children is one of the most widely accepted human rights. In many parts of the world, however, this right is ignored. 125 million children worldwide can't go to school either through poverty or because they are girls and the education of girls is not seen as important in their country.

In Afghanistan, between 1996 and 2001 a group called the Taliban, an extreme Muslim group, banned the education of all girls. Women and girls were all excluded from education – from primary school to university. Female teachers weren't allowed to work, all girls' schools were closed and girls and women risked being beaten if they went outside without a man and without being covered up from head to toe.

Some parents secretly educated their daughters at home. Some women and girls risked their lives to attend secret schools.

Today the situation in Afghanistan is better but not great for girls and for women. Women teachers and girls are still sometimes murdered for going to school – murdered because they value education. One girl, 16-year-old Anita, said 'It is difficult but we have to come to classes. It is our duty to be educated. Our families are happy that we come to school but they worry about our security.' Some of her classmates have stopped attending because of the threats though, she admitted.

For poor countries the education of girls leads to an increase in prosperity and in how long the whole population can expect to live. Education and learning has always been the real way out of poverty.

School facts:

- 4 to 5% of Afghan children had access to primary education under the Taliban, almost none of them girls
- 5.4 million children, about half, are enrolled in schools today
- 35% of the pupils are girls
- 28% of Afghans are literate
- 6% of schools have been closed due to terrorism

Opportunities to build Love of learning across the curriculum:

The aim of any school subject is to inspire a love of learning. Allowing students to follow their enthusiasms and to learn things that are NOT on the curriculum and which will NOT be examined can support a love of learning.

NINETEEN

Modesty

This may be the *best* introduction to the subject of modesty you will EVER read!!! Ah... whoops!

Modesty (or humility) is not top of the list of most people's preferred strengths. Modesty is one of the least common strengths universally, along with prudence and wisdom!

For centuries, pride was seen as wrong and modesty, its opposite, as a virtue. In our modern, 'feel good about yourself' culture it is possible we have swung too far the other way. While feeling good about oneself does lead to benefits like the confidence to pursue goals and positive emotions, there are also benefits to be obtained from a humble view of ourselves.

Modesty and/or humility are often confused with timidity. In fact, humility is an attribute of some of the greatest business leaders, people who lead their companies to greatness but avoid personal adulation. They direct praise to others, not to themselves. The co-founder of Hewlett-Packard, David Packard, is quoted as saying, 'You shouldn't gloat about anything you've done; you ought to keep going and find something better to do.' Modesty takes a quiet pride in its achievements but is not arrogant or boastful. It need not imply a negative view of the self, but an accurate, not over-inflated view of the self.

Modesty also implies an acceptance of one's own shortcomings, not an over-harsh view of the self. It can include a sense of wonder at the immensity of the universe, and of our own quite small place within it.

Key features of Modesty:

- An accurate (not underestimated) sense of our abilities and achievements
- The ability to own up to mistakes, weaknesses, gaps in knowledge
- Openness to new ideas, contradictory information and advice
- The ability to forget about the self and focus on others or on a greater goal
- Keeping own abilities and achievements in perspective
- Valuing other people and the world around us

Definition: You know your strengths and your weaknesses. You are always happy to learn from other people. When you do well you share your success with those who helped you.

Benefits: A modest person has a quiet strength – they don't need to impress others and are always willing to learn. They can forget about themselves and put others first. Modest people can be very popular – no one really likes people who are full of themselves.

Quotes:

'Humility is to make a right estimate of oneself.' – **Charles H. Spurgeon**

'Pride is concerned with who *is right. Humility is concerned with* what *is right.'* – **Ezra Taft Benson**

Thinking Questions:

- If somebody has NO humility, what are they like?
- Many religions value humility. Why?
- Is pride wrong?

Strengths Builders and Strengths Challenges:

Year 7

Strengths Builders:

1. Design a Modesty Superhero.
2. Find somebody in the class who is better than you at something. Ask them to tell you how you could improve. Work with them on getting better.

Strengths Challenge:

Make a list of your strengths and weaknesses.

Year 8

Strengths Builders:

1. Strength in Action Story – Can you remember a time when you or somebody you know used this strength? Do you know somebody who is never proud or boastful, no matter what they achieve? Write or draw or tell a story of Modesty in action.
2. Praising other people takes courage and modesty. Make a card for a friend or family member with a genuine compliment inside or a statement that recognises one of their strengths. Send it to them.

Strengths Challenge:

Hidden Actions – Plan an action that will help somebody, your family, or your school, that you can do in secret, without anyone knowing. Do it without telling them it was you.

Year 9

Strengths Builders:

1. Create your own Strength in Action Story – Make up a story that contains a character or characters who display the strength of Modesty or who use Modesty in a situation. Write or draw or tell your story of Modesty in action.
2. My Strengths and Weaknesses – Being modest means knowing your strengths and your weaknesses. Can you write a list of your own strengths and weaknesses in your journal?

Strengths Challenge:

For the whole day do not talk about yourself at all.

Closing activity

1. Tell a Modesty in Action story
2. Spend a few minutes quietly reflecting on people you need.

Display suggestion: Ordinary people

Collect images of the ordinary but vital people without whom society would fall apart – the cleaners, the shop assistants, the mothers pushing prams, the dads playing football in the park, the dustbin men, etc.

PSHE: Programme of Study for Key Stage 3 Links

Personal well-being

Key Concepts:

1.1 Personal identities

Humility is a true knowledge of our strengths and weaknesses.

While self-esteem is important, inflated self-esteem does not make us popular.

Key Processes:

2.1 Critical reflection

1.3 Developing relationships and working with others

A true estimate of our strengths and weaknesses helps us to see what we can contribute to others and what they can contribute to us. A willingness to let others shine is an important aspect of teamwork.

> **Story: A Coin Worth all the World**
>
> This story is set in China, long ago. It is the story of a statue of the Buddha which stands in a very old temple. It is a tall statue made of bronze, nearly ten feet high, and on its breast is a tiny copper coin, a coin that would buy almost nothing.
>
> It is also the story of a girl, a little girl whose parents were so poor that they sold her as a slave to a rich household. This girl was not unhappy. Though she had no one to play with – or time to play – no toys, no possessions of her own, no money and no freedom, she did have food to eat and clothes to wear and a mat to sleep on at night, and many people in China in those days had much less than that. No, she was not unhappy, but she did think, sometimes, that it would be good to have just one small thing to call her own.
>
> One day, she found that one small thing. While she was sweeping the yard early in the morning, she found a tiny copper coin. To most people it was almost worthless but to the little girl its worth was beyond price. It was dirty, it was tiny, it would buy her almost nothing, but it was hers, and to her it was worth the whole world.
>
> A few days later a young priest called at the household where the little slave girl lived. He was collecting gold and treasure and money for a new statue of the Buddha. The people of that country were Buddhists and they honoured the gentle teacher who had been loving, wise, and good, and they were eager to give what they could to make a new and beautiful statue of their teacher, the Buddha.
>
> The rich ladies brought their bracelets, the men brought their golden cups; even the servants found coins of silver or copper. And the great mound of treasure grew in the centre of the courtyard and the young priest smiled. Then the little slave girl stepped forward and happily held out her tiny copper coin, thrilled that she, too, had something to give for the statue of the Buddha.
>
> But the young priest frowned. He looked at the coin in her hand. It was dirty, it was tiny, it would buy almost nothing. 'This coin is worthless,' he said. 'It is certainly not worthy of a statue of the great Buddha.' And he shook his head at the girl and gathered up his load of treasure and proudly took it back to the temple to give it to the chief priest of the monastery.
>
> Other priests came back, bearing more treasure, and soon there was enough metal to melt down to make the statue, the statue to the wise, loving, and gentle Buddha. So the metal was melted down and poured into the mould and set to cool, but when the mould was taken away the statue was marked with ugly lines and patches. 'The metal must have been badly mixed,' they said. So they tried again, more carefully this time, but the same thing happened – the metal was marked with ugly lines and patches.
>
> Then the chief priest called the other priests together and asked, 'Was all of this metal given and received with love, for only love can make a statue of the one who taught us how to love?'
>
> And the young priest who had visited the slave girl hung his head in shame and told the chief priest how he had refused a dirty, tiny, gift of love. The chief priest sent him back to the slave girl.
>
> Once more the slave girl stood before the young priest, holding out her coin. It was dirty, it was tiny, it would buy almost nothing. But the young priest said, 'This coin is worth the whole world, please forgive me.' And the slave girl smiled and gave him her dirty, tiny gift of love.
>
> When the great statue was finished and the mould was opened, there it stood, beautiful and smiling and perfect. On the breast of the statue, just over the heart of the Buddha, was a tiny, copper coin. It was no longer dirty, but still a tiny gift of love, worth the whole world.

Opportunities to build Humility across the curriculum:

Perhaps the best way to encourage humility or modesty is for the teacher of any subject to be comfortable about admitting what they don't know and to acknowledge mistakes. In addition:

Science: *In science we seek to test hypotheses, to be open to contradictory evidence and to change our minds when new facts emerge. All of this requires us to accept that we don't know everything.*

RE: *Humility is explicitly taught by different faiths. Stories of humility can be explored in different faith traditions.*

PE: *Modesty in victory is a good habit to develop.*

History: *Students might research some of the unsung heroes of history, e.g., William Wilberforce is usually credited with the abolition of slavery, but in fact it was a small group of Quakers who persuaded him to get involved and to bring a bill before parliament. Quakers were not allowed to be MPs so they needed Wilberforce to be the public face of their campaign.*

TWENTY

Wisdom

Wisdom is defined by psychologists in different ways. Some see it as knowing what is truly important in life and how to obtain it (Baltes & Staudinger, 2000) – a wise person is one with expertise in how to live a meaningful life. Another view is that wisdom lies in balancing one's own interests with those of other people and society, and of living in a way that brings benefits to self and others (Sternberg, 1998).

Peterson & Seligman (2004) include wisdom in the list of 24 universal character strengths which form the foundation of *Strengths Gym*. They see wisdom as just another strength and argue that we should cultivate more of our top five strengths and use them as often and as much as possible. Other writers, however, take issue with this approach. They argue that more of a strength is not always better and that wisdom should be placed above the other strengths, as it is essential to the appropriate use of all the others. From this alternative perspective, without wisdom it is impossible to decide which strength a situation calls for – and how much of it we should use. Should we be honest when asked for an opinion about whether a friend looks good in a particular dress – or should we be kind? It is wisdom that helps us decide (Schwartz & Sharpe, 2006).

For many, wisdom is associated with age – but this is not necessarily the case. Young people and children can display wisdom and not all people grow wiser with age. Wisdom is not the same as intelligence – it is possible to be very clever but not very wise. Wise people possess clear insight into themselves and others, they possess good judgment and can give good advice, and they use their insight and abilities to promote their own well-being and that of other people. A wise person also knows their limitations – they know how much they do not know and will ask for help and advice when they need it.

It is how we meet the struggles and challenges of life that allows us to develop wisdom and it may be that wise friends, or mentors, can help us to become wiser ourselves. Reflection and dialogue can promote wisdom. The philosophical discussions that are a key part of *Strengths Gym* are intended to create the environment in which students can learn from each other and develop their own wisdom.

Key features of Wisdom:

- Is a key strength which allows us to use other strengths appropriately
- Is found in the young as well as the old
- Grows through overcoming challenges and through reflection

Definition: You understand what is really important in life. Somehow, you always know the right thing to do or say.

Benefits: Wisdom helps us enjoy life as we get older.

Quotes:

'True wealth is not measured in money or status or power. It is measured in the legacy we leave behind for those we love and those we inspire.' – **Cesar Chavez**

'A hundred times a day I remind myself that my inner and outer life depend on the labours of other people, living and dead, and that I must exert myself in order to give in the full measure I have received and am still receiving.' – **Albert Einstein**

'Wisdom is having humility, kindness, intelligence and understanding – and knowing how to deal with people who don't.' – **Johnny Nesbit**

Thinking Questions:

- What is wisdom?

- How do you become wise?
- Are there any disadvantages to wisdom?
- Is wisdom related to age or can anyone be wise?
- What other qualities or strengths do wise people have?

Strengths Builders and Strengths Challenges:

Year 7

Strengths Builders:

1. Design a Wisdom Superhero.

2. Play Agony Aunt (or Uncle). Work in threes. One of you makes up a 'problem'. Agony Aunt 1 gives some good advice. Agony Aunt 2 tries to give even better advice. Decide which advice is wisest. Then swap roles.

Strengths Challenge:

Who is the wisest person you know? Ask them what they think about something and listen hard to what they say.

Year 8

Strengths Builders:

1. Strength in Action Story – Have you or somebody you know ever been Wise enough to help a friend with a problem? In what ways did you help? Write or draw or tell a story of Wisdom in action.

2. Who do you think was the wisest person who ever lived and why? Join with a friend or friends who agree with your choice. As a group make a list of the facts you know about this person. Compare and discuss your person and list of facts with another group. What things do your lists have in common?

Strengths Challenge:

Find examples of two people from history that were considered wise, such as a religious leader, a famous writer/philosopher, or a politician. Find out an interesting fact about each of them. Share what you found out with a friend, family member, or teacher. Need help? Go to: http://en.wikipedia.org.

Year 9

Strengths Builders:

1. Create your own Strength in Action Story – Make up a story that contains a character or characters who use Wisdom in helping someone else. Write or draw or tell your story of Wisdom in action.

2. Name other qualities or other strengths that you think a person would need to possess in order to be considered Wise. Discuss and compare your choices with a friend and see if you can both come up with someone who fits the descriptions you have made.

Strengths Challenge:

Find examples of one or more people from history who were considered wise – for example, a religious leader, a famous writer/philosopher, or a politician. Make a list of the other strengths you think this person or people might have had in order to do their job well or to hold their position.

Closing Activity: Think of a wise person, one you know or one from a film. Have a conversation with them in your head about something you need to do or something that worries you. What advice do they give you?

Display Suggestion: Wisdom Quotes

Collect wise sayings from films, books, and teachers! Create a display based around these sayings.

PSHE: Programme of Study for Key Stage 3 Links

Personal well-being

All of the concepts and processes within the PSHE curriculum can be seen as contributing to, or benefiting from, the exercise of wisdom. To encourage wisdom in each distinct area, teachers might employ a philosophical approach that allows the expression of a range of opinions and time for reflection.

Key Concepts:

1.1 Personal identities

1.2 Healthy lifestyles

1.3 Risk

1.4 Relationships

1.5 Diversity

Key Processes:

2.1 Critical reflection

2.2 Decision-making and managing risk

2.3 Developing relationships and working with others

Wisdom requires self-awareness and awareness of others. It goes beyond knowledge of how to work with and motivate others, however, to the desire to benefit others as well as oneself.

Stories: The Smuggler

A man arrived at the border between two countries, leading a donkey with straw piled high on its back. The border guard stopped him. 'Are you carrying anything valuable that you plan to sell? If you are you must pay a fee.'

'Have a look,' said the donkey driver. 'If you find anything except straw I'll gladly pay your fee.' The suspicious border guard searched the straw bales thoroughly until the ground all around him was littered with straw. He found nothing so, reluctantly, he allowed the man to cross the border.

The next day the man returned to the border with a donkey piled high with more straw bales. The border guard, convinced that the man was a smuggler, searched every inch of straw bale but, once more, he found nothing and he had to let the man pass.

The next day and the next, for TEN years, the man arrived at the border with a donkey laden with straw and every day the border guard carefully searched the bundles but found – nothing.

At last the border guard retired, but he couldn't get the man with the donkey and the straw out of his head. He thought about him day after day, wondering what he had been smuggling and how he had hidden it. One day, walking along the street, the border guard saw the man's familiar face in the crowd and rushed over to him. 'Tell me,' he begged. 'I must know! You were smuggling, weren't you?' The man smiled and nodded. 'What?' asked the border guard frantically, 'what was it you were smuggling to the market?'

'Donkeys' said the man.

Opportunities to build Wisdom across the curriculum:

Science: *Studying the ethical issues behind science will provide opportunities for students to consider whether, just because we can do something, it is necessarily **wise** to do it.*

RE: *Proverbs is a book of the Bible that is sometimes called 'Wisdom' literature. Other scriptures also aim to build wisdom. Students might look at some scripture in translation and consider whether it encourages wisdom.*

Literature: *Literature helps us to consider what is important in life – what is wise and what is foolish.*

TWENTY-ONE

Self-Control

Self-control is about how we manage our impulses, emotions, desires, and actions so that we live healthily and happily, achieve our goals and bring benefits and not harm to those around us. Infants want instant gratification – they want what they want and they want it now. As we mature we learn to delay immediate satisfaction of our wants in order to achieve longer-term goals.

People with self-control set goals for themselves and monitor their thoughts and feelings, changing their behaviour as appropriate to achieve those goals. Self-awareness is an important aspect of self-control because many of our 'wants' start with a thought – 'I want that bar of chocolate', 'I want those trainers'. If we can become more aware of our thoughts we can choose whether or not to turn them into actions.

Research indicates that self-control is a little like a muscle – it becomes depleted after use. This means that if we have to use a lot of self-control in one situation we will have less of it to use in another. Conversely, also like a muscle, we can build our self-control – the more we use it, the more we are able to use it. This means that students who engage in a sport that requires self-discipline should be more able to show self-discipline in other settings. A study showed that people who worked on their self-control through daily exercises, like improving their posture, improved their capacity to show self-control in other areas. Paying attention to little things makes a difference.

Another interesting line of research shows that thinking through situations in advance and deciding what we are going to do makes actual self-control in that situation more likely. If we decide that, *if provoked by our neighbour we will keep calm and remain polite*, we are more likely to achieve this in real life. When set an essay, students who were asked to think about when and where they would write it were more likely to complete the assignment.

The implication of self-control being a limited resource is that, in order to live a well-regulated life, we need routine and structure and habit to guide many of our activities so that we can save conscious self-control for more challenging situations. Basically, if there are no biscuits in the house I don't have to exert self-control not to eat them; if I have formed a habit of exercising straight after work I don't have to think about whether I feel like it or not.

Self-control of our emotions is an important aspect of forming good relationships; students with good self-control are more popular and also do better academically.

Globally, we see the results of a lack of self-control in humanity's mismanagement of the earth – in overexploitation of natural resources, in global warming, in the extinction of species through over hunting, in overspending and debt, in rising alcohol abuse, in warfare and violence.

Self-control is a rather 'negative' strength in some ways in that it is characterised by what we don't do. It may be more helpful to focus on the positive qualities that we do want – moderation, appreciation, politeness and consideration for others – rather than on the excesses we don't want.

Key features of Self-Control:

- Is important for good relationships and success in life
- Is like a muscle that gets tired
- Can be increased through practice and effort
- Can be increased through rehearsing what we will (or won't) do in advance

Definition: You are in charge of your thoughts, feelings and actions. You can keep calm, you can do what you need to do.

Benefits: People with good self-control have higher self-acceptance and self-esteem, better relationships, better academic achievement and typically an absence of problems like debt, alcoholism, drug abuse.

Quotes:

'As far as your self-control goes, as far goes your freedom.' – **Marie Von Ebner-Eschenback**

'Kindness trumps greed: it asks for sharing. Kindness trumps fear: it calls forth gratefulness and love. Kindness trumps even stupidity, for with sharing and love, one learns.' – **Marc Estrin**

Thinking Questions

- What is self-control?
- What are the results of a lack of self-control? Personally or as a planet?
- Is self-control a good thing?

Strengths Builders and Strengths Challenges:

Year 7

Strengths Builders:

1. Design a Self-Control Superhero.
2. Draw three situations where you find it hard to keep calm. Imagine yourself being 'super cool' in each one.

Strengths Challenge:

Eat extra fruit or vegetables or do extra exercise this week.

Year 8

Strengths Builders:

1. Strength in Action Story – Can you remember a time when you or somebody you know used Self-Control in a difficult situation? Write or draw or tell a story of Self-Control in action.
2. Plan a new project, draw up a list of steps you will need to take, and take the first step in class if you can. Stick with your project until it is finished.

Strengths Challenge:

Watch no TV and play no computerised games at all for three days this week. Instead you could:

- Read a book
- Do some exercise
- Play with your little brother or sister
- Talk to your mum or dad
- Play a board game with your family

Year 9

Strengths Builders:

1. Create your own Strength in Action Story – Make up a story that contains a character or characters who use Self-Control in a difficult situation. Write or draw or tell your story of Self-Control in action.
2. With a friend make a list of situations where you can imagine yourself needing to use self-control. See how many different situations you can come up with together. Once you have your list, discuss what actions you will take in order to remain 'cool' in each of the situations on your list should they really occur.

Strengths Challenge:

For an entire week don't gossip or say anything unkind about anyone.

Closing Activity: Practise a **self-control-building thought**. Think of a situation where you would like to exercise more self-control. Tell yourself what you are going to do – you could even write the thought down. Say it to yourself a few times, say it to yourself regularly though the day.

Positive thoughts tend to work better than negative ones – e.g., *I **will** be calm* rather than *I **won't** lose my temper*. However, even negative self-control-building thoughts can help.

Display suggestion: Imagine a Fair Future.

Let the students imagine a world where we don't use more than our fair share of resources, where we conserve our natural species, control our aggression, and learn to lead peaceful and healthy lives. Use images from magazines, the Internet or draw your own to create such a future.

PSHE: Programme of Study for Key Stage 3 Links

Personal well-being

Key Concepts:

1.2 Healthy lifestyles

1.3 Risk

1.4 Relationships

Key Processes:

2.1 Critical reflection

2.2 Decision-making and managing risk

2.3 Developing relationships and working with others

Story: The Mythological Story of Midas

The story is told of how Midas, King of Macedonia, came across an elderly satyr, a creature half-man and half-goat, sleeping in his rose garden. The king took pity on the old creature, who was a servant of the god Dionysius, and fed him and cared for him. In return, Dionysius granted Midas a wish.

Now Midas was known for his love of beauty but not, perhaps, for his intelligence. Midas loved roses and he loved his beautiful young daughter, but perhaps more than all of this Midas loved gold.

'I wish,' he said, 'that everything I touch would turn to gold.'

'Are you sure?' the god asked, rather startled.

'I'm sure,' Midas replied.

'Are you absolutely, completely positive?' Dionysius went on.

Midas nodded enthusiastically.

'Very well,' said the god with a sigh. 'Your wish is granted.'

Midas rushed to a tree and touched it – and it turned to gold. He reached down to one of his beautiful roses and plucked it – and it turned to gold. 'Now I will be the richest and happiest man on earth!' he cried and he called to his servants to bring food and wine to celebrate. But when he picked up the food, it turned to gold.

> When he tried to drink, the wine turned to gold in his cup. And, worst of all, when his daughter ran to him and put her arms around him she, too, turned to gold.
>
> At last, hungry, thirsty, and heartbroken, the king went on his knees to the god Dionysius and begged him to take away his terrible curse. Dionysius took pity on the stupid king and told him to wash himself in the river Pactolus. The river washed away Midas's golden touch – and restored his daughter to life. From that day on the river gleamed gold in the sunlight – and from that day on Midas was a poorer but a happier man.

Opportunities to build Self-control across the curriculum:

PE: *Setting personal fitness goals and working towards them.*

Food technology: *Making healthy choices in terms of diet and nutrition.*

PSHE: Economic well-being and financial capability – *An understanding of the undesirability of debt, and of saving for the things we want.*

Any subject: *Using 'self-control-building thoughts' – to think through homework tasks to help us complete them.*

TWENTY-TWO

Social Skills

Social skills, or social and emotional intelligence, along with personal intelligence, are sometimes referred to by psychologists as 'hot' intelligences. They are used to process the feelings, cues, motives, and signals that occur in oneself and others. They are distinct from what is usually meant by IQ, abstract thinking and verbal abilities.

With younger students this strength can be referred to as 'friendship' – social intelligence is the strength required to make friends with others. Emotional and personal intelligence are the strengths required to be a good friend to yourself.

Personal intelligence refers to accurate self-assessment and self-understanding, social intelligence to the understanding and assessment of relationships, and emotional intelligence to the ability to understand, appreciate, and use emotional information and reasoning.

Social intelligence has been studied for many years, and has been called the ability to 'act wisely in human relations.' (Thorndike, 1920). Gardner's (1983) work on multiple intelligences introduced the concept of personal intelligence, which he divided into inter and intrapersonal intelligence. Emotional intelligence is a more recent subject of study, popularised by Goldman (1995).

Peterson & Seligman (2004) stress that these intelligences can be learned and improved upon. Intelligence is a combination of mental ability and accumulated knowledge, and knowledge about relationships, self-understanding, and emotions can certainly be increased. In the UK the Social and Emotional Aspects of Learning (SEAL) programme aims to improve students' functioning in this area.

There may be drawbacks to an overemphasis on social and emotional skills. For example, a focus on 'getting along' may stifle creativity, spontaneity, and healthy debate and disagreement. Further, a focus on oneself is not always the best way to improve mood or increase resilience.

Research into the benefits of social and emotional intelligence, particularly emotional intelligence, is in its early stages, but there are preliminary findings that suggest individuals with higher emotional intelligence have better social relationships, better coping strategies, and fewer problems with drugs, alcohol, and aggression.

Unlike many of the other strengths, social and emotional intelligence has no real moral aspect – it can be used for good or bad ends. A high degree of social and emotional intelligence is required to manipulate or defraud others, for example. There is no real link between emotional intelligence and happiness.

Women show higher degrees of social and emotional intelligence than men.

Key features of Social Skills:

- Can be improved
- Is a mixture of accurate self-understanding, understanding of others, and understanding of emotions

Definition: You know yourself really well and you know how to get on well with other people. You can fit in anywhere.

Benefits: Preliminary research suggests that higher emotional intelligence is linked to better relationships and better coping strategies and fewer problems with addiction or aggression.

Quotes:

'One's own self is well hidden from one's own self. Of all the mines of treasure, one's own self is the last to be dug up.' – **Nietzsche**

'Am I not destroying my enemies when I make friends with them?' – **Abraham Lincoln**

'If one is estranged from oneself, then one is estranged from others too. If one is out of touch with oneself, then one cannot touch others.' – **Anne Morrow Lindburgh**

'You have been my friend. That in itself is a tremendous thing. I wove my webs for you because I liked you. After all, what's a life, anyway? We're born, we live a little while, we die. A spider's life can't help being something of a mess, with all this trapping and eating flies. By helping you, perhaps I was trying to lift up my life a trifle. Heaven knows, anyone's life can stand a little of that.' – **Charlotte from *Charlotte's Web* by E B White**

'He is not strong and powerful, who throws people down, but he is strong who withholds himself from anger.' – **The Prophet Muhammad**

'Whoever suppresses his anger, when he has in his power to show it, Allah will give him a great reward.' – **The Prophet Muhammad**

'The most powerful person is the one who is victorious over his anger with his forbearance.' – **Imam Ali**

Thinking Questions:

- What are emotions?
- Why do we have emotions?
- Is social and emotional intelligence a good thing? Is it ever a bad thing?

Strengths Builders and Challenges:

Year 7

Strengths Builders:

1. Design a Social Skills Superhero.

2. Play a game of Circle Story – Make up a story with your friends. Each person says one line (or word) of the story. One by one each player adds a line to the story. Keep going round all the players as many times as you need to make a good story.

   Example:

   - First person – 'Once upon a time'
   - Second person – 'there was this cat'
   - Third person – 'named George'

   If you feel brave, tell the story to the class!

Strengths Challenge:

Say hello to someone at school who you don't know and try talking to them.

Year 8

Strengths Builders:

1. Strength in Action Story – Can you remember a time when you or somebody you know showed that they had good Social Skills? Write or draw or tell a story of Social Skills in action.

2. Group Strengths Poster – With a group of friends, create a poster that shows at least five strengths for each of you. Can you think of a 'group name' that reflects your strengths?

Strengths Challenge:

Make a real effort to find a new friend and get to know them.

Year 9

Strengths Builders:

1. Create your own Strength in Action Story – Make up a story that contains a character or characters who use good Social Skills in a situation. Write or draw or tell your story of Social Skills in action.

2. Play a game of Speakers and Listeners – Students work in pairs, with one being the Speaker and the other the Listener. The speaker talks for two minutes about their favourite holiday. The Listener needs to listen with their head, with their eyes, and with their face. When the Speaker has finished, the Listener feeds back what they heard. Then the Speaker 'marks' how their Listener has listened:

   - If they listened with their head (remembered what was said) they get one mark – one mark and you are an OK Listener.

   - If they listened with their eyes (kept looking) they get one mark – two marks and you are a Good Listener.

   - If they listened with their face (reflected the feelings of the speaker) they get one mark – three marks and you are a Very Good Listener.

Strengths Challenge:

Join a group of friends who are already talking and ask what they are talking about and then join in, but stick to the topic already being discussed. Listen first, talk last, and don't take over the conversation. Think about your body language and try and put others at ease by being relaxed.

Closing activity: Notice your emotions in the moment and name them to yourself. As you go through the day, simply notice the different emotions you feel at the beginning and end of each lesson.

Display suggestion: A Rainbow of Emotions

Use magazines and the Internet to find images of people (or animals) displaying as many different emotions as you can and create a spectrum or Rainbow of Emotions collage.

PSHE: Programme of Study for Key Stage 3 Links

Personal well-being

Key Concepts:

1.1 Personal identities

1.4 Relationships

1.5 Diversity

Key Processes:

2.1 Critical reflection

2.3 Developing relationships and working with others

Social, emotional and personal intelligence underscore successful relationships with others as well as growing maturity and self-awareness.

> **Story: An Islamic Story of Two Friends**
>
> There is a story that tells of two friends walking through a desert. As they walked they started to argue, and finally the first friend lost his temper and insulted the other. The second friend was hurt and knelt down and wrote in the sand, 'My best friend insulted me.'
>
> That night they came to an oasis where they could camp and sleep. The second friend decided to go for a swim in the cool water but he became stuck in the mud and nearly drowned. The first friend pulled him out and saved his life.
>
> That night, the second friend spent hours carving some words on a stone. In the morning the first friend saw what was written on the stone: 'My best friend saved my life.'
>
> He said, 'When I insulted you, you wrote about it in the sand. Now I have saved your life you have carved it on a stone. Why?'
>
> The second friend answered, 'When someone hurts us we should write in the sand where the wind can blow away the words and the hurt can be forgotten. When someone helps us we should carve it in stone so we remember it always.'

Opportunities to build Social Skills across the curriculum:

Any group work requires students to use social and emotional intelligence to achieve a goal. Letting students with a lot of this strength coach those with less can be effective. Philosophy for Children as an approach has been shown to increase social and emotional awareness in students.

Music: *Ensemble playing or choral singing cues students in to one another and is an opportunity to use this strength.*

PE: *Team games are a clear area where students can practise working with one another positively.*

TWENTY-THREE

Spirituality

All human beings have a spiritual aspect to them, whatever their religious beliefs or lack of them. We wonder about the meaning and purpose of our lives, we ask questions about pain and suffering, we believe in ideals and values. These are spiritual concerns, concerns that go beyond the here and now and beyond our immediate circle. For many people in the world their spirituality is closely linked or identical to their formal religious beliefs and many students may understand spirituality in this way. In the west, more people describe themselves as atheist or agnostic but would still want to acknowledge the spiritual side of their personality.

Spirituality has been linked by psychologists to positive outcomes for students, such as academic success, prosocial behaviour, and emotional adjustment. For adults, formal religious practice has been linked to better family relationships and to greater levels of health and happiness in old age. Prayer has been linked with coping with stress and with higher levels of well-being.

The opposites of spirituality are not atheism or agnosticism because these can be coherent beliefs. Rather they are pure materialism, a lack of awareness of any value to life beyond immediate physical concerns, banality, emptiness, purposelessness, and desperation.

There is debate about whether religious belief – or a tendency to believe – is inherited or learned. However, what is clear is that both the family and wider society have an important role to play in passing on values to the next generation.

Spirituality is linked to other strengths – gratitude, hope, and love of beauty. It is also linked with a sense of meaning, to our core values.

Spirituality and religion are without doubt contentious issues. While religion can lead to great humanity, forgiveness, compassion, and wisdom, it can also lead to bigotry, violence, and repression. The form that religion takes in an individual and a community greatly affects what kind of influence it has. It is worth noting that culturally grounded religious and spiritual beliefs may profoundly influence other strengths – such as intimacy, optimism, and emotional intelligence. Little is known about how young people influence one another's religious or spiritual beliefs and practices. Philosophical discussion and the use of *Strengths Gym*'s Thinking Questions may be of particular value in exploring some of these contentious issues in a safe and supportive environment.

Key features of Spirituality:

- Is sometimes, but not always, synonymous with 'religion'
- Is concerned with a sense of meaning and purpose
- Has positive outcomes – but not always!

Definition: Thinking deeply and often about God, life, love, and meaning.

Benefits: People who practise religion engage in less risky behaviour and may be happier and healthier.

Quotes:

'The best things in life are nearest: breath in your nostrils, light in your eyes, flowers at your feet, the path of right just before you. Then do not grasp at the stars, but do life's plain, common work as it comes, certain that daily duties and daily bread are the sweetest things in life.' – **Robert Louis Stevenson**

'The whole of the holy life is good friends.' – **The Buddha**

'Something precious is lost if we rush headlong into the details of life without pausing for a moment to pay homage to the mystery of life and the gift of another day.' – **Kent Nerburn**

'Holiness comes wrapped in the ordinary. There are burning bushes all around you. Every tree is full of angels. Hidden beauty is waiting in every crumb.' – **Macrina Wiederkehr OSB** *A Tree Full of Angels*

'Sometimes people get the mistaken notion that spirituality is a separate department of life, the penthouse of existence. But rightly understood it is a vital awareness that pervades all realms of our being.' – **Brother David Steindl-Rast**

'Don't hurry, don't worry. You're only here for a short visit. So be sure to stop and smell the flowers.' – **Walter C Hagen**

Thinking Questions:

- What is spirituality?
- Is spirituality different to religion?
- Is there a disadvantage to spirituality?
- Is there a good kind of religion and a bad kind of religion?

Strengths Builders and Strengths Challenges

Year 7

Strengths Builders:

1. Design a Spirituality Superhero.
2. Sit quietly for ten minutes, not speaking at all with your eyes shut. Spend this time thinking about life and your place within the world.

Strengths Challenge:

Find out more about a religious faith. You could:

- Ask a Jewish friend what they believe about God
- Ask a Muslim friend what they believe about God
- Ask a Christian friend what they believe about God
- Ask a Hindu friend what they believe about God

Do you know people of other faiths? Can you ask them about what they believe?

Year 8

Strengths Builders:

1. Strength in Action Story – Can you remember a time when you or somebody you know used their Spirituality or beliefs to get them through something that was difficult? Write or draw or tell a story of Spirituality in action.
2. Imagine you are very old. Make a list of all the things you have done in your lifetime (for example, did you travel, get married, have children, move away, go to university, get a great job?). What will people say about you after you die?

Strengths Challenge:

Meditation is said to increase creativity and brings us health benefits, as well as helping us to grow spiritually. Sit quietly, comfortably, and listen to the sound of your breath for five minutes each day this week. Go to: http://www.millionmeditators.com and click on their 'How To Guides' to find out more about meditation.

Year 9

Strengths Builders:

1. Create your own Strength in Action Story – Make up a story that contains a character or characters who use their Spirituality or beliefs to get them through something difficult. Write or draw or tell your story of Spirituality in action.

2. With a friend, or in a group, talk about God. Can you come up with reasons to believe in God? Can you come up with reasons not to believe in God? Remember – respect the views you don't agree with!

Strengths Challenge:

Go to the library or search on the Internet and investigate a faith that you know nothing about, such as Buddhism, Shinto, or Taoism. Need help searching? Go to: http://en.wikipedia.org. Has what you have found out changed your perception of people of other faiths? What did you learn?

Closing activity: Stillness and Silence

Sitting and listening to a simple sound – a rain stick, a singing bowl, or just the quiet sound of one's own breath – is a classic form of meditation and a satisfying end to a lesson.

Students who want to go further and learn to meditate can find a lot of help at http://www.calmcentre.com or http://www.millionmeditators.com.

Display suggestion: What's Important?

Ask students to bring in images of what *they* think life is about – about what is important to them – and create a class collage.

PSHE: Programme of Study for Key Stage 3 Links

Personal well-being

Key Concepts:

1.1 Personal identities

For many students, their self-identity is intimately connected with their spiritual or religious beliefs.

Key Processes:

1.2 Critical reflection

Values are a key aspect of religion and of spirituality.

For some students, how they feel about themselves and how they understand concepts like optimism and hope, intimacy and emotion will be rooted in their religious and cultural identity.

Story: A Dreamtime story from Australia: Tiddalik the Frog

The indigenous people of Australia, the Aborigines or Torres Straits Islanders, had their own culture and beliefs before white men brought religions with them from Europe. Their beliefs were based on a sense of belonging to the land and the sea and to their people. These beliefs were handed on through stories called *The Dreaming* or *Dreamtime*, a form of spirituality that is unique to Australia.

'So the sad thing about it all was the missionaries didn't realise that we already had something that tied in with what they'd brought to us. They saw different as inferior, and they didn't ask us what it was that we had. And it's very sad because if they had asked ... things may have been different today.

Our people, before the white man came were very spiritual people. They were connected to land and creation through the Great Spirit; there was a good great and a great evil spirit ... And Satan was the great evil one. So there wasn't much difference in what the missionaries brought and what we already had...'

Wadjularbinna Doomadgee
Gungalidda Leader
Gulf of Carpentaria, 1996

The Dreaming means different things to different Australians. It is a network of knowledge, faith and practices that come from creation stories. These stories lay down guidelines for behaviour and for society and for how people should behave. During the Dreamtime the ancestral spirits walked on the earth, creating the land, the sea, the animals, and the rivers. The Aborigines did not own the land – it was part of them and it was their duty to protect it.

Tiddalik the Frog

During the Dreamtime, Tiddalik, the largest frog that ever lived, woke up. He was thirsty. VERY thirsty. He drank from a puddle and drained it dry. But he was still thirsty. He drank from a pond and drained it dry. But he was still thirsty. He drank from a river and a water hole and a lake and drained *them* dry. But he was still thirsty. He found more rivers and more lakes and more water holes and he drank and drank and drank until there was no water left anywhere.

By then, Tiddalik was HUGE and the land was dry, the grass was shrivelled and the trees were dying. None of the other animals had anything to drink. They begged Tiddalik for some of his water but he just sat there, with his mouth shut.

Worried, they gathered to decide what to do. Somehow they had to get their water back. Then Wise Wombat said, 'We've got to make him laugh. Then the water will come out of him!'

So they tried to make Tiddalik laugh. Kookaburra told jokes, Lizard walked on his hind legs, Kangaroo and Emu played leapfrog. But Tiddalik just sat there, with his mouth shut.

Finally, Eel crept out of the dry river bed and began to twist and turn and weave himself into such fantastic knots that at last he tied himself so tight he got stuck. The other animals laughed and laughed, and finally Tiddalik started to smile, and then to grin, and at last he opened his mouth and laughed and laughed and laughed and the water gushed out and flowed back into the water holes, back into the rivers, back into the lakes, and the land turned green once more. And Eel – he slithered into the water, untied himself and slipped away in relief.

Opportunities to build Spirituality across the curriculum:

Science and Maths: *For some students, the wonder of science or the beauty of numbers provide a sense of meaning.*

RE: *For many people around the world, spirituality is synonymous with religion.*

Art and Music: *Beauty can provide a route into spiritual development.*

Literature: *Poetry, especially, is concerned with the expression and exploration of meaning.*

TWENTY-FOUR

Enthusiasm

Enthusiasm, vitality, and zest for life describe a strength that is marked by a feeling of energy and aliveness. It is a positive feeling, not to be confused with tension or nervous energy. A sense of mental and physical vigour is associated with good health and happiness and is a mark of optimal human functioning. It is more often found in children and young people than in adults. Enthusiasm and vitality may not just be associated with good health but may actively promote it.

Psychologists have linked enthusiasm and vitality to the basic psychological needs for autonomy, competence, and relatedness. It is affected by both physical and psychological factors; enthusiasm and vitality may be diminished by poor diet, smoking, lack of exercise or ill health, and by conflict, or feeling powerless or unappreciated.

Vitality and enthusiasm are linked to the Chinese concept of chi or energy and the Indian concept of prana. A person with a lot of enthusiasm or vitality lives life to the full and enjoys each moment fully. They have the energy to implement their plans, they believe in their own abilities, they are confident they will achieve their goals.

In the workplace, low enthusiasm is associated with a feeling of lack of support and high stress. It increases the risk of ill health and absenteeism. Conversely, higher enthusiasm and vitality is associated with individuals who achieve radical innovation in the workplace.

Exercise has been reliably shown to increase vitality, as has contact with nature. A ten-minute walk in the fresh air increases vitality two hours later. By contrast, a sugary snack increases tension immediately and two hours later leads to lower energy levels than before the snack.

Enthusiasm is one of the strengths that most predicts happiness. (The others are hope, gratitude, curiosity, and love.)

Key features of Enthusiasm:

- Is increased by good diet and exercise
- Contributes to physical and mental health
- Is encouraged by autonomy, competence and relatedness

Definition: You are eager, full of energy and raring to go.

Benefits: Enthusiasm leads to greater well-being and contributes to physical and mental health. Enthusiastic individuals are more likely to achieve their goals.

Quotes:

'It is a mark of intelligence, no matter what you're doing to have a good time doing it' – **Anon**

'Courage is going from failure to failure without losing enthusiasm.' – **Winston Churchill**

'Nothing great was ever achieved without enthusiasm.' – **Ralph Waldo Emerson**

Thinking Questions

- What makes us enthusiastic?
- What is enthusiasm?
- Where does enthusiasm come from?
- Is there a disadvantage to enthusiasm?

Strengths Builders and Strengths Challenges:

Year 7

Strengths Builders:

1. Design an Enthusiasm Superhero.
2. Make a list of your favourite activities. Do one of them with a friend this week.

Strengths Challenge:

Try an activity you have never done before.

Year 8

Strengths Builders:

1. Strength in Action Story – Can you remember a time when you or somebody you know was full of life and energy? Write or draw or tell a story of Enthusiasm in action.
2. Give It A Go. Think of a book you love, a film you really enjoyed, a food you find delicious, or a song you think is great. Find somebody in your class and see if you can use your enthusiasm to persuade them to try these things for themselves. If you feel brave, try to persuade your whole class to 'Give It A Go'.

Strengths Challenge:

Try to do one new activity every day for a week. You could:

- Eat a food you've never eaten before
- Read a book you've never read before
- Go to an after-school club you've never tried before

Year 9

Strengths Builders:

1. Create your own Strength in Action Story – Make up a story that contains a character or characters who are full of life and energy. Write or draw or tell your story of Enthusiasm in action.
2. Passion Pairing – Decide what your passion or enthusiasm is. Go round the class asking other people 'What's your passion?' and find a Passion Pair – someone you share a passion with! Find out how many different passions there are in the class.

Strengths Challenge:

For one week, keep track of how many hours of TV you watch and how many hours you spend indoors on the computer or playing computerised games. What do you think about how much time you spend doing stationary activities? Could you have done something more exciting with your time, like an outside activity or joining a sports team or club?

Closing activity: What are you enthusiastic about? Imagine yourself doing something you really enjoy. Close your eyes and picture yourself full of energy, full of life, full of enthusiasm.

Display suggestion. Things we most enjoy. Create a visual display of the students' enthusiasms.

PSHE: Programme of Study for Key Stage 3 Links

Personal well-being

Key Concepts:

1.2 Healthy lifestyles

1.3 Risk

A healthy lifestyle promotes vitality, but so does knowing when to take risks. Success is usually only achieved by taking risks.

Key Processes:

2.2 Decision-making and managing risk

2.3 Developing relationships and working with others

Feeling supported and connected to others enhances our vitality and enthusiasm for life.

Story: The Simon Bolivar Youth Orchestra

Life can be grim in any inner city, and the slums of Venezuela in South America are no exception. For some children and teenagers, though, there is a way out of the slums – a way out of drug-running, burglary, and violence – and it is music – classical music.

Forty years ago there were only two orchestras in Venezuela, staffed mainly by foreigners. It was impossible for young Venezuelans to play in them. That was changed by the passion and enthusiasm of one man, a man called Jose Antonio Abreu. He was a conductor, an economist, and a politician, and he had a dream – he started a youth orchestra. He started with just seven children. Two weeks later he had 150 children. Then he started another orchestra, and then another. Now, 30 years later, about 250,000 children receive four hours of music tuition after school EVERY DAY, and there are 200 youth orchestras. Because the children and teenagers play for 20 hours a week they have become extraordinary musicians. Knives and guns have been exchanged for violins and clarinets.

The lead orchestra is the Simon Bolivar Orchestra, with players as young as 14 and a conductor who is now 24 but who began conducting when he was 12. They have taken concert halls all over the world by storm. These young people rehearse for hours and hours, year after year. Music has become their passion, their life – and their hard work has created a world-leading orchestra.

They have fulfilled their dreams because of their passion, enthusiasm and hard work and because of the passion and enthusiasm of one man who knew young people could be great musicians.

Opportunities to build Enthusiasm across the curriculum:

PE: *Exercise increases vitality and enthusiasm, but only if it is exercise we enjoy. Challenge students to find one form of exercise they feel enthusiastic about.*

Food technology: *Explore the links between diet and vitality.*

PSHE: *Economic well being and financial capability.*

Students learn more effectively when they feel enthusiasm for a subject. Challenge them to find an aspect of every subject that they enjoy.

APPENDIX

Sources for Stories Included

1. **Love of Beauty**

    The Moon Can't Be Stolen

    Can be found at http://www.nozen.com/stolenmoon.htm

2. **Courage**

    The Rescue of the Danish Jews

    Adapted from Sandy Toksvig (2006). *Hitler's Canary*. Corgi.

3. **Love**

    The Story of Violette Szabo

    Can be found at http://en.wikipedia.org/wiki/The_Life_That_I_Have

    Internet movie database http://www.imdb.com/title/tt0051454/plotsummary

4. **Prudence**

    The Biblical Story of Joseph and Pharaoh (Genesis 37–41)

5. **Teamwork**

    Working All Night

    Personal Communication

6. **Creativity**

    The Yoruba Creation Myth

    Can be found at http://www.mythicjourneys.org/bigmyth/myths/english/2_yoruba_full.htm

    http://en.wikipedia.org/wiki/Creation_myth

    http://www.gly.uga.edu/railsback/CS/CSGoldenChain.html The version at this site is by David A. Anderson/Sankofa (1991). *The Origin of Life on Earth: An African Creation Myth*. Mt. Airy, Maryland: Sights Productions.

7. **Curiosity**

    John Rae

    Can be found at http://en.wikipedia.org/wiki/John_Ray

8. **Fairness**

    Rosa Parks

    Can be found at http://en.wikipedia.org/wiki/Rosa_Parks

9. **Forgiveness**

The Forgiveness Project

http://www.theforgivenessproject.com/stories/andrew-rice

Murdoch, A., & Oldershaw, D. (2008). *16 Guidelines for a Happy Life: the basics*. London: Essential Education.

10. Gratitude

The Spirit of the Corn

Scott Littleton, C. (ed.) (2002). *The Illustrated Anthology of World Myth & Storytelling*. London: Duncan Baird.

11. Honesty

The Quakers

http://www.en.wikipedia.org/wiki/Quaker_history

12. Hope

A Cow Named Tutti

Heiney, Paul. *The Times* Wednesday 10 September 2008

13. Humour

The Parrot and the Conjurer

Adapted from the parrot joke.

14. Persistence

Thomas Edison

Can be found at http://www.en.wikipedia.org/wiki/Thomas_Edison

15. Open-mindedness

Oskar Schindler

16. Kindness

A Bowl made of Wood

From *The Old Man and his Grandson* by the Brothers Grimm

Grimm, The Brothers (1984). *The Complete Illustrated Stories of the Brothers Grimm*. London: Chancellor Press.

17. Leadership

A Wise Ring and a Good King

Adapted from *This Too Shall Pass*, from Forest, H. (1996). *Wisdom Tales from Around the World*. Little Rock: August House Publishers.

18. Love of Learning

Afghanistan

Can be found at http://www.timesonline.co.uk/tol/news/world/asia/article3882980.ece

The Times, Wednesday 7 May 2008

19. Modesty

A Coin Worth all the World

Can be found at http://www.sln.org.uk/storyboard/stories/b4.htm

20. Wisdom

The Smuggler

Forest, H. (1996). *Wisdom Tales from Around the World.* Little Rock: August House Publishers.

21. Self-control

The Mythological Story of Midas

Can be found at http://www.primaryresources.co.uk/english/kingmidas.htm

22. Social Skills

An Islamic Story of Two Friends

Can be found at http://www.ezsoftech.com/stories/mis16.asp

23. Spirituality

Tiddalik the Frog

Michael J Connolly Dreamtime Kullilla-Art

http://www.dreamtime.net.au

http://www.dreamtime.auz.net

24. Enthusiasm

The Simon Bolivar Youth Orchestra

Can be found at http://entertainment.timesonline.co.uk/tol/arts_and_entertainment/musical/classical/article6094174.ece

Bibliography

Baltes, P.B, & Staudinger, U.M. (2000). Wisdom: A metaheuristic (pragmatic) to orchestrate mind and virtue toward excellence. *American Psychologist, 55*, 122–136.

Bargh, J.A., Chen, M., & Burrows, L. (1996). Automaticity of social behavior: Direct effects of trait construct and stereotype priming on action. *Journal of Personality and Social Psychology, 71*, 230-244.

Egan, K. (1990). *Romantic Understanding: The Development of Rationality and Imagination, Ages 8–15*. New York: Routledge.

Egan, K. (2005). *Imaginative Teaching*. San Francisco: John Wiley & Sons.

Forest, H. (1996). *Wisdom Tales from Around the World*. Little Rock: August House Publishers.

Frederickson, B. (2009). *Positivity*. New York: Crown Publishing Group.

Gardner, H. (1983). *Frames of Mind: The Theory of Multiple Intelligences*. New York: Basic Books.

Goldman, D. (1995). *Emotional Intelligence: Why it Can Matter More Than IQ*. London: Bloomsbury.

Goleman, D. (2003). *Destructive Emotions and How We Can Overcome Them*. London: Bloomsbury.

Kashdan, T.B., & Fincham, F.D (2004). Facilitating Curiosity: A Social and Self-Regulatory Perspective for Scientifically Based Interventions. In P.A. Linley & S. Joseph, S. (Eds.), *Positive Psychology in Practice* (pp. 482-503). New Jersey: Wiley.

Morrison, R. (2007). True Class: South America's Lightning Conductor. *The Times*, 17 February.

Murdoch, A., & Oldershaw, D. (2008). *16 Guidelines for a Happy Life: The Basics*. London: Essential Education.

Niemiec, R.M., & Wedding, D. (2008). *Positive Psychology at the Movies*. Cambridge MA: Hogrefe & Huber.

Peterson, C. (2006). *A Primer in Positive Psychology*. Oxford: Oxford University Press.

Peterson, C., & Seligman, M.E.P. (2004). *Character Strengths and Virtues*. Oxford: Oxford University Press.

Schwartz, B., & Sharpe, K.E. (2006). Practical Wisdom: Aristotle Meets Positive Psychology. *Journal of Happiness Studies, 7*, 377–395.

Sternberg, R.J. (1998). A balance theory of wisdom. *Review of General Psychology, 2*, 347–365.

Thorndike, E.L. (1920). Intelligence and its use. *Harper's Magazine, 140*, 227–235.

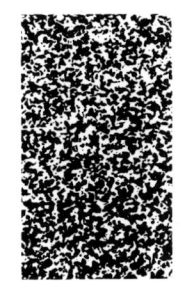

PATTERNS FROM YOUR FAVOURITE CLOTHES

also of interest

Pattern Cutting and Making Up   Martin Shoben and Janet P. Ward

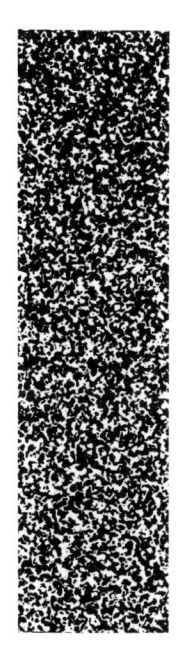

PATTERNS FROM YOUR FAVOURITE CLOTHES

Martin Shoben

Heinemann Professional Publishing

For Barbara and Richard

Heinemann Professional Publishing Ltd
Halley Court, Jordan Hill, Oxford OX2 8EJ

OXFORD   LONDON   MELBOURNE   AUCKLAND

First published 1988

© Martin Shoben 1988

British Library Cataloguing in Publication Data
Shoben, Martin
 Patterns from your favourite clothes.
 1. Dressmaking – Pattern design
 I. Title
 646.4'072   TT520

 ISBN 0 434 91847 4 cased
    0 434 91843 1 paper

Printed by Imago Publishing Ltd, Hong Kong

Fashion illustrations by Stephen Worth
Photographs by Eric Balmer

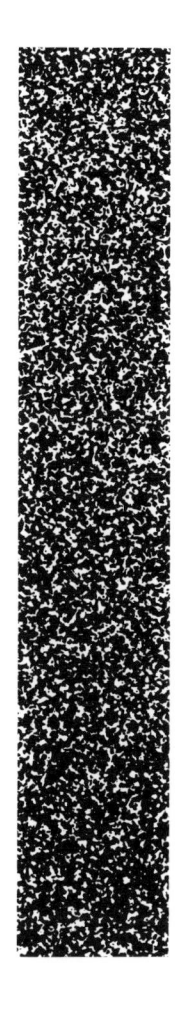

CONTENTS

Garment suppliers — vi
Acknowledgements — vi
Introduction — 1
How to use this book — 2
Preparation notes — 3
Equipment — 4

STYLE 1 Casual shirt – fold and spike method — 6
STYLE 2 Dirndl skirt – direct measurements — 26
STYLE 3 Unlined summer jacket – fold and spike method — 32
STYLE 4 Six-gored A-line skirt – direct measurements — 46
STYLE 5 Denim jeans – fold and spike method — 52
STYLE 6 Blouse with raglan sleeve – overdrape method — 66
STYLE 7 Classic tailored skirt – fold and spike method — 76
Patterns from drapes and gathers – overdrape method — 82
Reproducing darts – spike and pivot method — 87

Further reading — 89
Index — 90

Garment suppliers

Morplan Garment Trades Supplies Service
56 Great Titchfield Street
London W1 8DX

Franks
Market place
London W1P 8DY

Acknowledgements

I would like to thank Caroline Croxford, Janet Ward, Irena Kovar, Eileen Lane, Sue Hadden and my editor, Anne Martin, for their advice and help in producing this book.

I would also like to thank Design Intelligence Ltd for permission to reproduce the fashion sketches on pages 22, 23, 25, 44, 45, 62 and 63.

INTRODUCTION

This book is aimed at the home dressmaker who can make up clothes from commercial patterns but who would like to be a little more creative and begin to adapt and style their own patterns. Everyone has a favourite dress or shirt or pair of trousers that is very comfortable to wear but is slightly faded or the wrong length or in an out-of-date colour. This book offers you the facility to remake your old favourite into an up-to-date garment. It illustrates in detail how to take patterns from your clothes, and how to take these patterns and change their silhouette and length – and to add collars and pockets as well.

The seven basic styles have been selected because they are most likely to be found in the average woman's wardrobe. Each style has an interesting set of style variations specially selected to illustrate some simple pattern cutting techniques and some exciting ways of using fabric. The last sections of the book concentrate on cowls and drapes and darted styles and show how to reproduce patterns from them.

*Working through the following styles will be an interesting and creatively rewarding experience. However, this book has **not** been written for people making clothes for profit; it has been written for those making clothes for themselves in their own homes. It is both illegal and immoral to copy other people's designs for personal gain.*

HOW TO USE THIS BOOK

Select the garment from your wardrobe that you want to copy – one that suits you but is perhaps somewhat out of fashion and in need of updating. Simple alterations such as lengthening or shortening, or slightly more difficult adjustments like adding flare or gathers, will dramatically affect the appearance of your old favourite dress and turn it into something really up to date.

Find a fabric that will be suitable for the style. Each style will advise on fabric selection, and will also indicate a fabric layout and provide simple rules which will enable you to use your fabric to the full. This will undoubtedly enhance the finished appearance of your garment.

Next look through the book and find the style that is nearest to your style. This book is made up of designs that can be found in most wardrobes, so you should not have any difficulty. Remember to examine your garment carefully before making your choice of the style in the book. Before starting to make the pattern, assemble all the necessary equipment, i.e. paper, pins, pencils, tape measure etc. Then make up the basic style pattern.

Restyle the pattern at this stage if desired. The design ideas found at the back of each style will advise on interesting adaptions to your original pattern. All the techniques illustrated are within easy reach of the inexperienced pattern cutter, and should be interesting and rewarding to follow, and they can also be applied to shop-bought patterns. *Note that in this book* the alterations are made to produce a new *pattern*, not direct on the material. Remember to alter the basic style pattern *without* seam allowances.

Cut out the garment and start to assemble it. Making-up instructions are not included in this book, except for trouser zip openings. If you are stuck, you should be able to get help from the making-up guides listed at the end of this book.

Try on the finished garment and make any adjustments necessary. Remember to alter your pattern so that for future attempts your pattern will be correct. Keep the pattern with a drawing of the style on it for future reference.

PREPARATION NOTES

After selecting the garment from your wardrobe, follow these preparation notes.

Pressing

Carefully press your garment as flat as possible. Creases in the wrong places will reduce the garment size and make copying difficult.

Locating key points

Figure 1 illustrates the points that must be located on a garment before starting to cut the pattern from it. Certain points such as the centre front and centre back should be marked with pins so that they are clearly defined.

Sketch the garment

The following details must be noted: seam positions, darts, grains for each section, facings etc. Also, is the garment symmetrical or asymmetrical? If it is symmetrical, i.e. both left and right sides are the same design, only half a pattern need be made; think about it at this stage. Remember to consider the fabric that has been purchased for the style; is it suitable?

Assemble equipment

The equipment list in the next section is very comprehensive, but not all the items are essential. All the same, the better the equipment the easier the job.

Selecting the book style

Choose the book style nearest to your garment and carefully work through the instructions stage by stage. There are several methods of producing patterns from garments, and each style will indicate the best method for that style.

EQUIPMENT

It is very wise to begin working through the styles with a good basic set of equipment. The craftsman is well aware of the importance of this. Having the correct equipment to hand saves time and the wear and tear on nerves. The recommended equipment listed here will help to achieve the best results.

A *Metre stick*   Essential for drawing long straight lines for skirts and dresses.
B *Set square*   For 90 and 45 degree angles.
C *French curves*   For armholes and other curved lines.
D *Pattern master*   This combines the above functions in one instrument and is available from Morplan (56 Great Titchfield St, London W1 8DX).
E *Scissors*   The larger the better. If possible have two pairs, one for paper and one pair for fabric.
F *Tape measure*   Metric, with a metal end with a hole. This is useful for swinging arcs as well as for measuring.
G *Pencils*   Soft and hard leads. Black and colours.
H *Fine spike*   This will be used all the way through the book.
I *Pins*   Dressmaker's pins, the finer the better.
J *Map pins*   For pinning down patterns on paper.
K *Weights*   There are special flat pattern weights available, but any heavy flat object will do.
L *Pattern paper*   Available in large sheets. However, a large roll of paper, sold by weight, is cheaper in the long run.
M *Dress stand*   A very useful piece of equipment to have. There are many types available on the market.
N *Tracing wheel*   For tracing through lines from one pattern to another as well as marking through seam *lines* on to paper.

Plus all the usual dressmaker's equipment for sewing up.

5

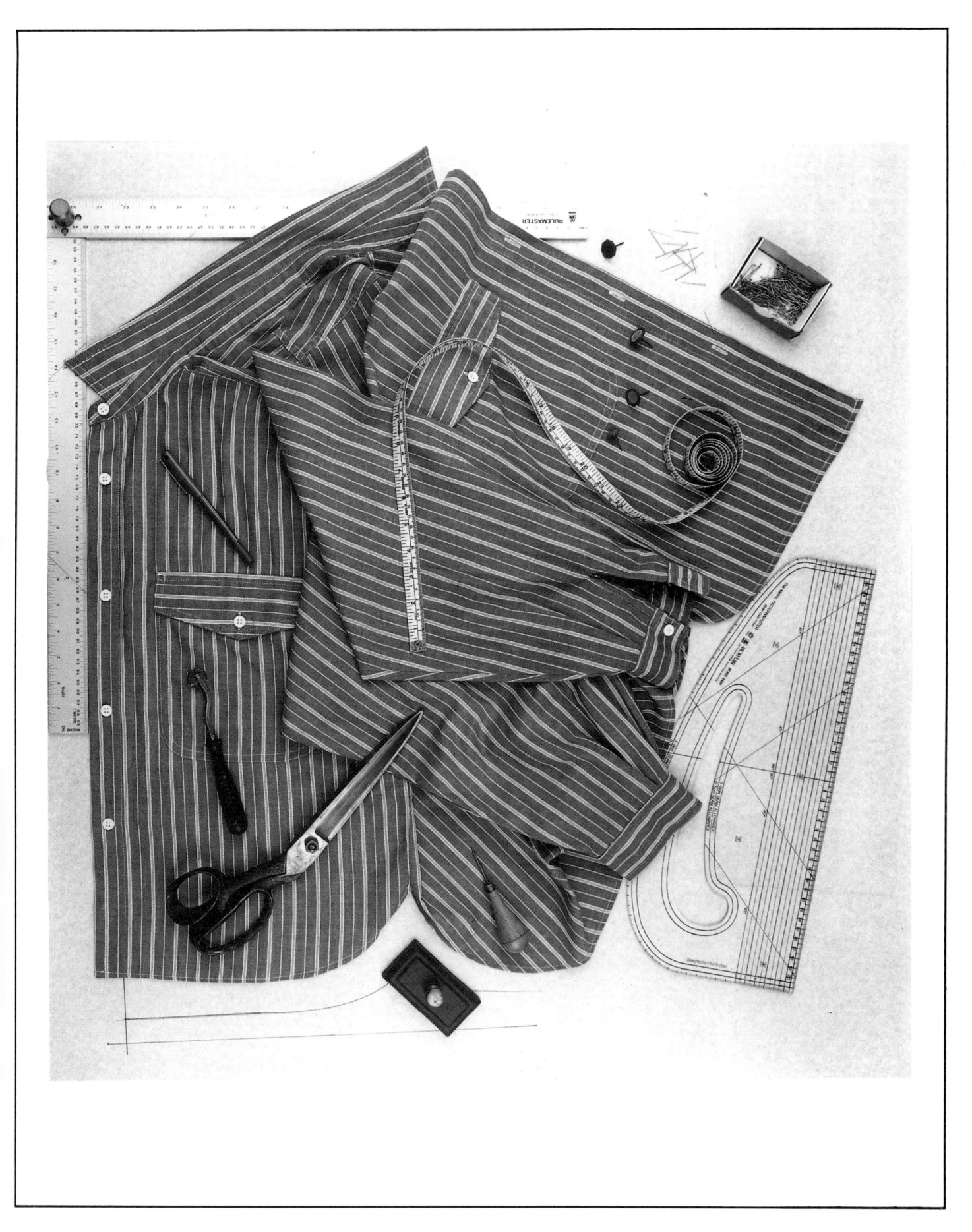

STYLE 1

CASUAL SHIRT – fold and spike method

This highly fashionable all-purpose shirt shape is an easy style to start with because it is simple to copy and easy to sew and also extremely versatile. It can be lengthened into a dress and cut in all types of printed fabrics which will add new life to your personal wardrobe.

What to look for

First neatly press the shirt. Examine the shirt very carefully and draw a simple sketch of it, noting all the seam positions, pleats, pockets etc. (see Figure 1). At this stage it is possible to leave out certain features such as the pocket, or even to add two pockets. Note on which fabric grain each section of the shirt is cut.

Method to choose

When pressed, the shirt will lie completely flat on the table. This means that there are no darts to give shape to the shirt. The best method of taking a pattern from this garment is the fold and spike method.

Equipment needed

White paper, fine spike, tracing wheel, tape measure, set square, sharp, fairly hard pencils, scissors etc.

Locating the key points

The first key points to locate are the centre front and the centre back (Figure 1). The centre front is where the buttons and the buttonholes are positioned. Place a line of pins carefully along the centre back of the shirt.

The back shirt

Draw a long straight line on a large sheet of paper (Figure 2).

1

2

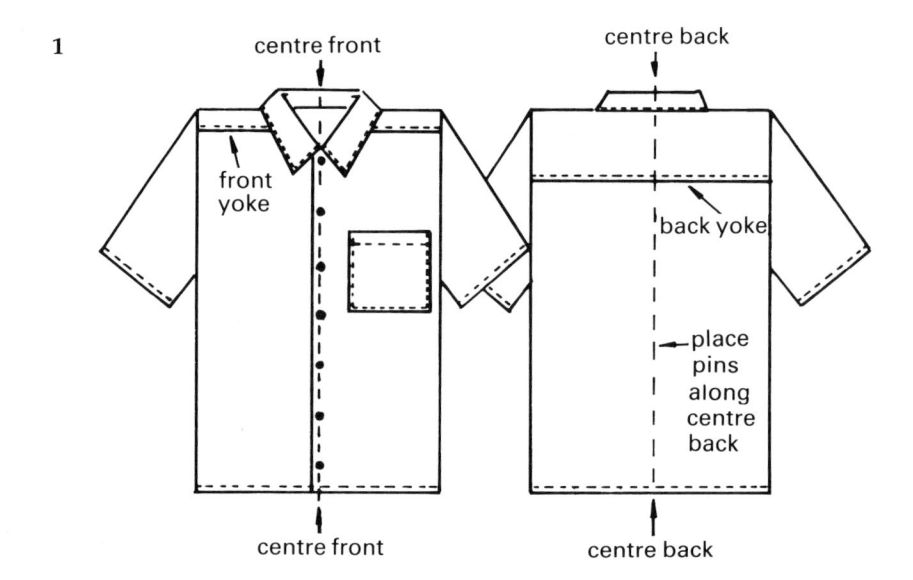

draw parallel line 6 cm edge

Lay the centre back (marked by the line of pins) on this line (Figure 3). Smooth the fabric out from A to B (the yoke/back seam) and down to C at the hem, and place a weight to hold point C firmly on the fabric. Spike point B.

Smooth out the fabric from C to D. Using a pencil, draw line C around to D, very close to the shirt hem.

Place a weight on point D and carefully flatten out the side seam. Make sure that E from F is flat. Mark the side seam from D to E. Spike through point E.

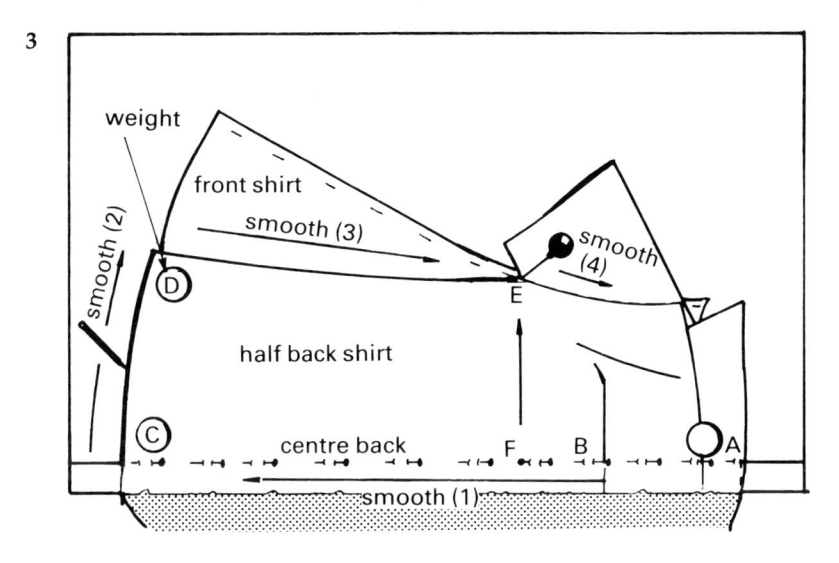

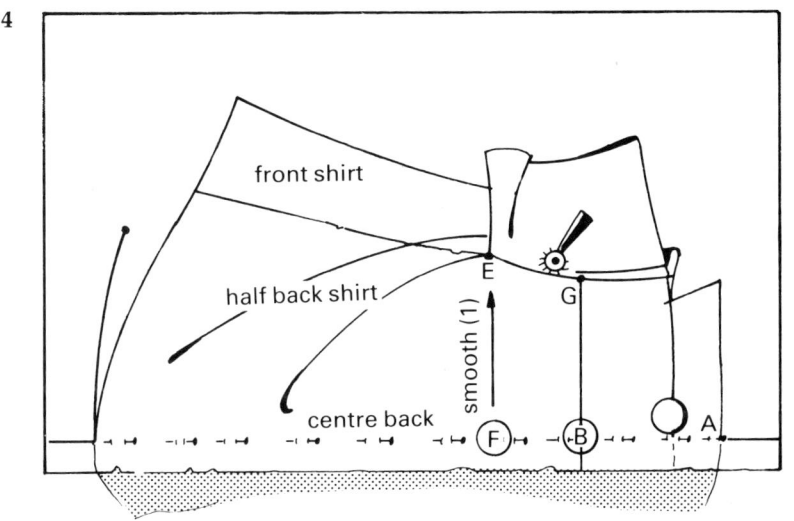

Holding point E firmly down and making sure that point F does not move from the original line, flatten out the back armhole. Using a tracing wheel or spike, mark through the armhole from E to G (Figure 4).

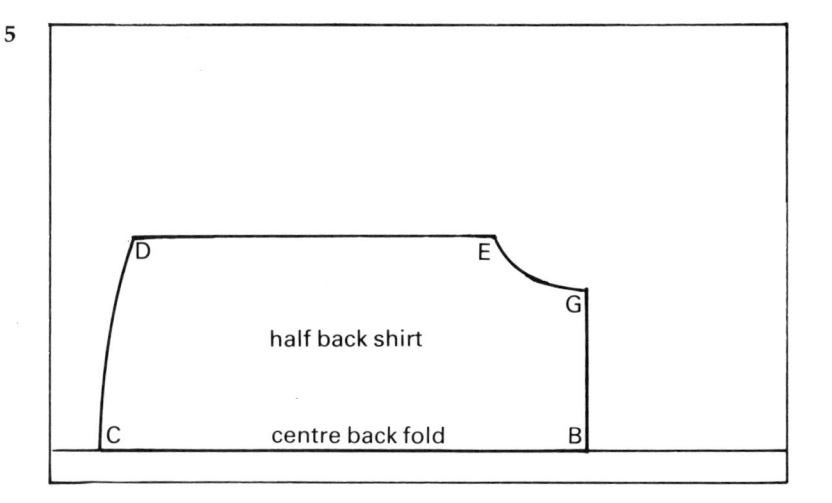

Remove the shirt and connect up points E–G–B using a ruler and a curve (Figure 5).

Do not cut the pattern out yet.

The back yoke

Draw a straight line on a fresh sheet of paper.

Place the centre back of the yoke on the straight line. Holding point B (the yoke seam) firmly down on the paper, spike through points B and G (Figure 6).

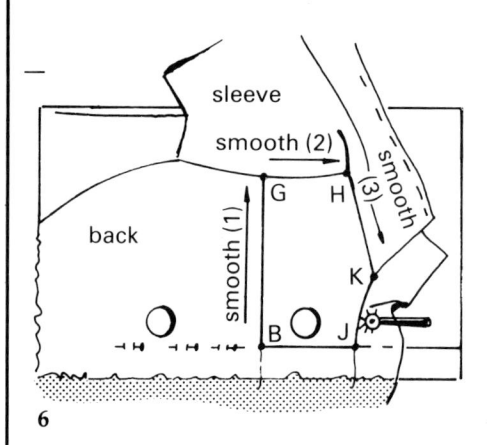

Smooth out the shirt to point H at the shoulder end. Spike through point H. Holding point J (the centre back) on the straight line, smooth out point K and then spike through point K. Trace wheel the back neck from K to G.

Remove the shirt and connect up points B–G–H–K–J (Figure 7).

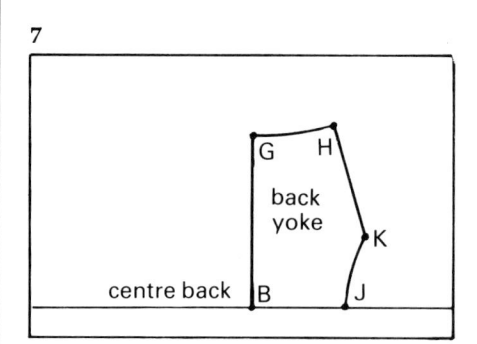

The front shirt

Draw a straight line on a fresh sheet of paper, leaving a 10.0 cm margin (Figure 8).

Lay the centre front of the shirt on the straight line. Smooth the fabric out from A down to C at the hem and place a weight to hold point C firm.

Draw around the shirt front.

Smooth out the fabric from C to D, and using a pencil draw line C–D to follow the shirt hem.

Place a weight on point D and carefully flatten out the side seam up to point E. Point E from point B must be held firmly down. Spike through point E.

Holding point E firmly down and making sure that point B has not moved from the original line, smooth out the front armhole. Using a spike or tracing wheel mark through to point G at the shoulder (Figure 9).

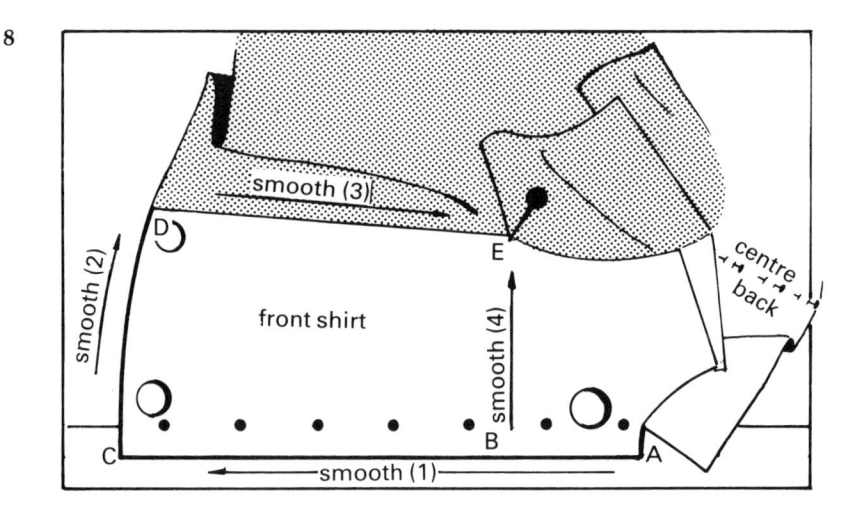

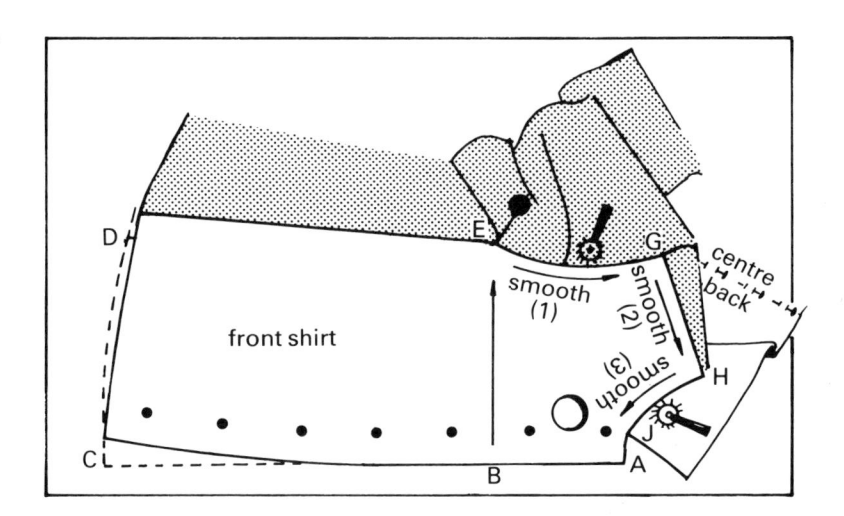

6

7

8

9

8

Holding point G firmly down, smooth out the shoulder seam and spike through point H. Using a tracing wheel, mark the front neckline around to the collar. J is where the collar starts.

Remove the shirt and connect up points D–E–G–H–J–A (Figure 10).

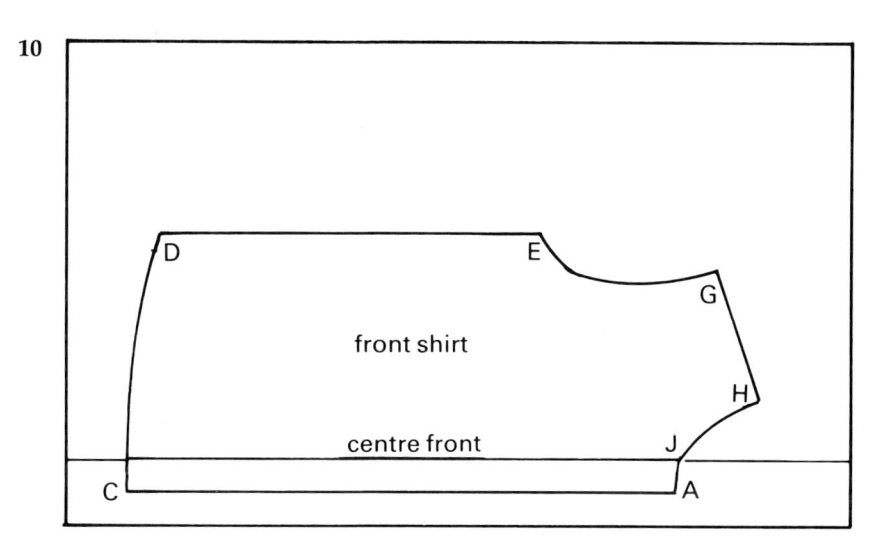

10

The collar

Draw a straight line on a fresh sheet of paper.

Fold the shirt down the centre back so that the collar is exactly folded in half. Pin securely.

Place the folded centre back edge on the straight line and smooth the collar out so that the exact shape is visible (Figure 11). Wheel through points A–B–C.

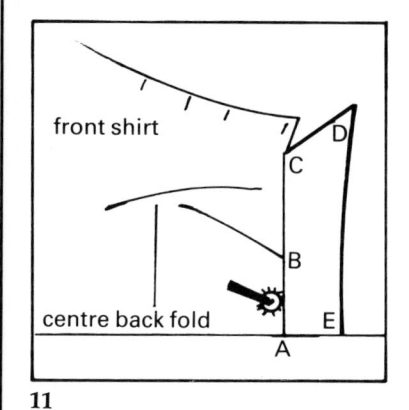

11

Using a pencil, draw around the edge of the collar from E to D to C.

The sleeve

The sleeve is usually the hardest part to copy. However, a shirt sleeve like this is quite straightforward.

Draw a straight line, leaving a large margin on both sides of it.

Fold the sleeve in half and lay the folded line on the straight line (Figure 12). Note that the sleeve may not lie completely parallel to the line at point A; the small gap at the shoulder end is the sleeve ease amount.

Hold point A on the line and smooth down to point B, along to C and around to D. Draw B–C–D.

Place a weight on D to hold firmly. Trace wheel through from D to A for the sleeve head curve.

Remove the sleeve from the paper and connect B–C–D–A. Fold the paper along the line and trace through to form the complete sleeve pattern (see Figure 12).

The pocket

Simply measure the pocket and draft accordingly.

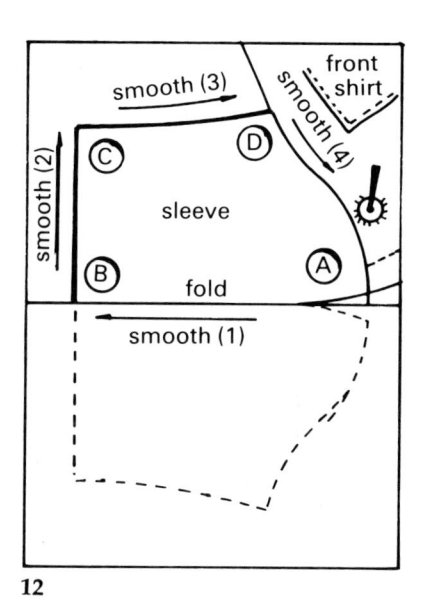

12

The pattern now consists of the following five pieces: back, back yoke, front, collar and sleeve (plus pocket). All that remains to be done is

1. Check that the pattern has been accurately drawn.
2. Add seam allowances.
3. Add or cut a front facing.

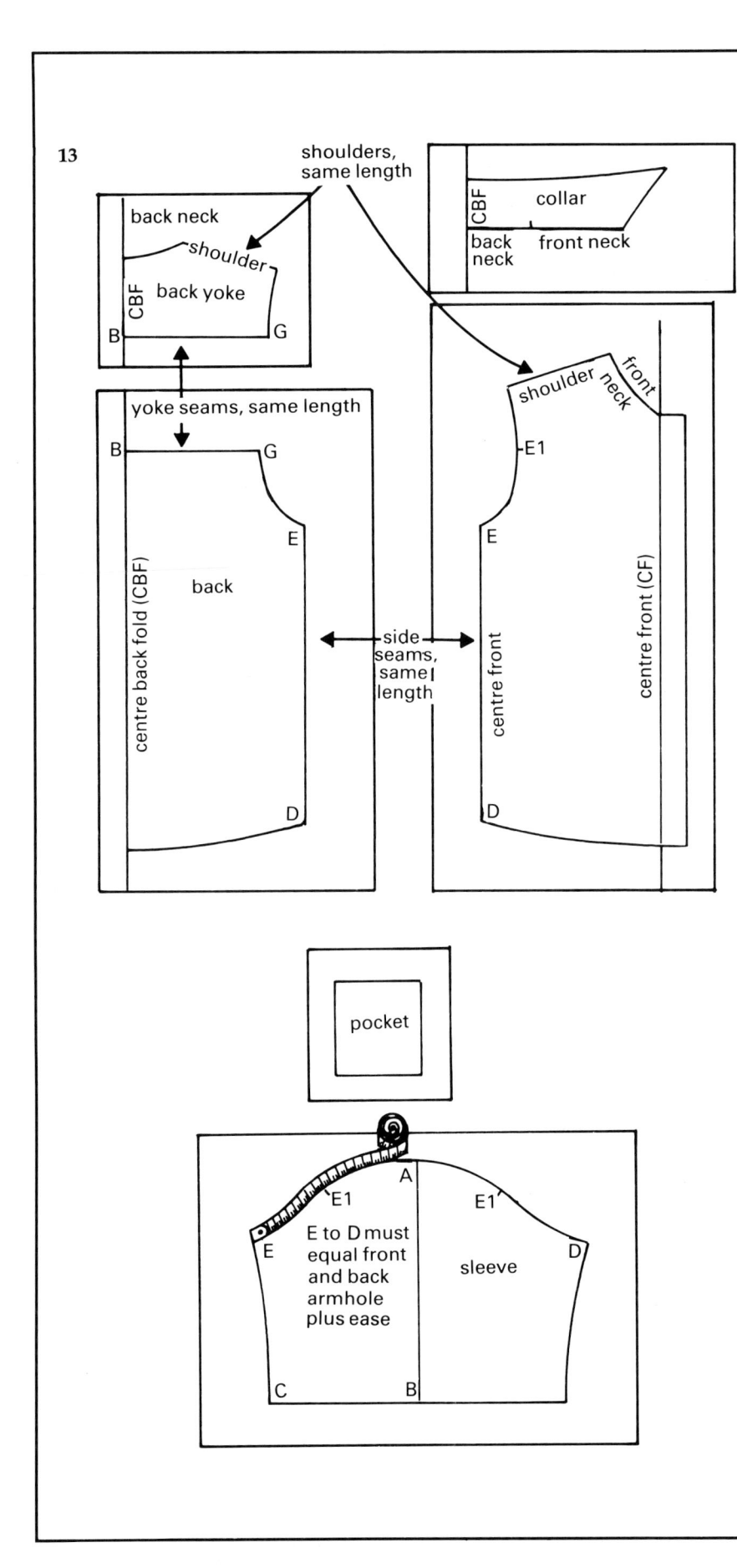

Checking the pattern

The seams that sew together must measure the same length. Figure 13 illustrates the areas that must be measured and compared. If any errors are discovered, *recheck the shirt*.

Sleeve setting

To aid the sleeve setting, measure E–E1 and place a balance mark on the front shirt armhole of the same measurement. Also apply the same measurement from point D on the sleeve underarm.

Adding seam allowances

Add seam allowances as indicated in Figure 14. Also add a turnback facing of about 8 cm to the shirt front, or cut a separate facing (see shaded area of front shirt on Figure 14). Check all the seam lengths carefully.

Cutting

Carefully cut out each pattern section (note the material grain directions indicated on Figure 14).

Alterations

The basic style pattern can be adapted to produce new patterns. Remember to alter the basic pattern *before* adding seam allowances; in this case, therefore, start with Figure 13.

14

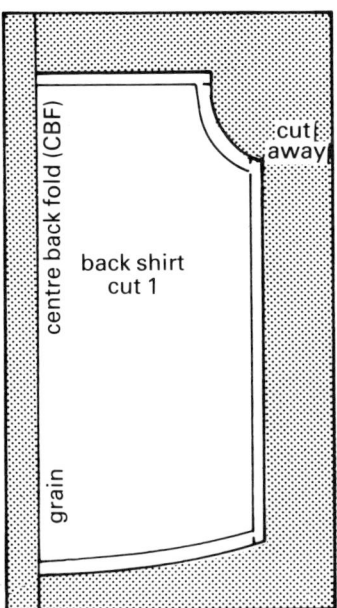

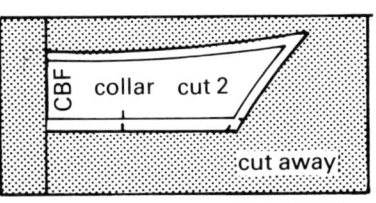

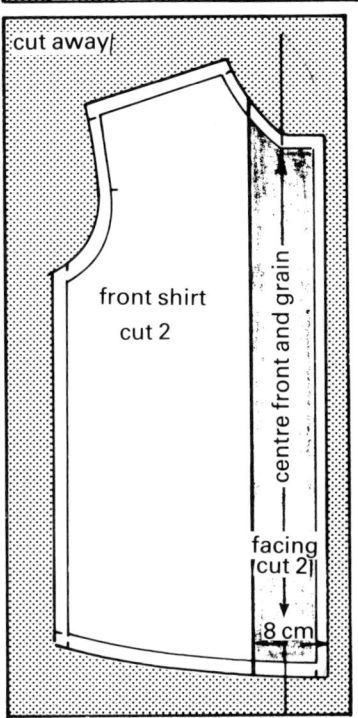

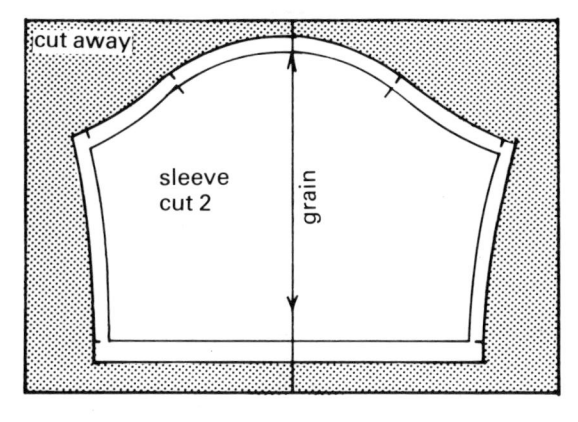

Simple dress: lengthening the basic pattern

The shirt can be transformed into a dress by lengthening the side seams.

Figure 15 shows how to establish the required length by measuring the body. When applying length alterations to the pattern, always measure from the nape of the neck (point A in Figure 15) to whatever length is required.

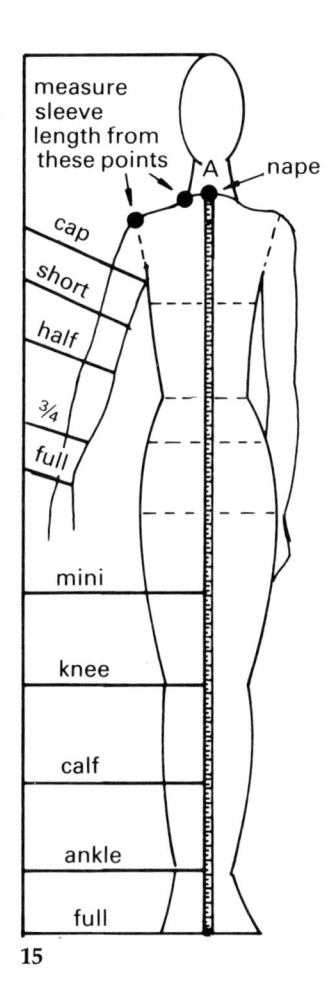

15

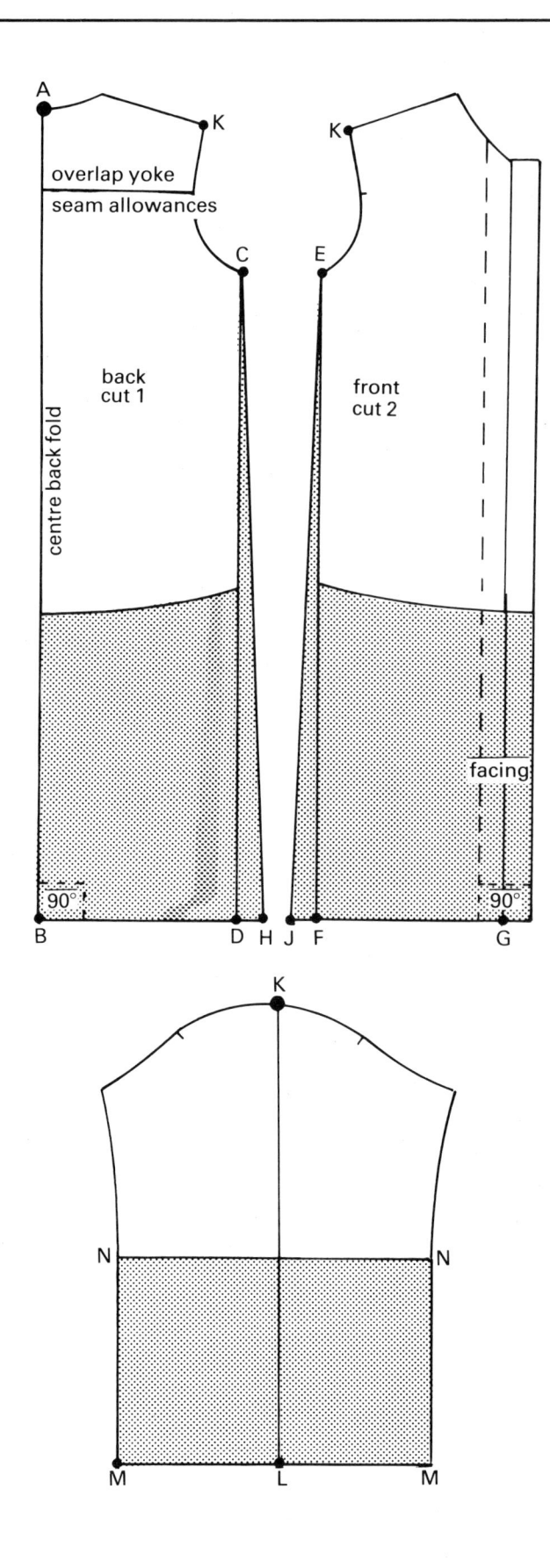

Apply this measurement from point A on the back pattern to the hem point B in the following way (Figure 16). Overlap the yoke seams at the back pattern and extend the nape down to the required length (A–B) on fresh pattern paper. Using a set square, draw a 90 degree line from B. Extend the side seam from C to D. Measure the length C–D. Drop a line of the same length from E to F on the front pattern, and square across to G.

If a wider hem is required, add extra flare from D to H. For example, D–H might be 5 cm. Connect H to C. Repeat this for J from F. Connect J to E.

Adjust the sleeve in a similar manner (Figure 16). Measure K at the shoulder end to the required length. Apply this measurement to the sleeve pattern; K to L equals the sleeve length. Square L to M and connect M to N.

Add seam allowances as before.

Gathered top or dress

In this variation on the garment silhouette, softly hanging gathers fall from a yoke and the sleeve head (Figure 17).

Divide the back pattern evenly into four sections (Figure 18) and cut out the pattern. Draw line A–B on the new pattern paper to maintain the straight seamline. To increase the back, slash up the (three) divisions to the yoke seam and open out the pieces about 4 cm into each cut. This will gather back into the yoke. Make up the new pattern.

Divide the front pattern (Figure 19). Draw line C–D on the front pattern and draw a corresponding line on the new pattern paper. When opening

17

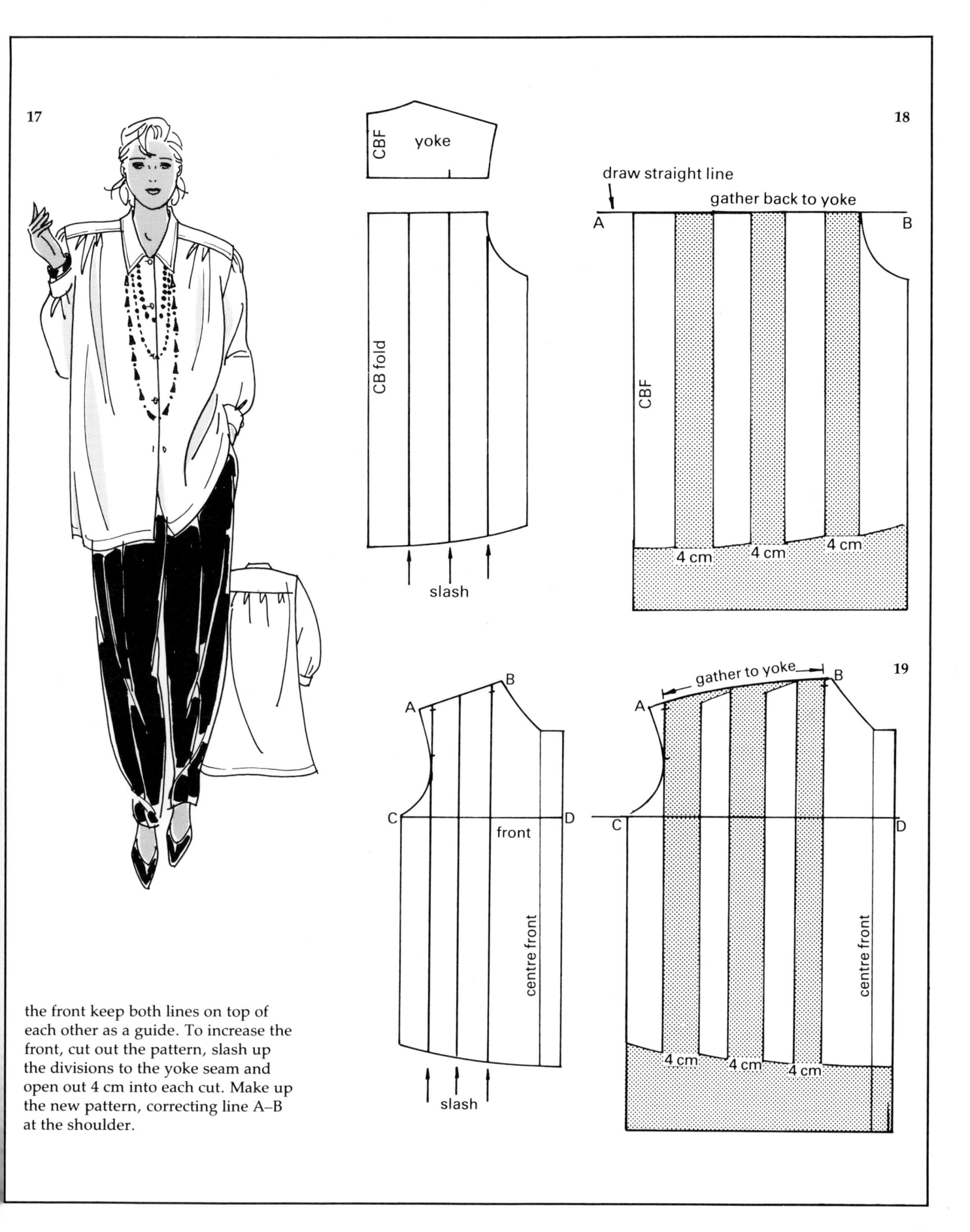

18

CBF yoke

CB fold

slash

draw straight line

gather back to yoke

A   B

CBF

4 cm   4 cm   4 cm

19

A B

C   front   D

centre front

slash

gather to yoke

A   B

C   D

centre front

4 cm 4 cm 4 cm

the front keep both lines on top of each other as a guide. To increase the front, cut out the pattern, slash up the divisions to the yoke seam and open out 4 cm into each cut. Make up the new pattern, correcting line A–B at the shoulder.

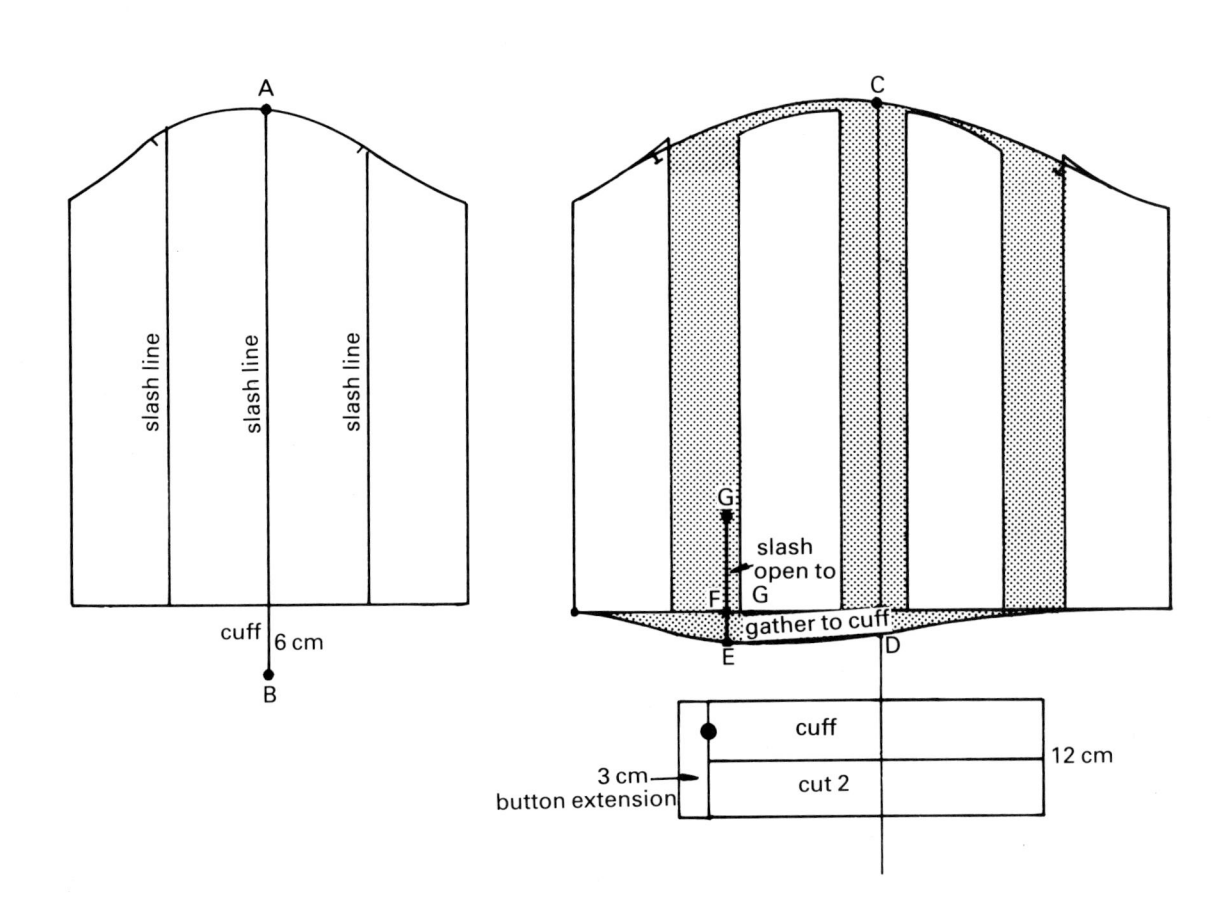

On Figure 20, A–B is the required sleeve length including the cuff. Mark the cuff depth (6 cm) back from B, and cut out the sleeve pattern. Draw slash lines on the sleeve. Slash up the sleeve and open out 4 cm into each slash. This will gather back into the cuff and also into the armhole. Make up the new pattern, correcting the sleeve head through C.

Form the sleeve opening and the style at the sleeve bottom using the following measurements: E from D is half the back sleeve, E from F is 3 cm, and G from E is 12 cm. The material will be cut from G to E and hemmed on both edges.

To form the cuff pattern, double the cuff depth to 12 cm (the fabric pieces will be folded to 6 cm). Measure the wrist size, and add a 3 cm tolerance and a 3 cm button extension to give the cuff pattern length (Figure 20).

Add seam allowances as before.

Flared dress

This adaptation alters the silhouette from a straight box shape to a flared outline (Figure 21).

To prepare the new front and back patterns, lay out a large sheet of paper. Mark around the basic front and back shirt patterns (Figure 22). Extend the shirt lengths if required to a dress length. Draw slash lines up to the back yoke seam and up to the front shoulder seam. Trace the front and back outlines on another sheet of paper.

21   22

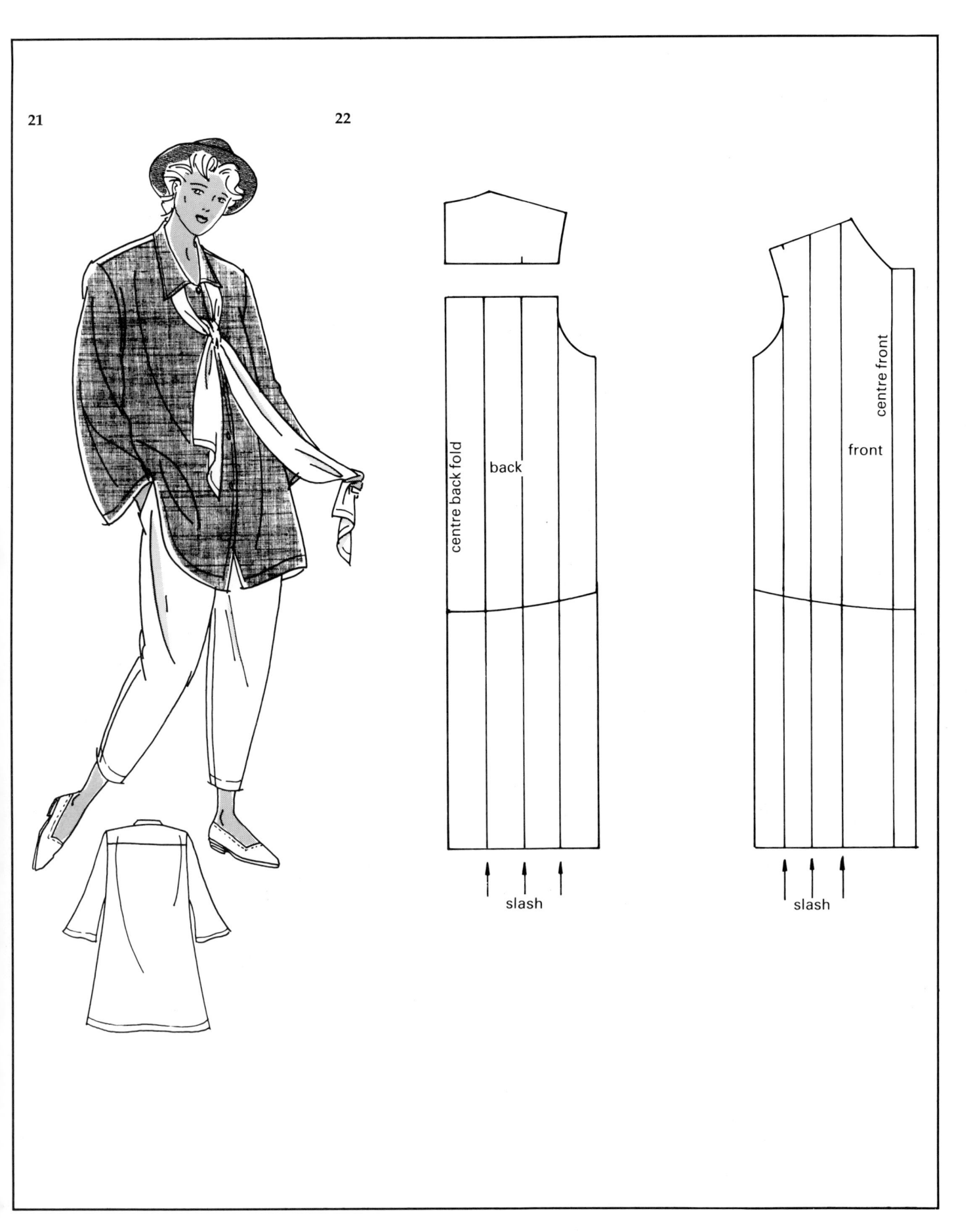

centre back fold | back

centre front | front

slash

slash

23

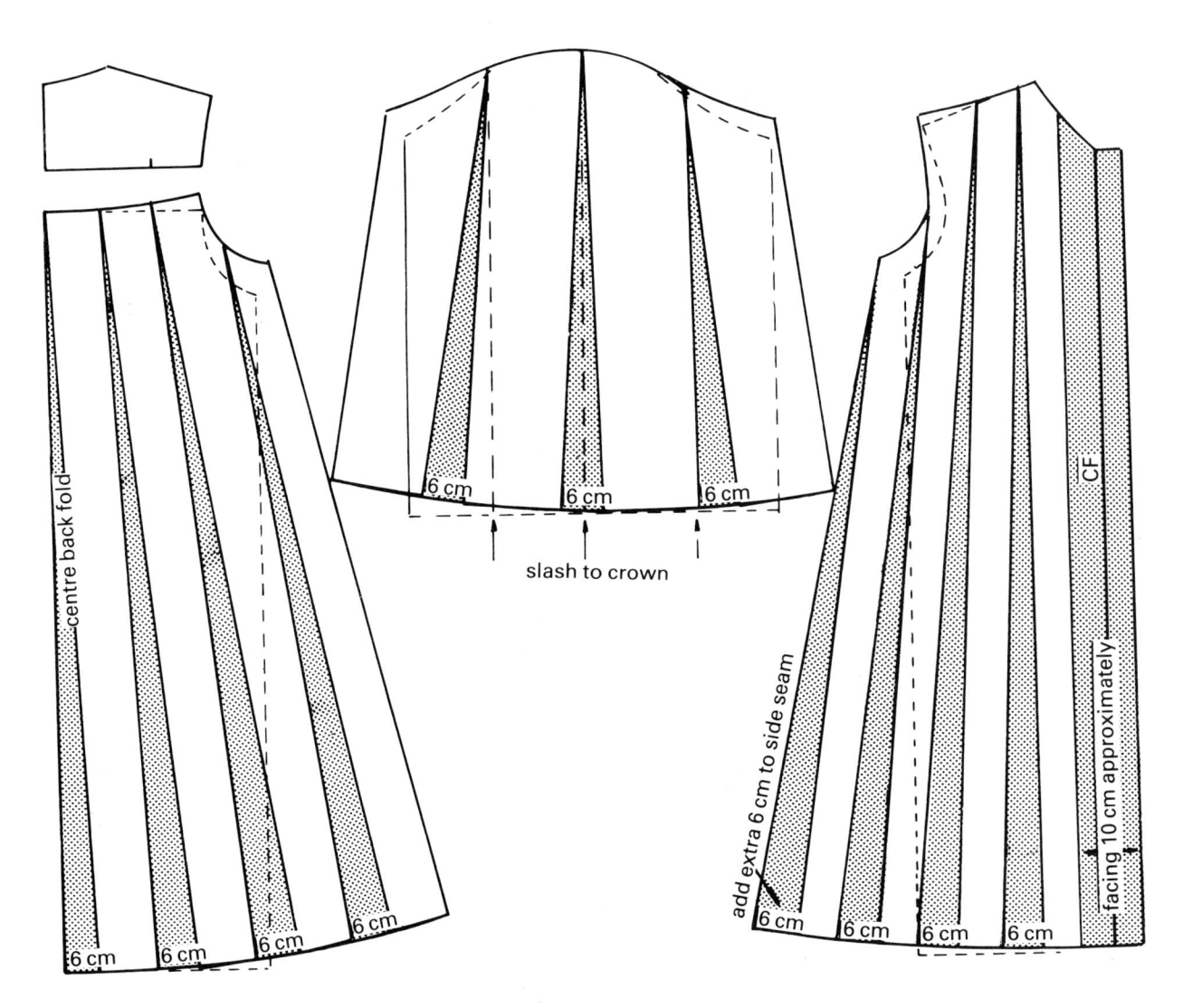

Cut out the patterns, slash up the slash lines and open out the patterns as indicated in Figure 23, approximately 6 cm into each cut. Pin these pattern sections down on the second paper. Redraw hemlines and cut out the new pattern.

Repeat this process with the sleeve. Add seam allowances.

Different fabric effects

By varying the direction in which the pattern is laid on the fabric, different visual effects can be obtained. These effects can virtually change the whole appearance of the garment.

Stripes and whom they suit

Figures 24 and 25 illustrate the shirt cut in a striped fabric. The stripes have been positioned vertically and horizontally to create different effects. Vertical stripes will appear to add height to the wearer, whereas horizontal stripes will appear to increase width. Therefore a short person should avoid horizontal lines on the body, and should wear vertical stripes to appear taller; the reverse applies to a tall person.

What to avoid when buying striped fabric

Avoid fabric with 'bowed' stripes. Check this by folding the material from selvedge to selvedge. If the stripes are 'bowed' it will be impossible to match up the stripes, which will result in great difficulty when attempting to match the stripes across the garment.

How to position the pattern on the striped fabric

Lay out the striped fabric and assess the stripe. If the fabric design has a very bold stripe in it, try to make use of the bold stripe by positioning it down the centre front and the centre back. If the stripe is not centrally positioned the garment will often look badly cut and off balance.

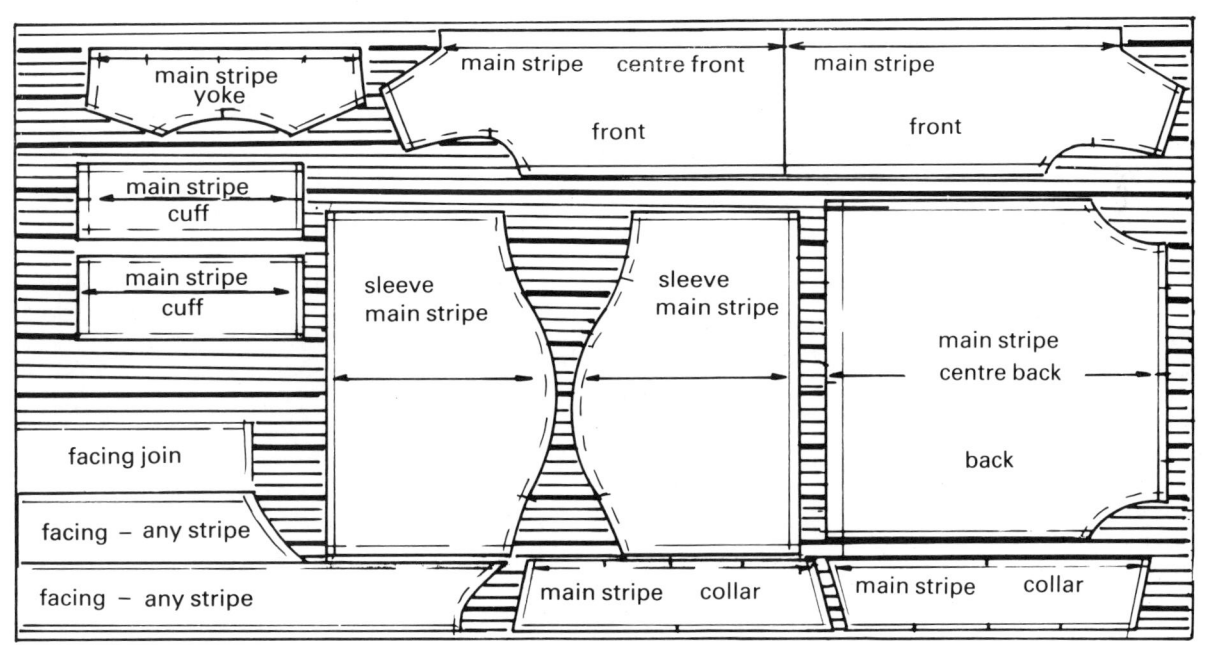

Figure 26 illustrates how to position a pattern on vertically striped fabric. With vertical stripes the side seam does not have to be matched. Notice the bold stripe down the centre front. Position pockets on opposite stripes to achieve a bold positive affect.

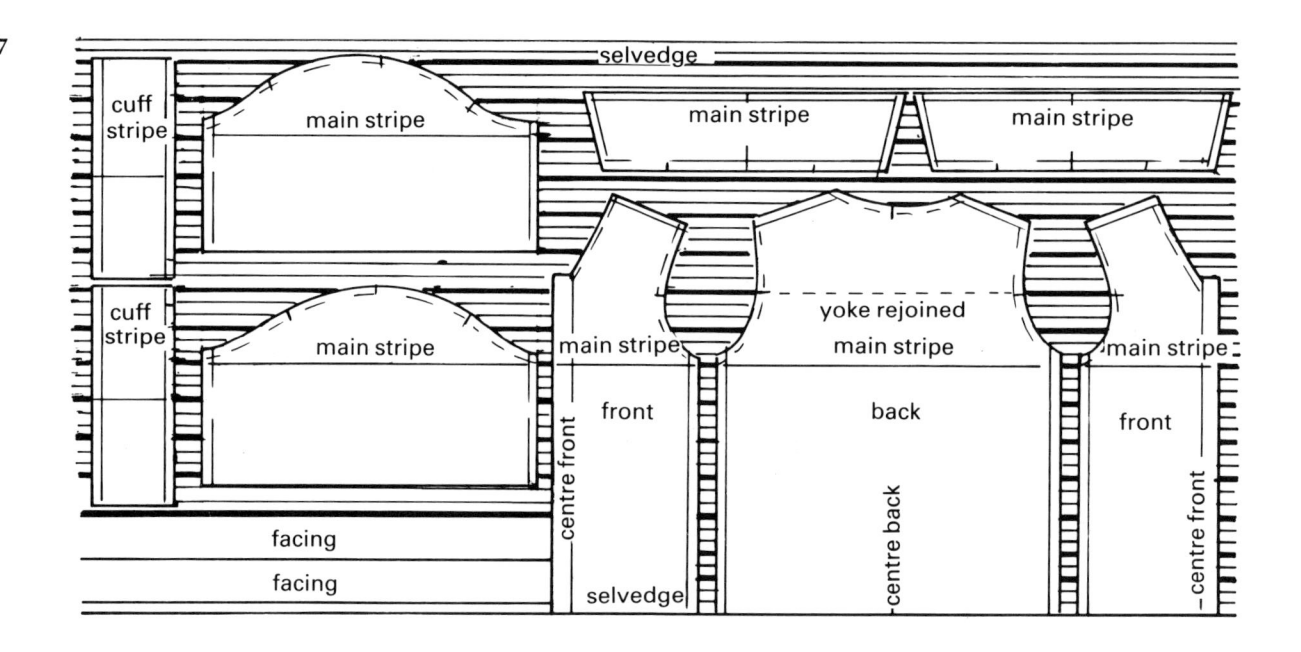

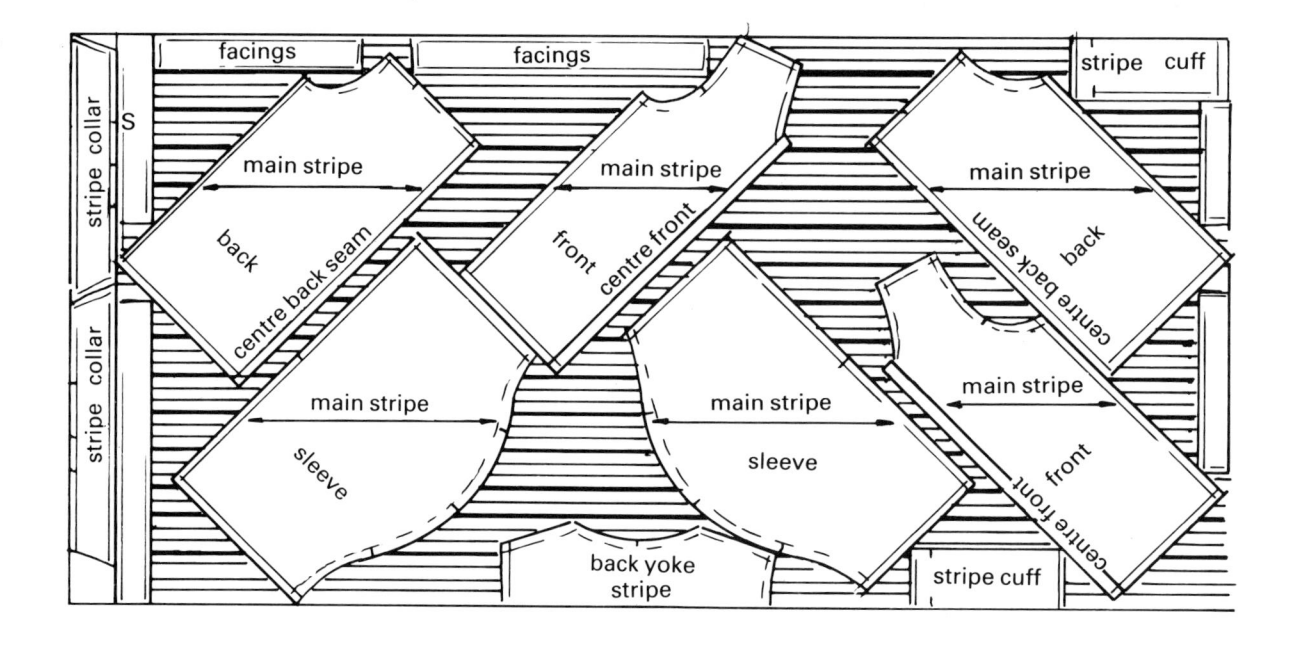

Horizontal stripes (Figure 27) are more difficult because the side seams at sleeve and underarm *must* be matched if a professional look is desired.

Always consider the fabric; never leave the pattern position on the fabric to chance.

Crossway stripes

Figure 29 illustrates the use of crossway stripes, which can create a very striking effect. However, note that fabric cut on the cross-grain is liable to 'drop' at the hem, and also uses more fabric than the previous examples.

Figure 28 shows how to position the pattern on the fabric to obtain this effect. Side seams and centre back and front must be matched to have the full chevron effect. Check that the stripes are evenly woven or printed; if they are not it will be almost impossible to match them as illustrated.

Asymmetrical use of stripes

This unusual arrangement (Figure 30) is quite an economical one for saving fabric, because patterns can be arranged tightly and the matching of stripes is avoided. However, a complete pattern is necessary (i.e. two of everything) to accurately plan the fabric layout (see Figure 31).

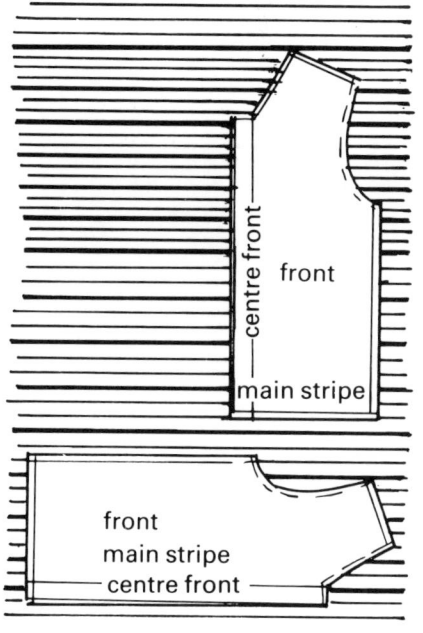

Large patterns such as geometric designs and flowers

Geometric and floral patterns are usually easier to use than stripes or checks because they do not have to be matched up at seam junctions. However, it is important to note that some designs can be termed 'one way'. This means that the pattern is non-reversible. The floral pattern in Figure 32 illustrates this. It would look wrong if the flower pointed upwards on the left front and downwards on the right front, so carefully select the direction in which the 'one-way' pattern should run. Figure 33 illustrates the incorrect and correct use of a geometric one-way fabric design, and Figure 34 illustrates the same for a floral one-way fabric.

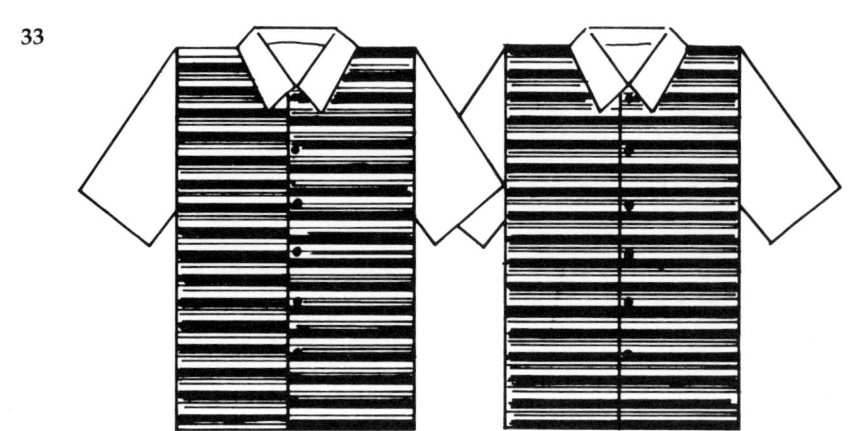

32

33

34

Another point to note is that a large flower should be positioned in a prominent place to make the most of the design. Large floral and geometric patterns are not suitable for designs that have lots of seamlines, as this breaks up the fabric design and gives a cut-up appearance to the garment. The centre front of the shirt can illustrate how to deal with this (Figure 35). Place the centre front of the right shirt on the centre of the large circle. Place the centre front of the left shirt on the centre of the large circle.

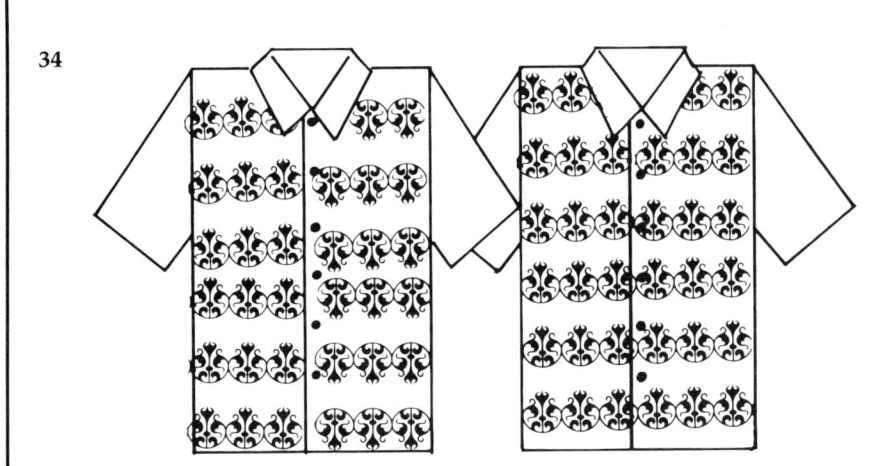

Always calculate the pattern positions on the fabric from the sewing line, *not* the seam allowance edge.

It would be advisable to eliminate the back yoke seam by joining it to the lower shirt to make one back piece; this will avoid distorting the floral pattern on the back and therefore use the beauty of the fabric to the full.

35

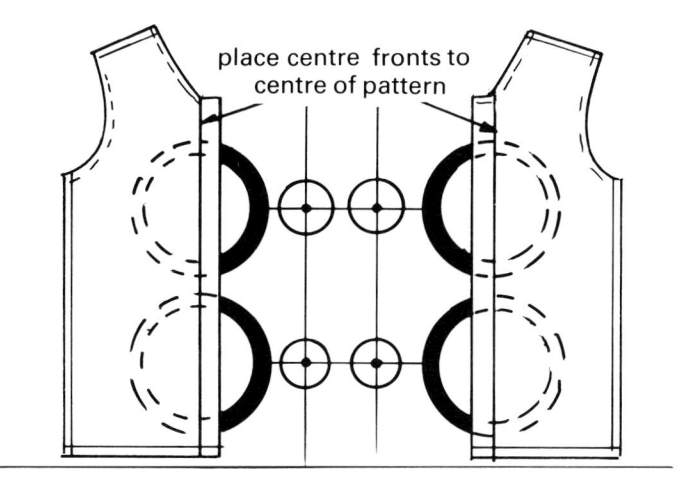

place centre fronts to centre of pattern

Border prints

These kinds of prints are ideal for shirts, skirts and dresses. Figure 36 shows how the various effects of the border design can be used. Usually the heavier part of the print is positioned around the hem of the shirt and sleeve. Utilize the selvedge of the fabric to neaten the hem. Collars and pockets should also be positioned on the bold part of the print. Style 2, which is a gathered skirt, illustrates some suitable fabric layouts.

36

37

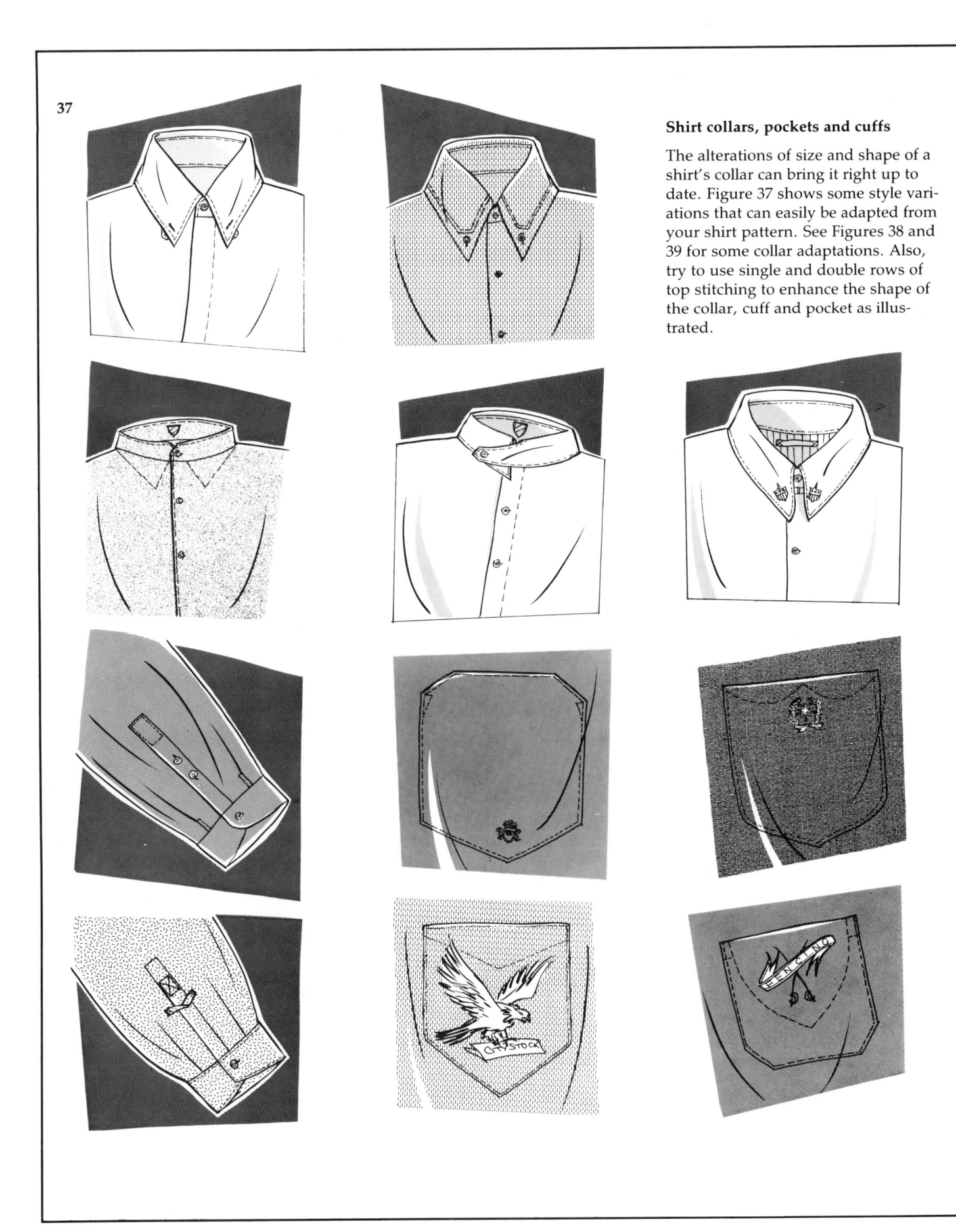

Shirt collars, pockets and cuffs

The alterations of size and shape of a shirt's collar can bring it right up to date. Figure 37 shows some style variations that can easily be adapted from your shirt pattern. See Figures 38 and 39 for some collar adaptations. Also, try to use single and double rows of top stitching to enhance the shape of the collar, cuff and pocket as illustrated.

22

23

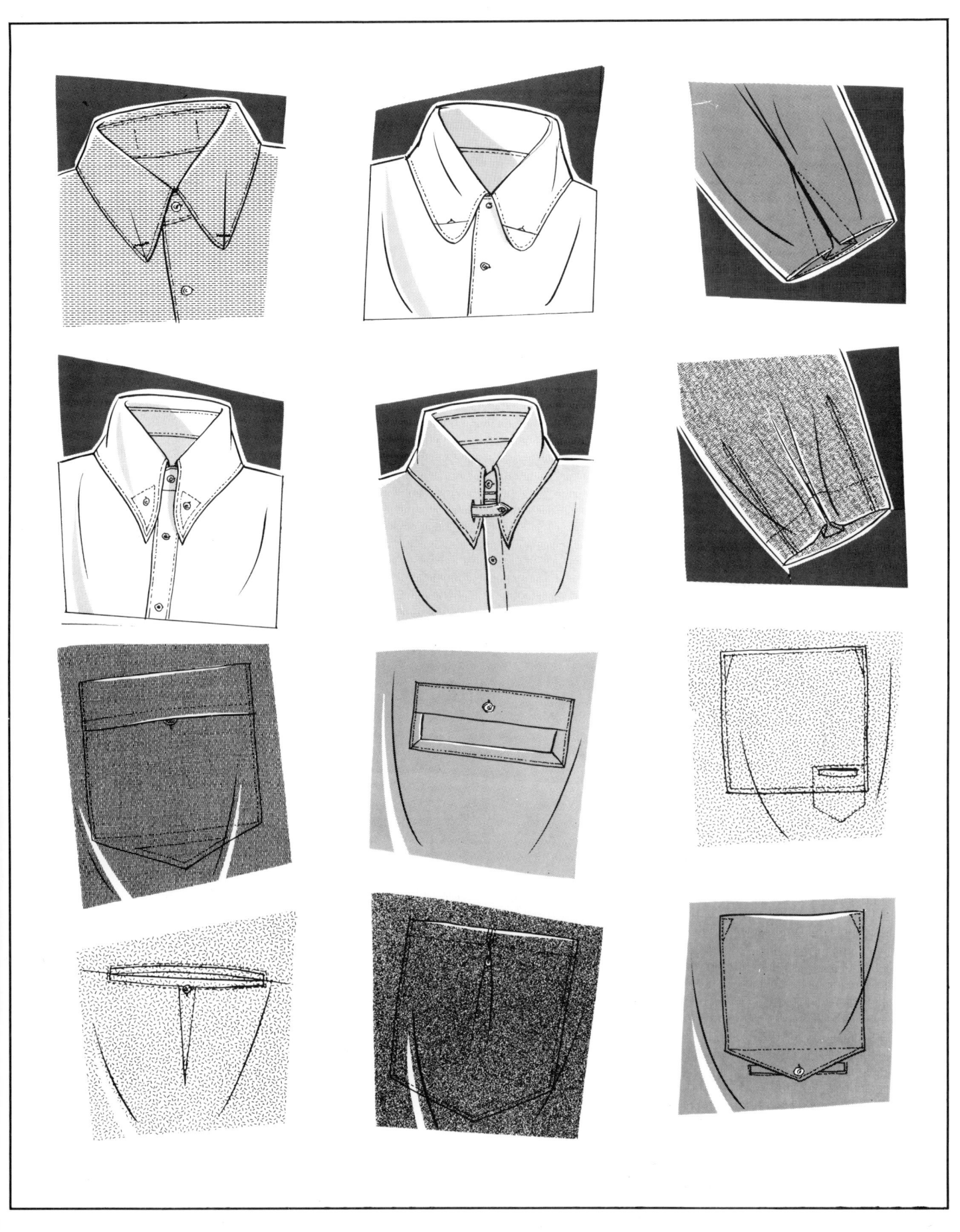

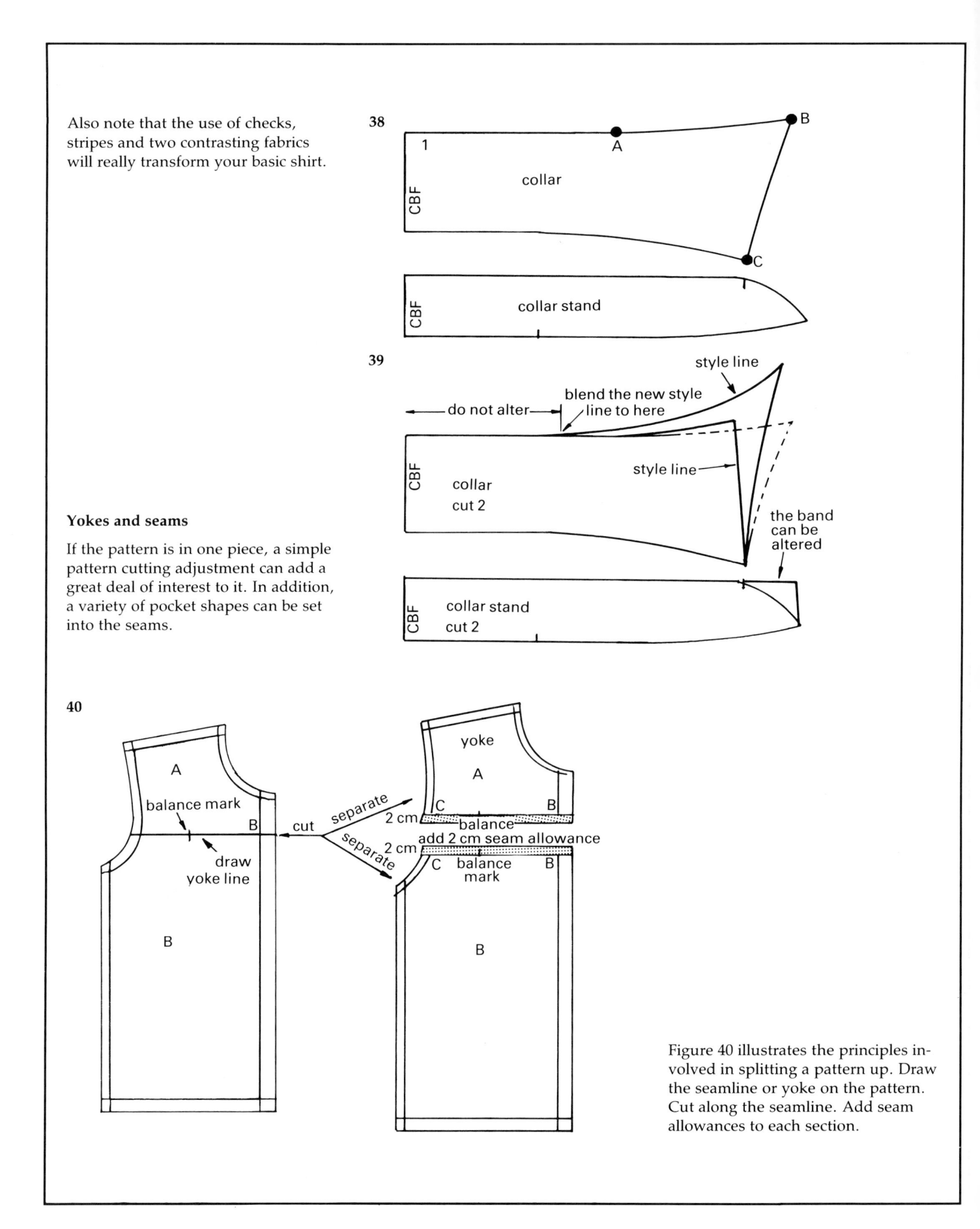

Also note that the use of checks, stripes and two contrasting fabrics will really transform your basic shirt.

38

39

Yokes and seams

If the pattern is in one piece, a simple pattern cutting adjustment can add a great deal of interest to it. In addition, a variety of pocket shapes can be set into the seams.

40

Figure 40 illustrates the principles involved in splitting a pattern up. Draw the seamline or yoke on the pattern. Cut along the seamline. Add seam allowances to each section.

41

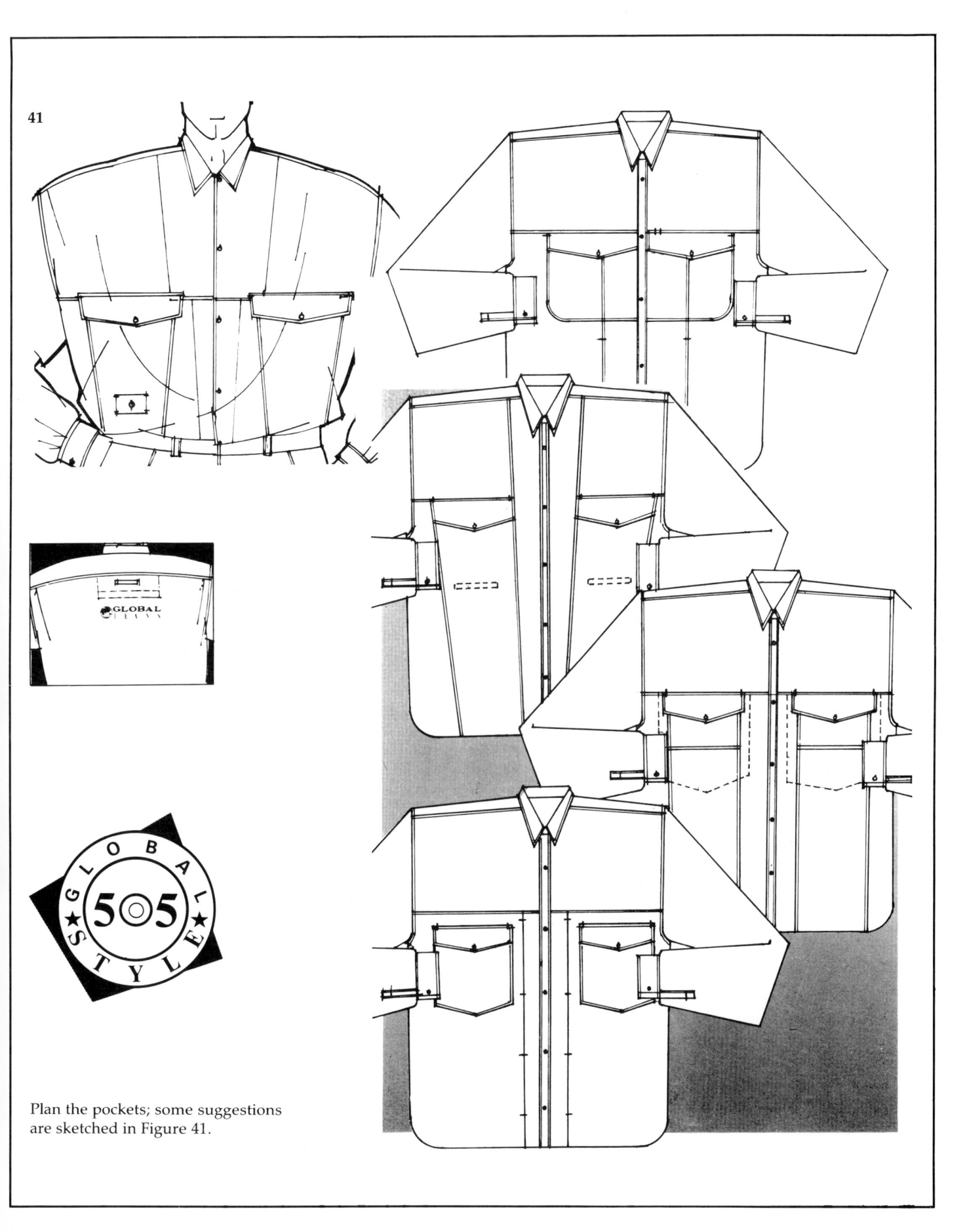

Plan the pockets; some suggestions are sketched in Figure 41.

STYLE 2

DIRNDL SKIRT – direct measurements

This skirt, which is based on a traditional Eastern European folk costume, is extremely easy to reproduce and will look good and up to date in any number of fabrics.

What to look for

First neatly press the skirt. Examine the skirt very carefully and draw a simple sketch of it (Figure 42), noting all the seam positions, pockets and other interesting points and also the grain positions.

The skirt is cut in three sections (front, separated back: see Figure 43), and can easily be copied. First it is necessary to measure the amount of fabric used to gather back into the waistband – that is, to decide whether the skirt has been made from a straight or a shaped piece of fabric.

In Figure 42, A to B is the skirt length. Pull the skirt taut and measure C to D. In Figure 44, measure E to F about 20 cm below the waistband. If the two measurements are the same, the skirt has been cut from a rectangle of fabric. However, if C–D is wider than E–F the skirt is cut from a shaped piece of fabric.

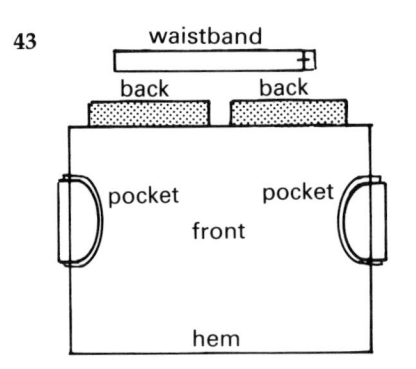

Method to choose

The dimensions of this skirt can be established by directly measuring the fabric around the skirt hem.

Equipment needed

Paper, tape measure, set square, pencils, scissors etc.

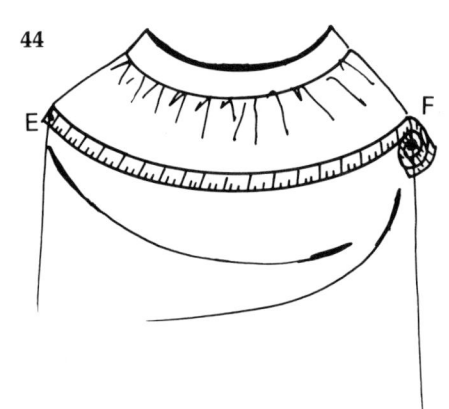

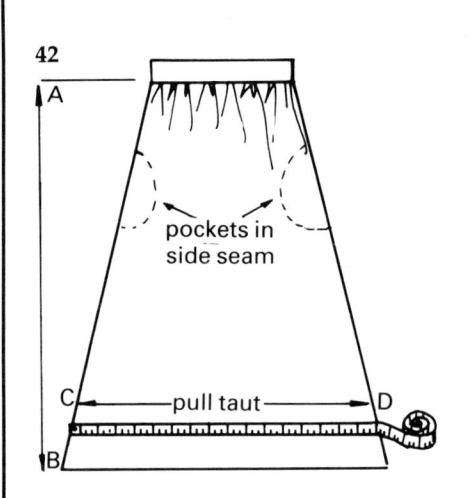

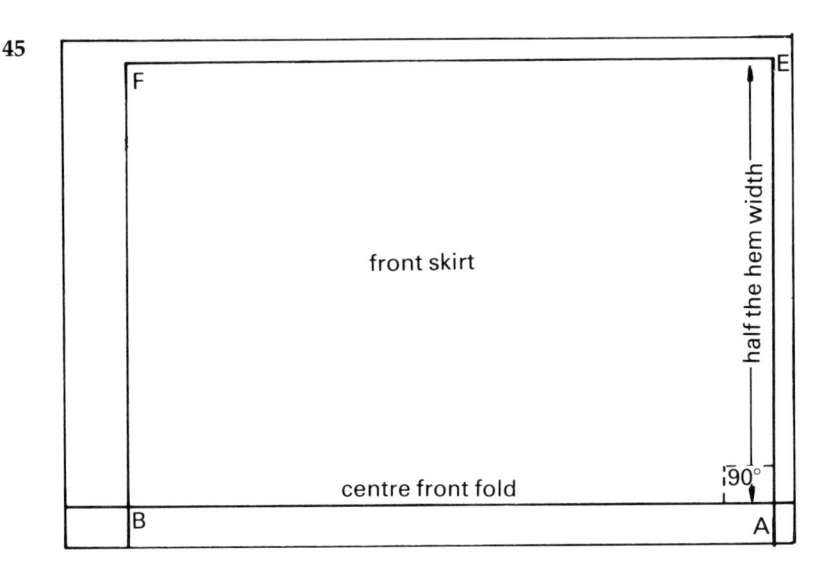

26

Front and back skirt

Lay down a large sheet of paper and draw line A to B 3 cm in from the edge (Figure 45). A to B should equal the skirt length.

Measure C to D on Figure 42, making sure the fabric is pulled taut. Then E from A on Figure 45 should equal half of C from D (the front skirt will be cut on the fold), and should be a right angle from A–B. Square from F and connect to B.

Add seam allowances around the edge of the pattern (Figure 46). This can be used for both the front and the back skirt; a centre back seam allowance is simply added to the back section when laying on to the fabric.

46

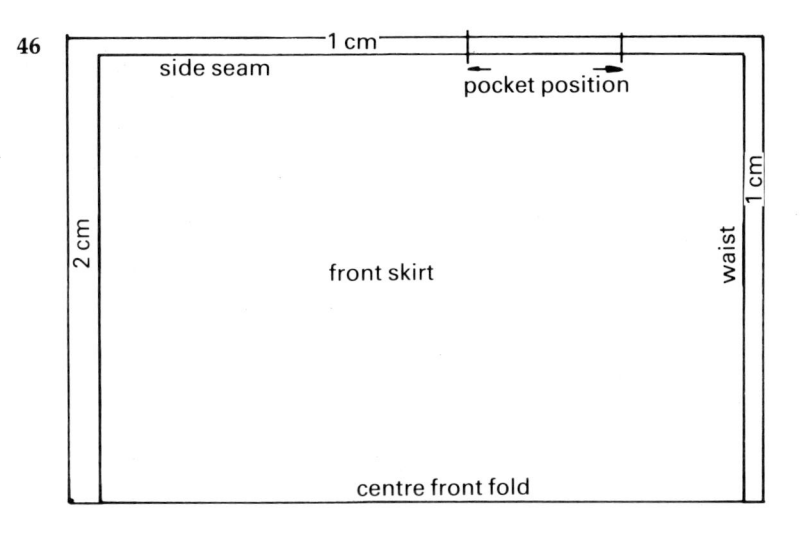

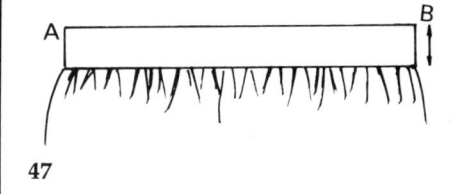

The waistband

Measure A to B on Figure 47 for half the waistband measurement. Draw a line of equal length on a sheet of paper, shown as C–D on Figure 48. Draw E to D, the finished waistband width. Square from G to E.

H from D is for the overlap, which contains the button and buttonholes or hooks and eyes. It is usually about 2.5 cm.

Add a 1 cm seam allowance all around the waistband, as shown in Figure 48.

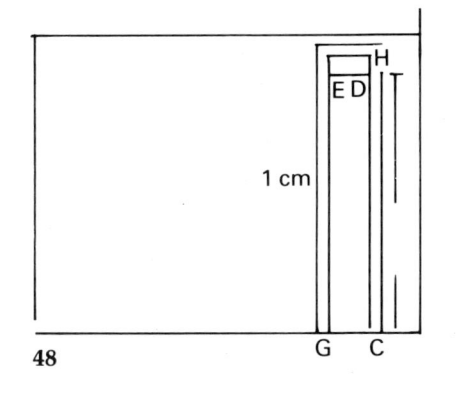

The pocket

Turn the skirt inside out and measure the pocket down from the waistband to give the pocket position which should be marked on to the pattern (Figure 46).

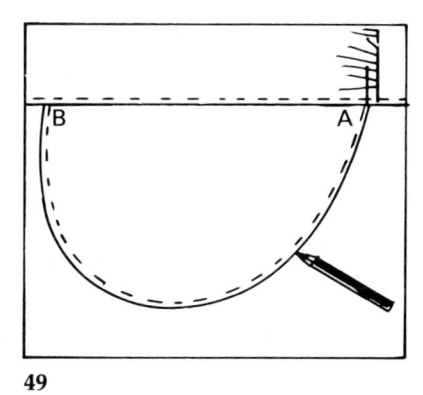

Lay the pocket flat on a sheet of paper and draw around the outline from A to B (Figure 49). Remove the skirt. Connect A to B with a straight line, and add seam allowances to give the pocket pattern (Figure 50).

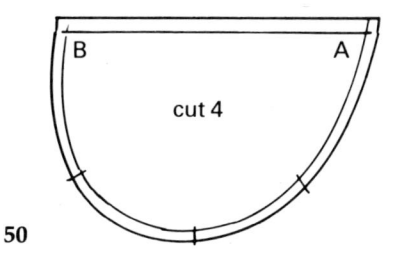

51

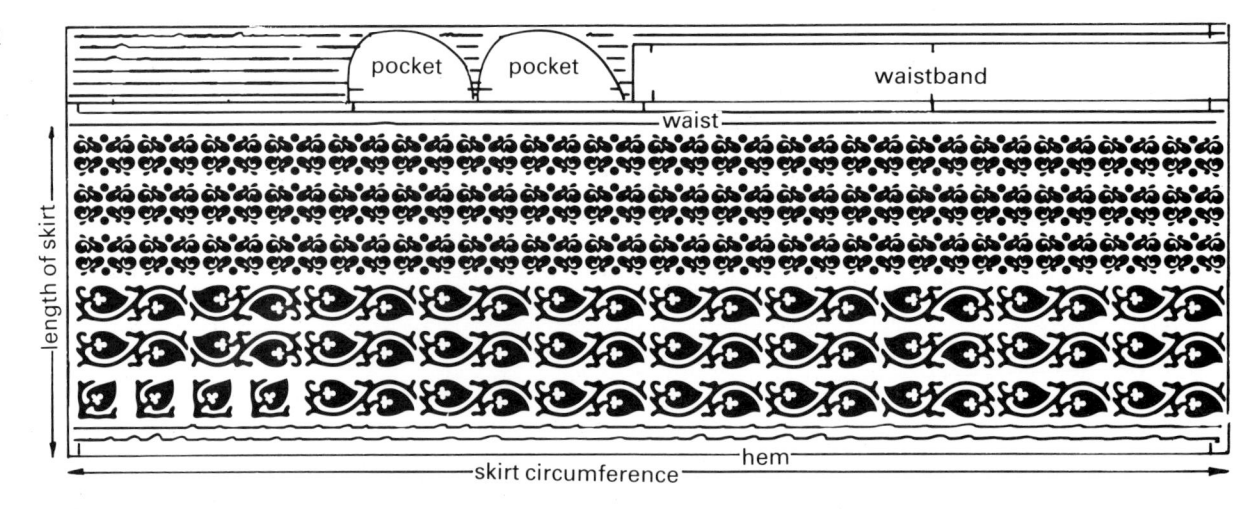

Alterations

Length adjustments

To adjust the size of this skirt is a simple process. The length is easily adjusted by cutting out a longer skirt. The waistband can be altered to make it larger or smaller by adding appropriate amounts to each edge.

Fabric effects

There are various ways in which this skirt can be cut (see Style 1 for ideas). In addition, some interesting effects can be achieved by varying the pattern placement on the fabric. Note that these styles can be marked directly on the fabric; a paper pattern is not needed.

Border prints

Rather than cut the skirt in three pieces, as for the original, it is simpler to cut it in one continuous length. This will be very helpful if the fabric is a border print (Figure 57), because it avoids cutting into the fabric design. Always position the larger print around the hem to add design balance to the garment. Figure 51 illustrates a typical border print fabric layout.

Joined widths

Figure 54 illustrates a method of adding extra fullness to the skirt without using extra material. This can be achieved by joining fabric widths which are cut 'across' the fabric, i.e. from selvedge to selvedge. The wider the fabric the more fullness will be gathered or pleated back into the waistband. This will be suitable for a small print or a plain fabric rather than a stripe, as it will avoid matching fabric patterns. Figures 52 and 53 illustrate how to cut a skirt of this type.

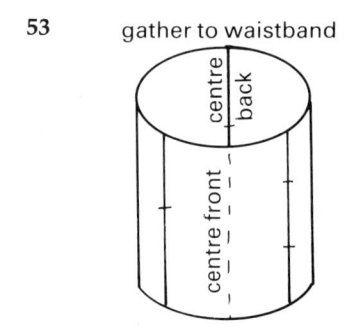

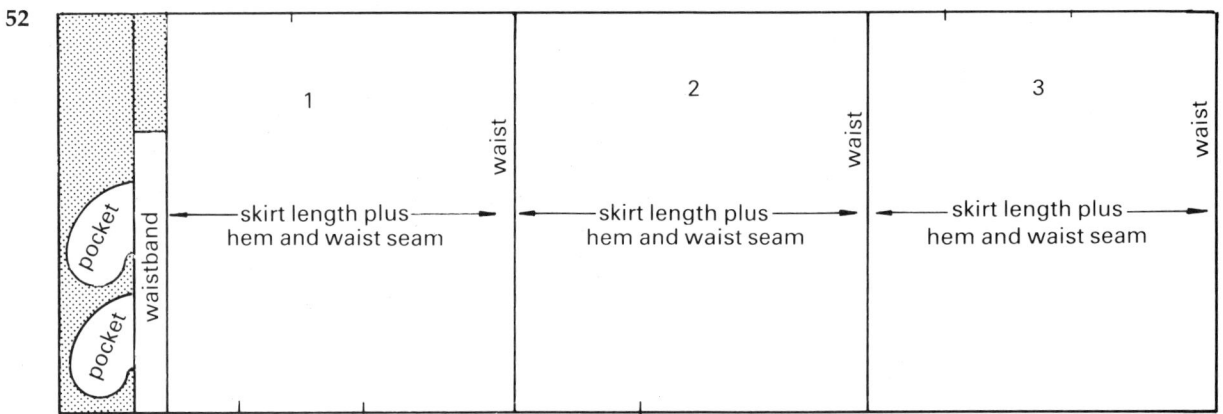

53

52

54 55 56 57

29

58

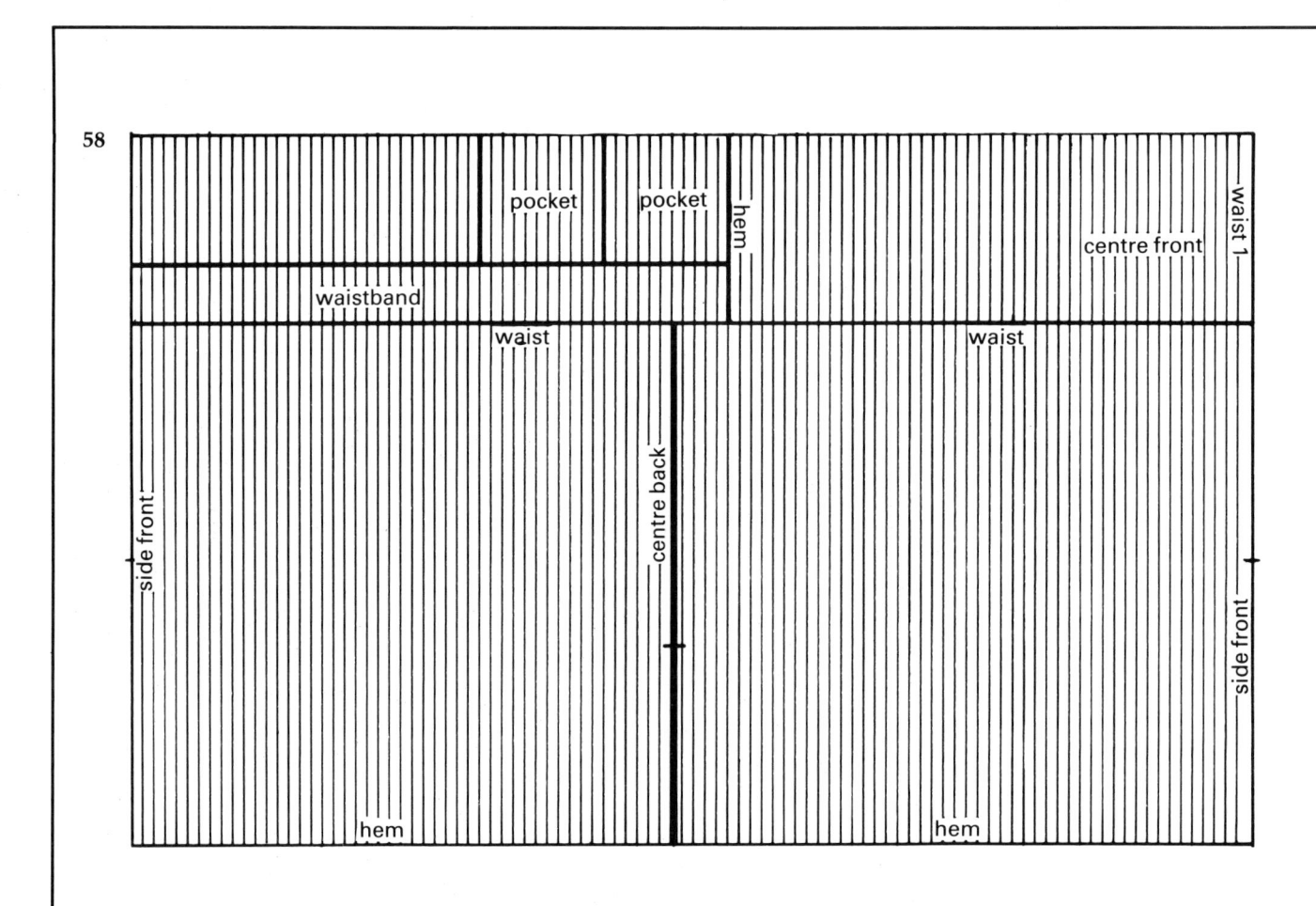

- pocket
- pocket
- hem
- centre front
- waist 1
- waistband
- waist
- waist
- side front
- centre back
- side front
- hem
- hem

60

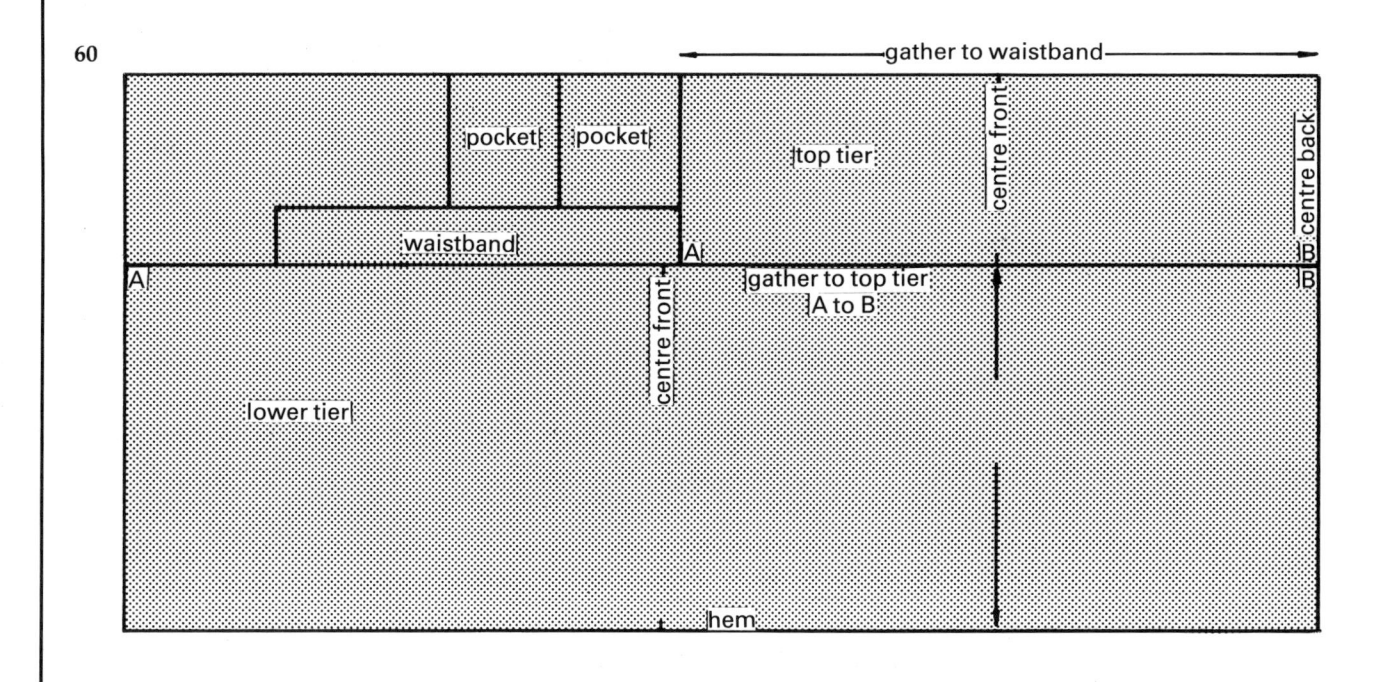

- gather to waistband
- pocket
- pocket
- top tier
- centre front
- centre back
- waistband
- A
- A
- B
- B
- centre front
- gather to top tier A to B
- lower tier
- hem

59 gather to waistband

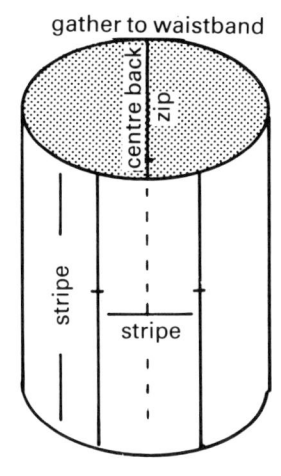

Reverse stripes with front panel

Figure 56 illustrates an effective way of using striped fabric. However, this style is only suitable for a wide fabric which is soft and easy to gather. Figure 58 illustrates a typical striped fabric layout, and Figure 59 shows the arrangement of the pieces. Position the zip into the centre back seam.

Two-tier gathered skirt

Figure 55 illustrates an interesting way of using soft fabric. The fabric needs to be very soft so that the lower skirt can be gathered into the upper tier. Figure 60 gives the fabric layout. Care should be taken when cutting this type of skirt to consider the proportions between the upper and the lower tiers. If the proportions are not correct, the result will be a skirt, that looks out of balance.

STYLE 3

UNLINED SUMMER JACKET – fold and spike method

This casually smart popular summer jacket can be made longer or shorter according to the 'length of the moment'.

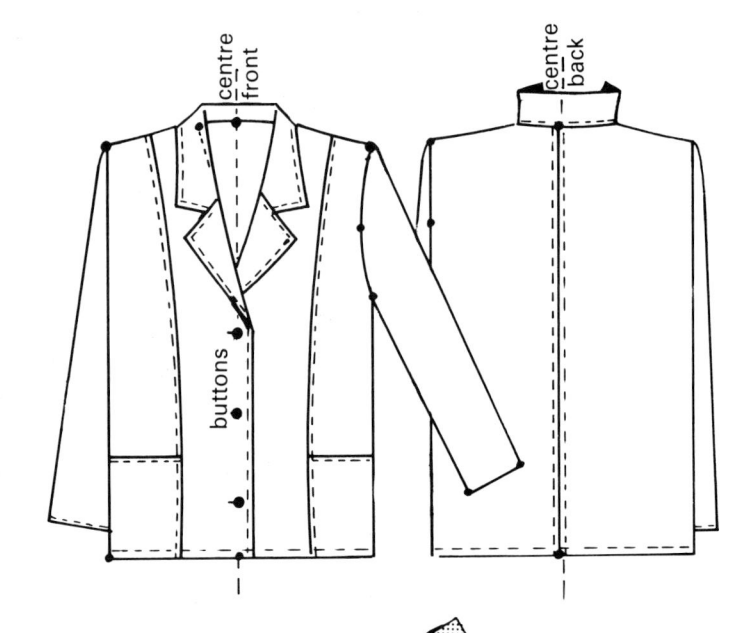

What to look for

First neatly press the jacket. Do *not* press a crease down the centre sleeve.

Examine the garment very carefully and draw a simple sketch of it (Figure 61), noting all the seam positions, pockets etc. Fasten up the jacket and lay it flat on the table. If it lies completely flat, it can be assumed that there is no bust dart, which would complicate the pattern.

Method to choose

The fold and spike method is the best method of reproducing this type of flat garment.

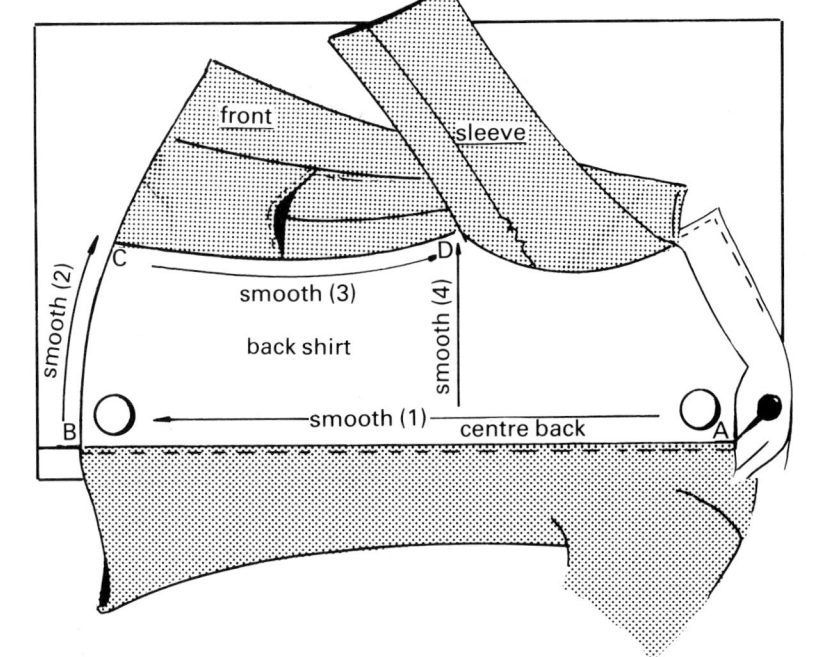

Equipment needed

Paper, fine spike, tracing wheel, tape measure, set square, pencils, scissors, etc.

Locating the key points

Locate the key points on the jacket, shown by the large dots on Figure 61. They define the shape of the garment.

The back jacket

Draw a line on a large sheet of paper.

Lay the centre back seam of the jacket on the line (Figure 62). Smooth the fabric from A to B. Place a weight on A and B to hold the jacket firmly down on the paper. Spike through point A.

Smooth out from B to C and draw in the hemline with a pencil.

Smooth out from C to D and from the centre back to D. Spike through point D for the side seam.

Holding point D firmly, smooth out the armhole to point E at the shoulder (Figure 63). Using a tracing wheel, wheel through the armhole from D to E.

Spike through points E and F for the shoulder line. Wheel through from F to A for the back neck.

Remove the back jacket and connect up all the points (Figure 64).

The front jacket collar section

Draw a straight line on a large sheet of paper.

Lay the front jacket edge to this straight line (Figure 65). Mark point A at the hem. Smooth out the fabric edge until it begins to leave the straight line at B. Smooth out the lapel from B to C. Make sure that the shape of the lapel is retained; B–C will not be on the straight line. Draw from B to C and up to D for the lapel point.

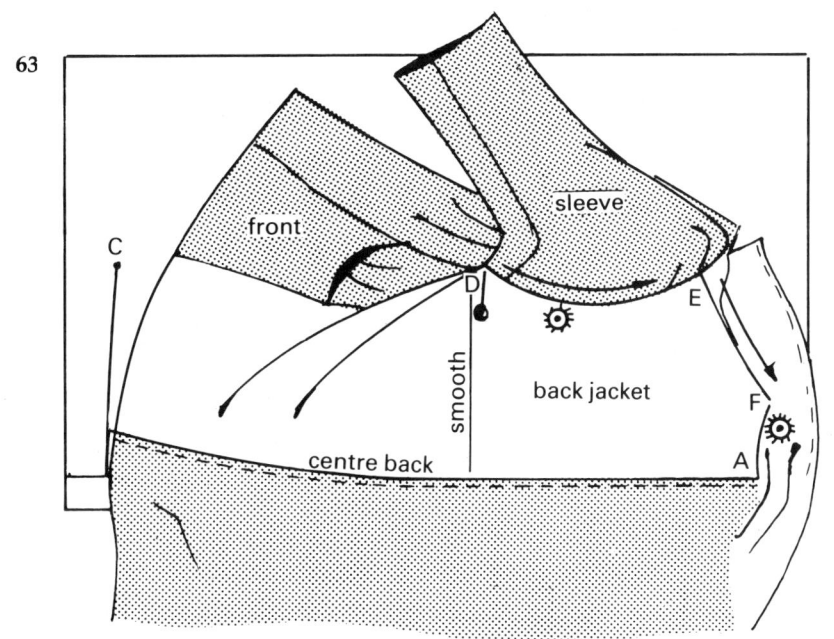

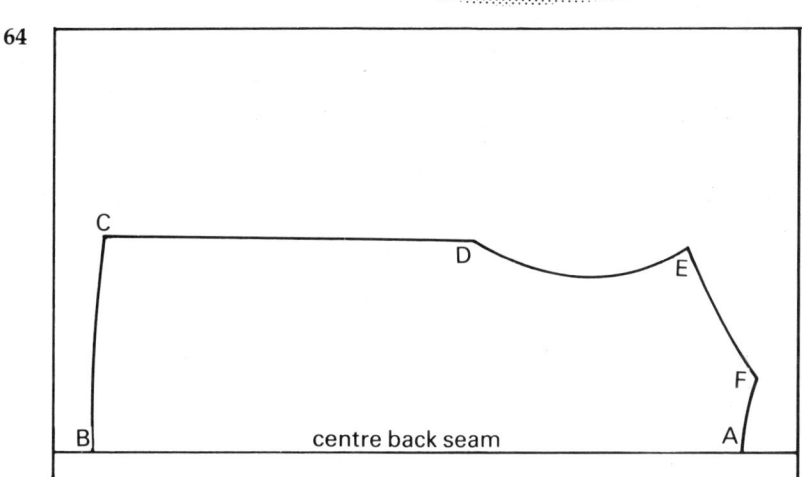

Smooth out the neckline and seamline. Using a tracing wheel, mark the neckline shape.

Spike through points E, F and G and down to H. Draw along the hem from H to A.

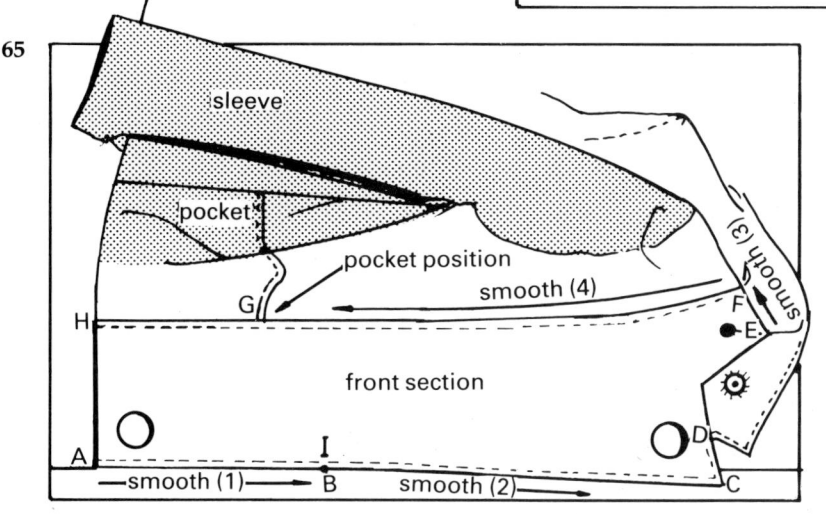

Remove the jacket. Connect up points D–E–F–G–H (Figure 66).

This pattern will also be used as a front facing.

The side front

Examine the jacket side front and place pins into the straight grain at the hem and shoulder (and middle if required).

Draw a straight line down the centre of a large sheet of paper.

Lay the pinned line of the jacket on the straight line (Figure 67). Mark point H at the hem. Smooth out the jacket on the straight line, and along the seam to point G at the pocket and upwards to F at the shoulder. Using a tracing wheel, mark along line H–G–F.

Place a weight on point H and smooth to point J. Smooth out along the side seam to K. Mark along the hemline H to J with a pencil and use a spike to mark point K.

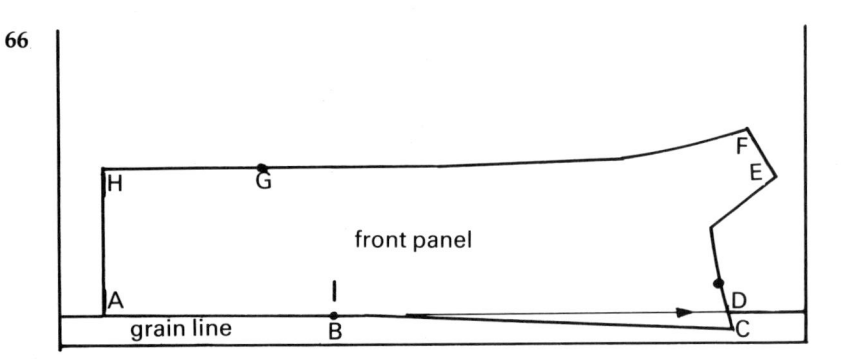

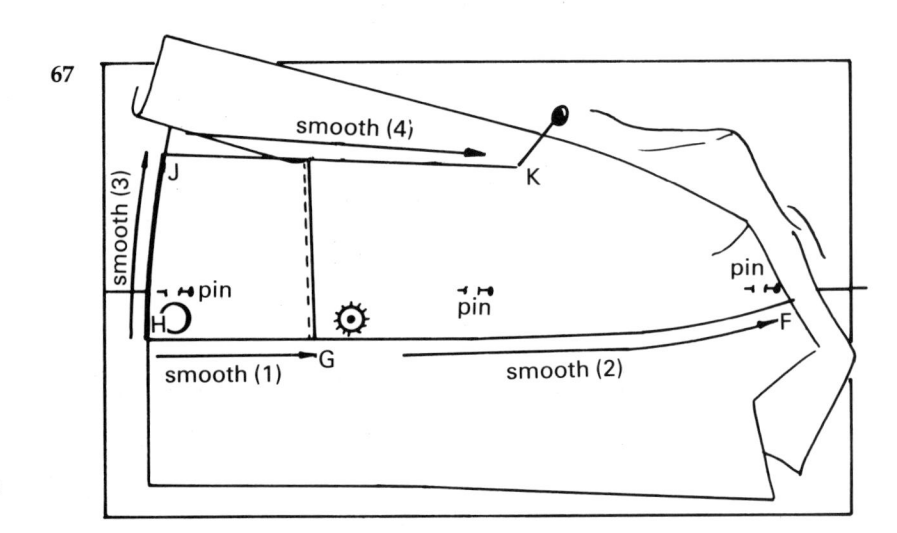

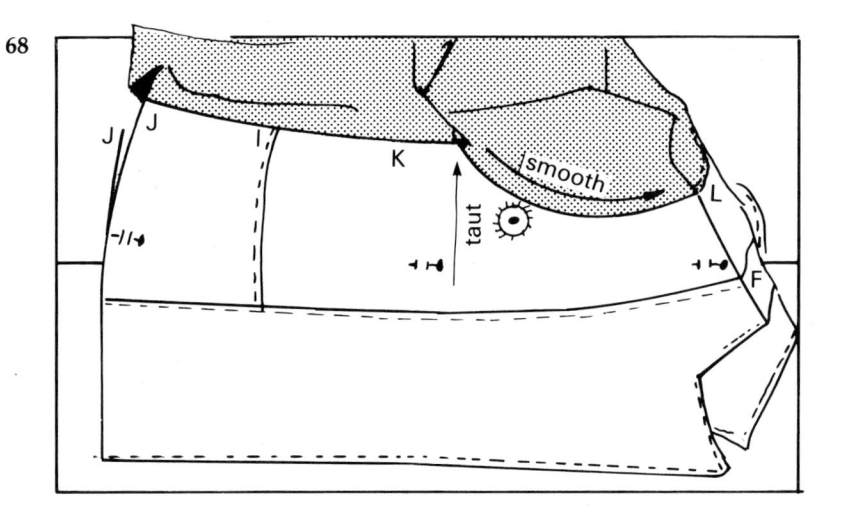

Holding point K taut from the original pinned grain line, smooth out the armhole to point L at the shoulder (Figure 68). Use a tracing wheel to trace through line K–L. Spike through point I.

34

Remove the jacket and connect up points J–I–K–L–F (Figure 69).

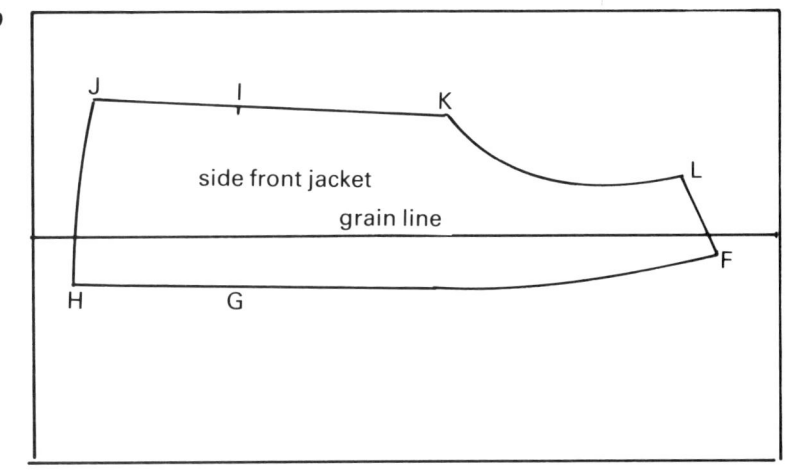

The collar

Fold the collar at the centre back so that the front edges are exactly together.

Draw a straight line on a small sheet of paper and lay the centre back of the collar on it (Figure 70). Pencil around the outer edge from A to B to C. Spike through points D, E and F.

Remove the jacket and connect up all the collar points (Figure 71).

The sleeve

Most jacket sleeves are cut in two pieces – that is, they have a top sleeve and an under sleeve. This type of sleeve gives the garment a more tailored appearance.

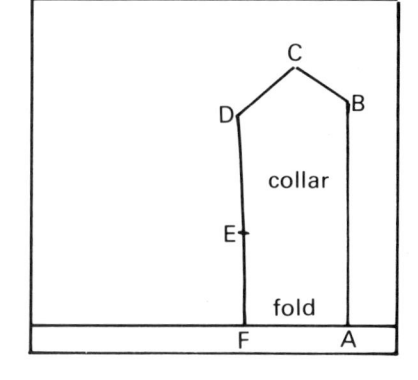

The under sleeve

Fold the sleeve along the front under sleeve line, which will probably be slightly curved. Place pins into the straight grain.

Draw a straight line on the paper and place the straight grain on this line (Figure 72). Flatten the sleeve out at its front edge A–B.

Draw line B–C.

Using a tracing wheel, wheel line C–D (the back under sleeve line) and then the part of the sleeve head from D to A.

Remove the sleeve and finish connecting points C–D–A–B.

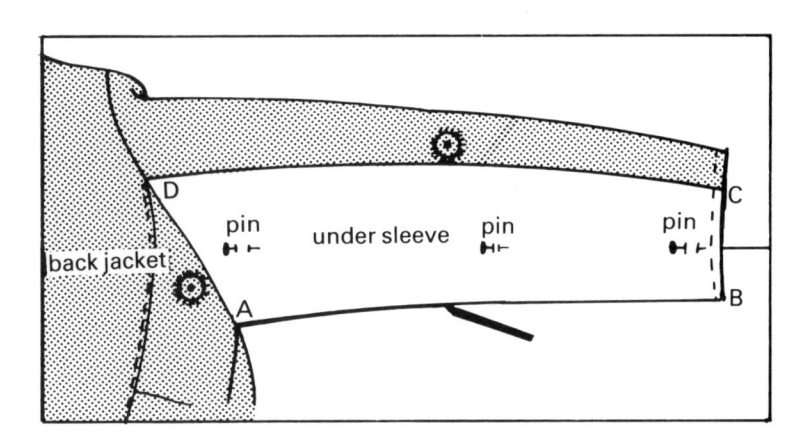

The top sleeve

Most sleeves have fullness in the sleeve head which is eased into the armhole. The exact amount can be established as follows.

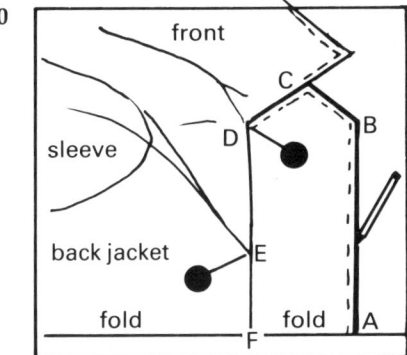

Fold the sleeve in half (which is a continuation of the jacket silhouette at the top).

Draw a straight line on paper. Lay the folded line on the straight line and mark points E–F–G (Figure 73).

Draw line E–B at the wrist and trace wheel line B–D (front top sleeve line). Also trace wheel the sleeve head D–G.

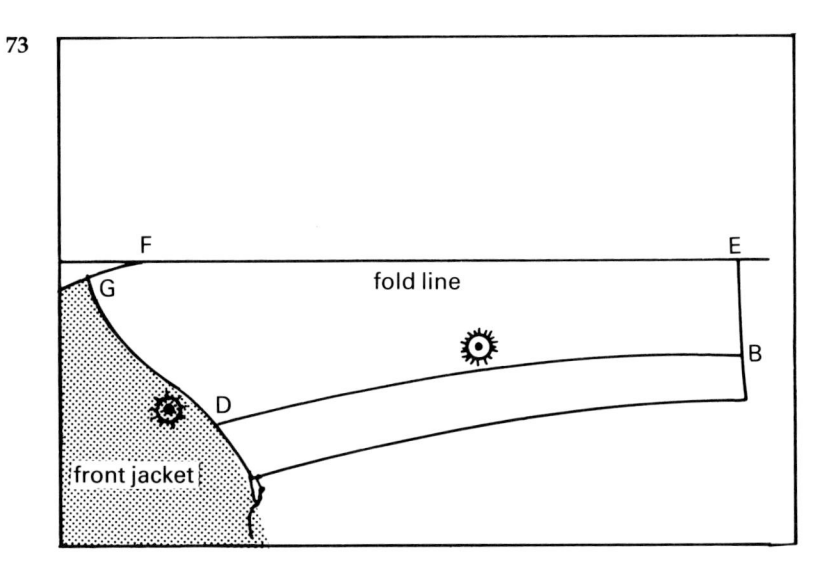

73

Reverse the sleeve on line E–F and wheel through points H–A–B1 (back line) to E (Figure 74).

Remove the sleeve and connect up all the points.

Note that the space between H and G is the ease in the sleeve head. Connect H to G with a curved line.

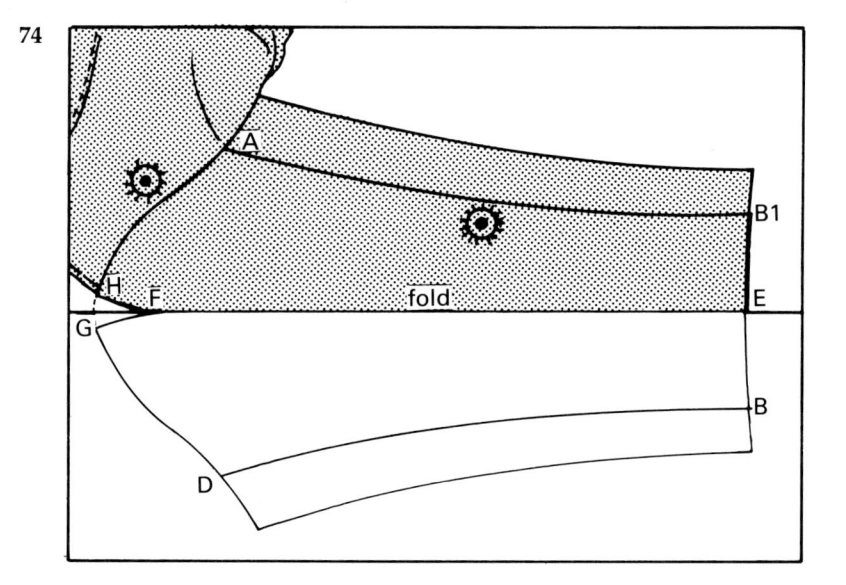

74

75

back jacket cut 2
4 cm hem

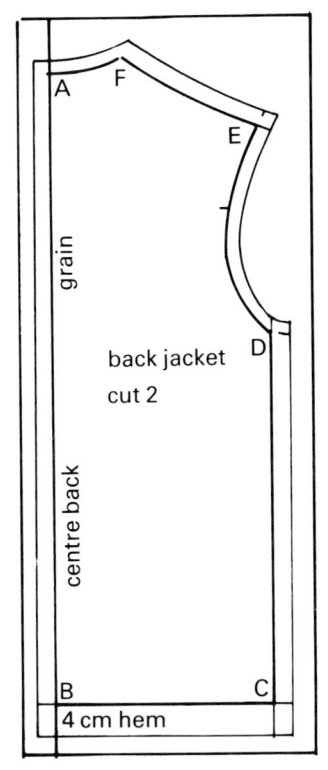

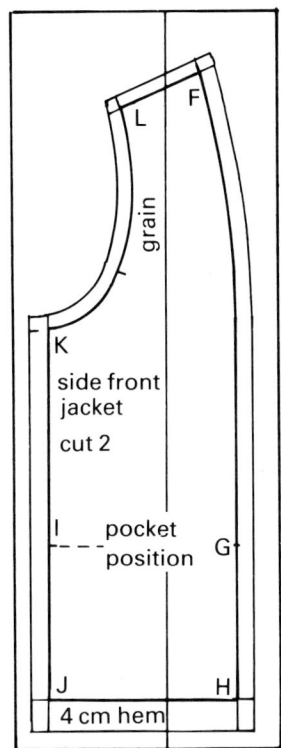

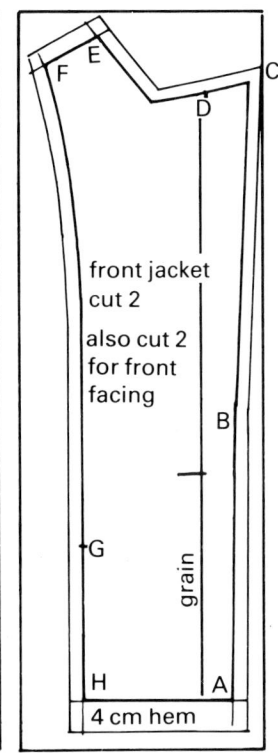

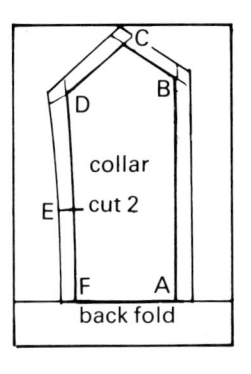

side front jacket cut 2
pocket position
4 cm hem

front jacket cut 2
also cut 2 for front facing
4 cm hem

collar cut 2
back fold

plan the pocket by measuring the side front pocket position

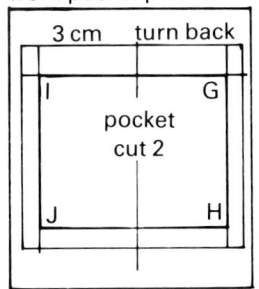

pocket cut 2
3 cm turn back

Adding seam allowances and checking the pattern

Before adding seam allowances to the pattern, measure the jacket and check that the pattern is the same size. For example, measure the half across the back pattern and check it against the half across back measurement of the jacket.

Check that D–C on the back jacket equals K–J on the front jacket, and that F–E equals L–F plus F–E (Figure 75). Repeat this checking at all areas that have to be sewn together. Check the sleeve (Figure 76) against the jacket armhole.

Add seam allowances as in Figures 75 and 76.

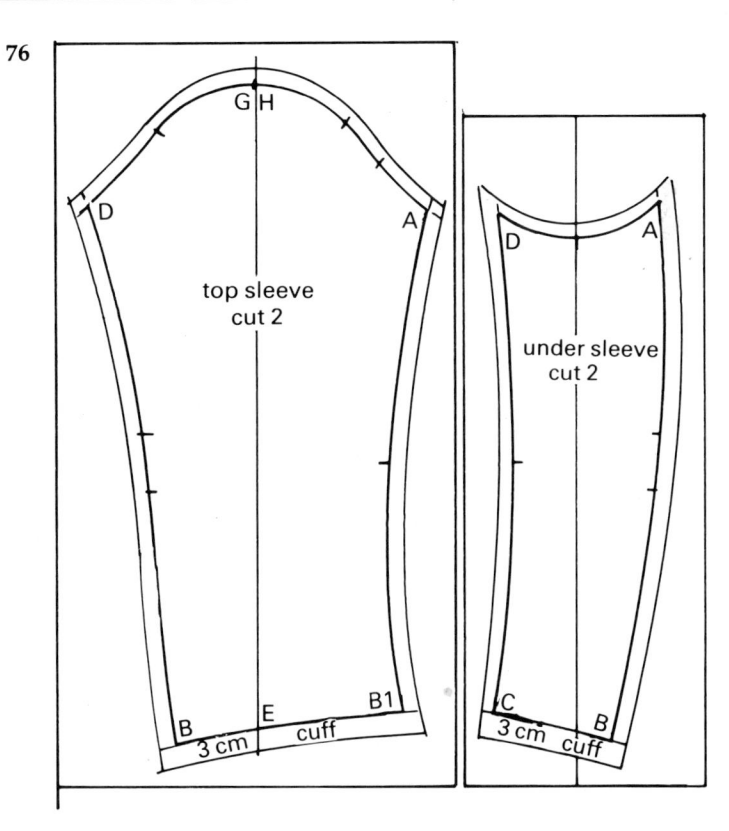

76

top sleeve cut 2
3 cm cuff

under sleeve cut 2
3 cm cuff

77

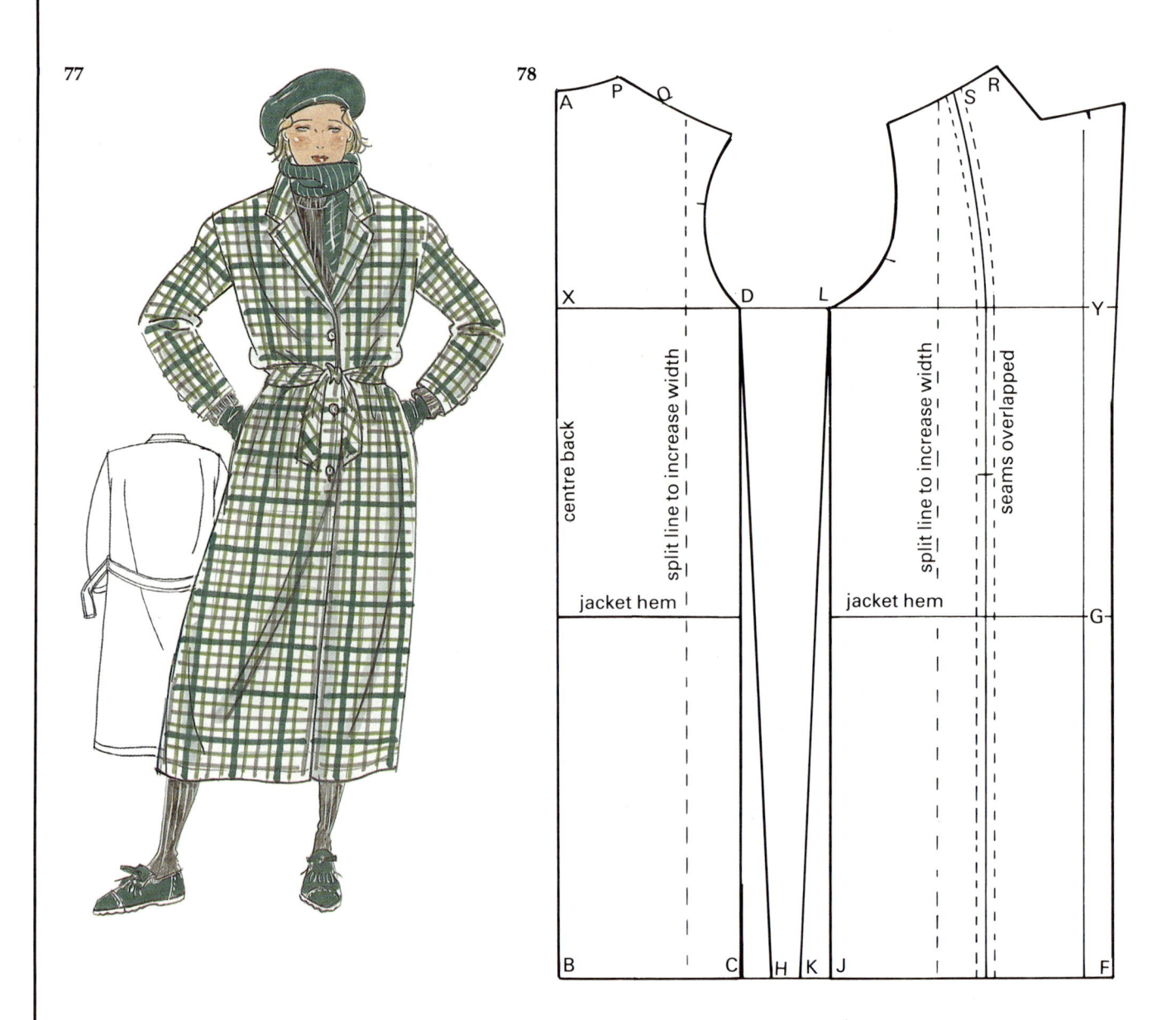

78

Alterations

Long, loose coat

The basic jacket shape can be adjusted to form the stylish unstructured coat shown in Figure 77.

The first stage is to lengthen the pattern.

The back

Draw a straight line X–Y across a large sheet of paper. Lay the back jacket on the straight line (Figure 78). Extend line A–B to the required length. Square across to C and connect to D.

The front

The original front pattern has a vertical seam which has to be removed in order to cut the coat in Figure 77. These seams can be eliminated by overlapping the two patterns on line X-Y on the draft. Lay the front patterns down on the paper, overlapping the front seams. Extend line B–C across to J–F on the front hem. Connect to F and G.

Add flare into the hem: H from C and K from J are both 5 cm. Connect H to D and connect K to L.

As this is a coat it needs to be larger and therefore looser. To make the pattern larger, complete and cut out the patterns from figure 78 and draw vertical lines down from the shoulder to the hem (Figure 79). Cut along these lines and open the sections out so that the pattern is wider by approximately 4 cm, depending on how large the coat is required to be. Remake the pattern on fresh paper.

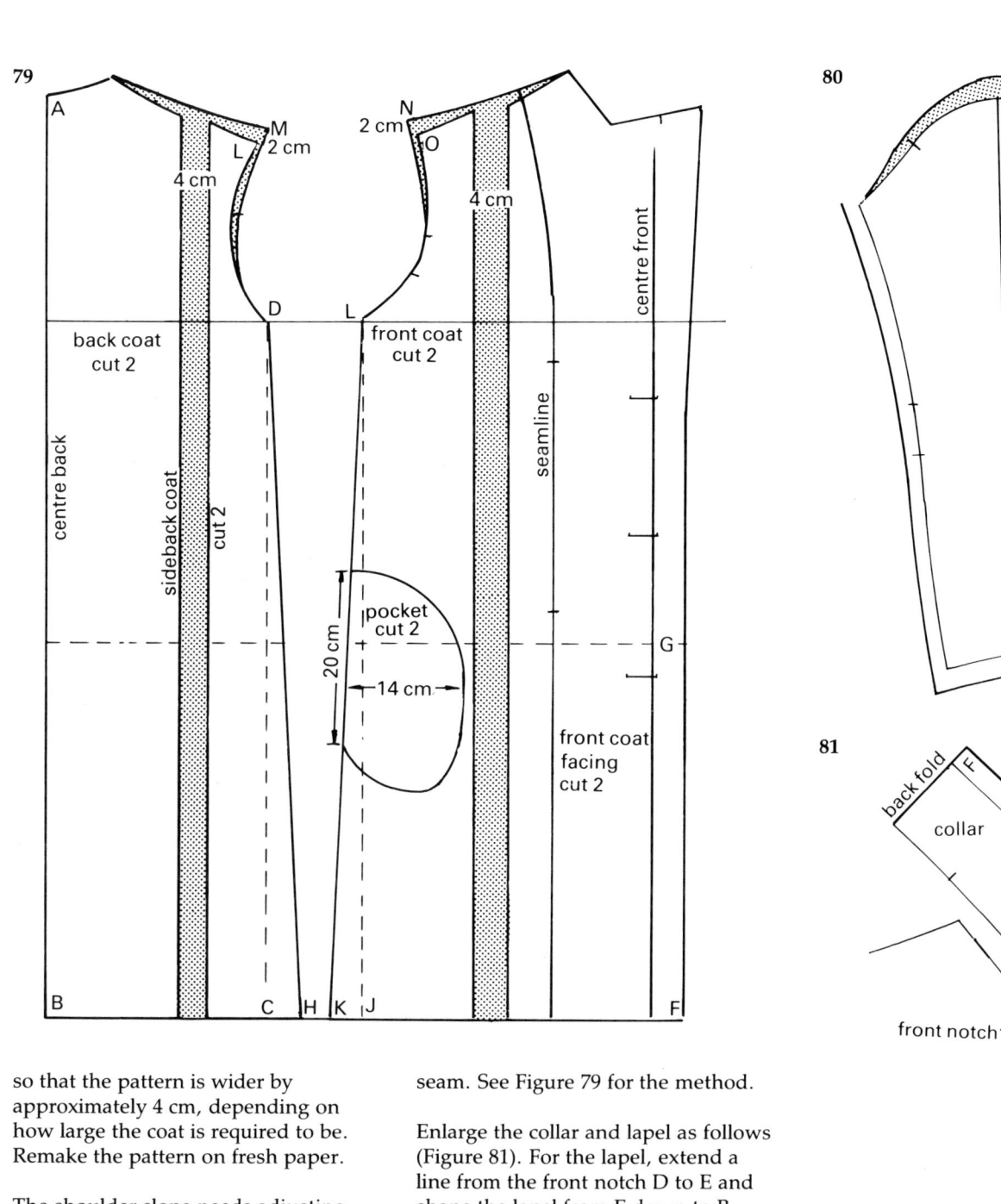

The shoulder slope needs adjusting so that pads can be inserted. Raise the shoulder angle by the width of the shoulder pad. On Figure 79, M from L and N from O are both 2 cm. Raise the sleeve head by the same amount (Figure 80).

A pocket can be inserted into the side seam. See Figure 79 for the method.

Enlarge the collar and lapel as follows (Figure 81). For the lapel, extend a line from the front notch D to E and shape the lapel from E down to B. Measure D–E. Extend D on the collar to E by the same amount as on the lapel. Connect E to F at the centre back of the collar.

Trace off each pattern section and add seam allowances as before. Remember to cut a new facing.

39

82

main stripe on centre back

match underarm and side seams

main stripe down centre sleeve

match underarm and side seams

main stripe down centre front

main stripe across bust line

main stripe above hem allowance

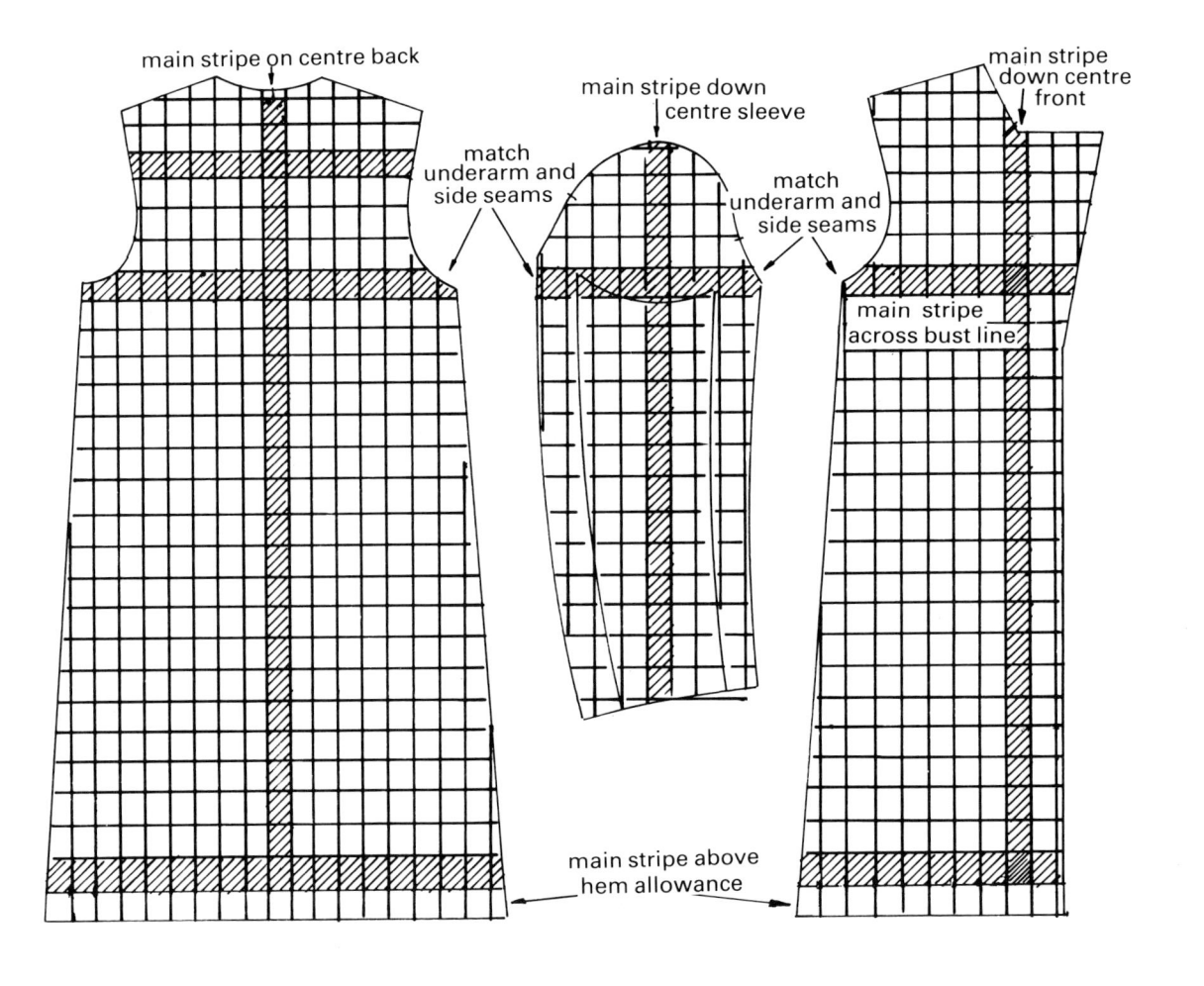

The coat shown in Figure 77 is cut from a large check design and a contrast collar. When cutting out this coat, note the following:

1. Match the checks at the side seam and sleeve.
2. Place the dominant stripe down the centre front and centre back so that the coat will not appear off centre when worn.
3. The horizontal dominant stripe should be positioned across the bust line and hemline (allowing for the turn-up) if possible. This will give the garment a balanced, professional appearance.
4. *Always* match horizontal stripes.

Panel dress

The dress shown in Figure 83 is a very simple variation of the basic pattern. Start with the pattern produced in Figure 79.

To form the cap sleeve, extend the front shoulder line from A to B, in Figure 84. Connect C at the hem to B. Measure A–B. On the back pattern, extend D to E the same length as A–B on the front. Connect E to F at the hem.

Remember that the original jacket seamlines have been overlapped. In this variation the seamlines are used for the neckline and to insert the ties at the hip.

On the front, draw line G–H as in Figure 84. The neckline is J–K, and J is as low as you wish it to be. K is located on the centre front. Square J to K.

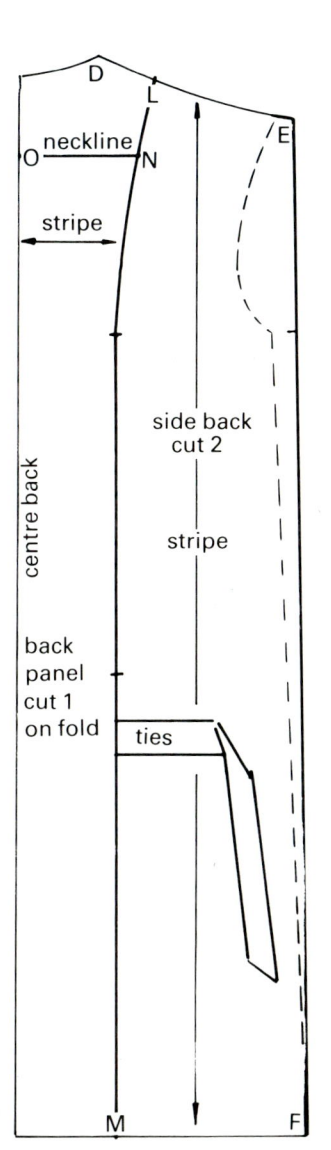

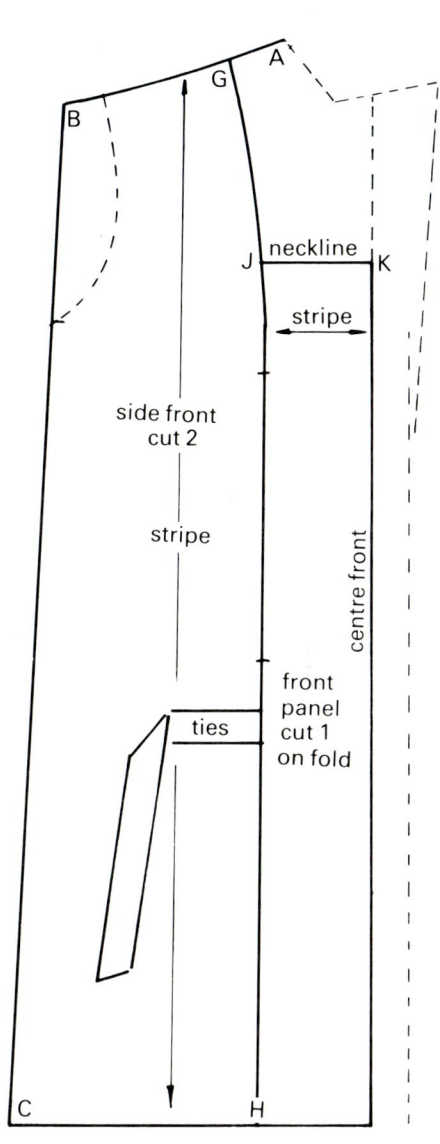

83

84

Measure A–G, and on the back make L from D the same (approximately 8 cm). Connect L to M at the hem. N from L is about 6 cm. Square N to O.

The ties are inserted on lines G–H and L–M at whatever point suits you the most; it could be hip, knee or mid-calf.

Trace off each pattern section and add seam allowances. Note that facings are not required; simply use a piping or binding to finish off the armhole and neckline. Measure around the armhole and neckline to calculate how much crossway is required. The ties should be cut double the finished measurement plus seam allowances.

41

85

belts cut 2

crossway for neck and armholes

The arrangement of stripes on the pattern illustrated in Figure 85 will produce a dress with the stripes horizontal on the back and front panels and vertical on the side panels. The belt and crossway are cut at 45 degrees to the selvedge. If the fabric is cut accurately the effect will be a chevron at the side seams.

Safari jacket

This safari jacket has back and front yokes and patch pockets (Figure 86). Use the pattern taken from the original jacket (Figure 75). If a very large, loose fit is required, enlarge it as for a coat (Figure 79).

86

The back

Draw a straight line X-Y across a large sheet of paper. Lay the original back jacket pattern on the line and draw around it (Figure 87). Extend line A–B to the required jacket length. Square across to C and up to D.

The front

Lay the front jacket on the straight line in Figure 87, overlapping the vertical seam. Draw around it. Continue line B–C across to the front to points E and F. Connect to G and H.

Raise the back and front shoulder lines for the pads if required (see instructions for the long, loose coat in Figure 79).

The front yoke line L–M (Figure 87) is parallel to the shoulder seam and is about 5 cm down.

For the back yoke, J from A is about 15 cm. Square J across to K. Use a curve to draw the yoke point at N from J. Connect N to K. Draw line O–P 5 cm above J.

The back and front yoke patterns can be joined together at the shoulder, which will eliminate the shoulder seam.

The sleeve can be made less fitted as follows (Figure 88). Draw around the top sleeve. Cut the under sleeve in half along line C–D. Join sections A and B to the top sleeve. Straighten off the sleeve seamlines as in the diagram.

If a cuff is required, cut a rectangle. The length is the wrist measurement plus 2 cm, and the width is double the cuff width (Figure 88).

The belt pattern is a rectangle. Calculate this as the waist measurement plus at least 25 cm for tying.

43

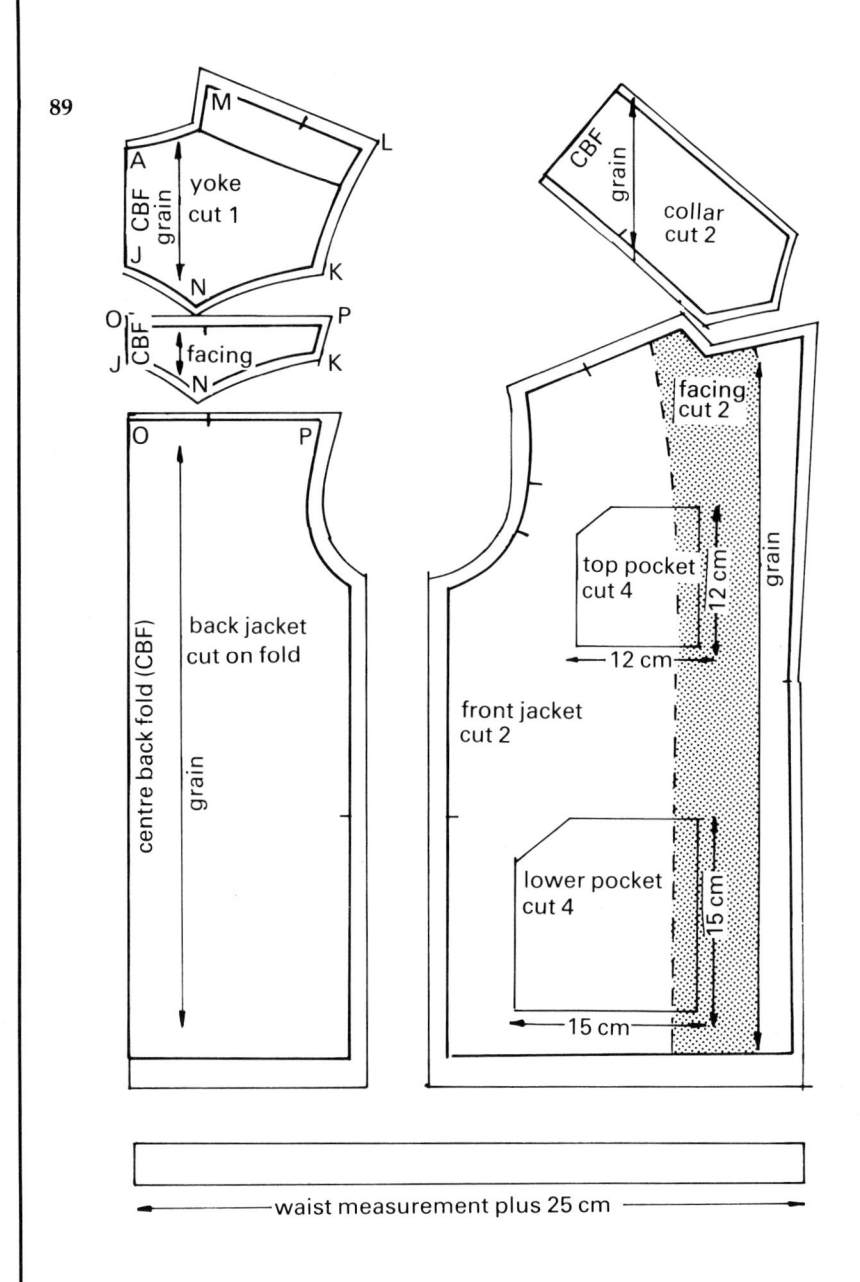

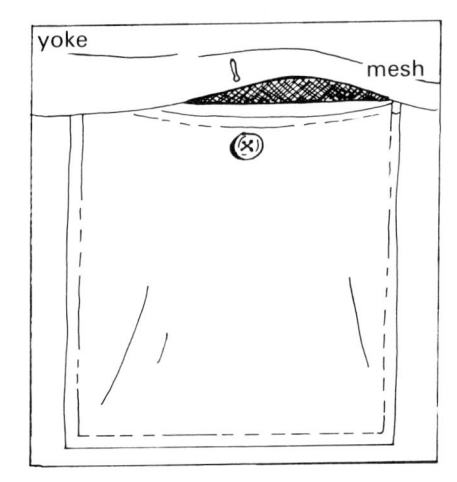

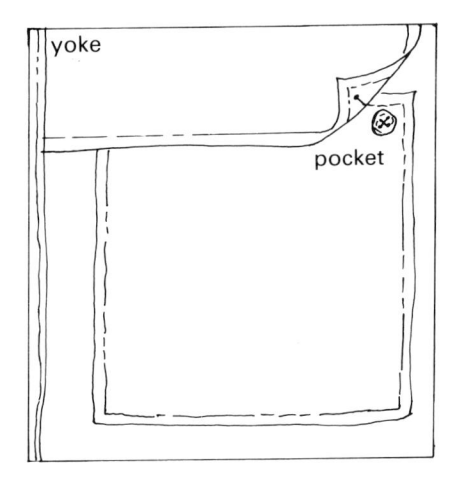

Figure 89 illustrates the finished pattern complete with seam allowances.

When making up:

1. Cut a single back yoke. Sew the front yoke to the front jacket. Sew the facing to the back yoke and then stitch line O–P to the jacket line O–P.
2. Bag the pockets out and stitch them on the jacket fronts.
3. Top stitching on seams is very much in character for this garment.

A variety of pocket details are illustrated in Figure 90. These interesting pockets can be added to the garment quite simply. Their construction may be a challenge, but they will make the garment more practical and attractive especially when used with yokes and top stitching. The book *Pattern Cutting and Making Up* (Martin Shoben and Janet P. Ward; Heinemann, 1987) provides a whole section on the manufacture and cutting of pockets that will be very helpful.

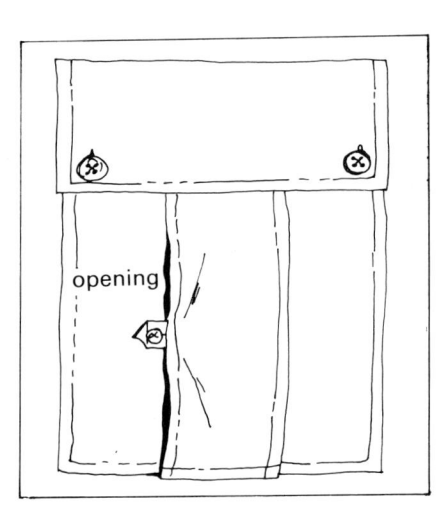

90

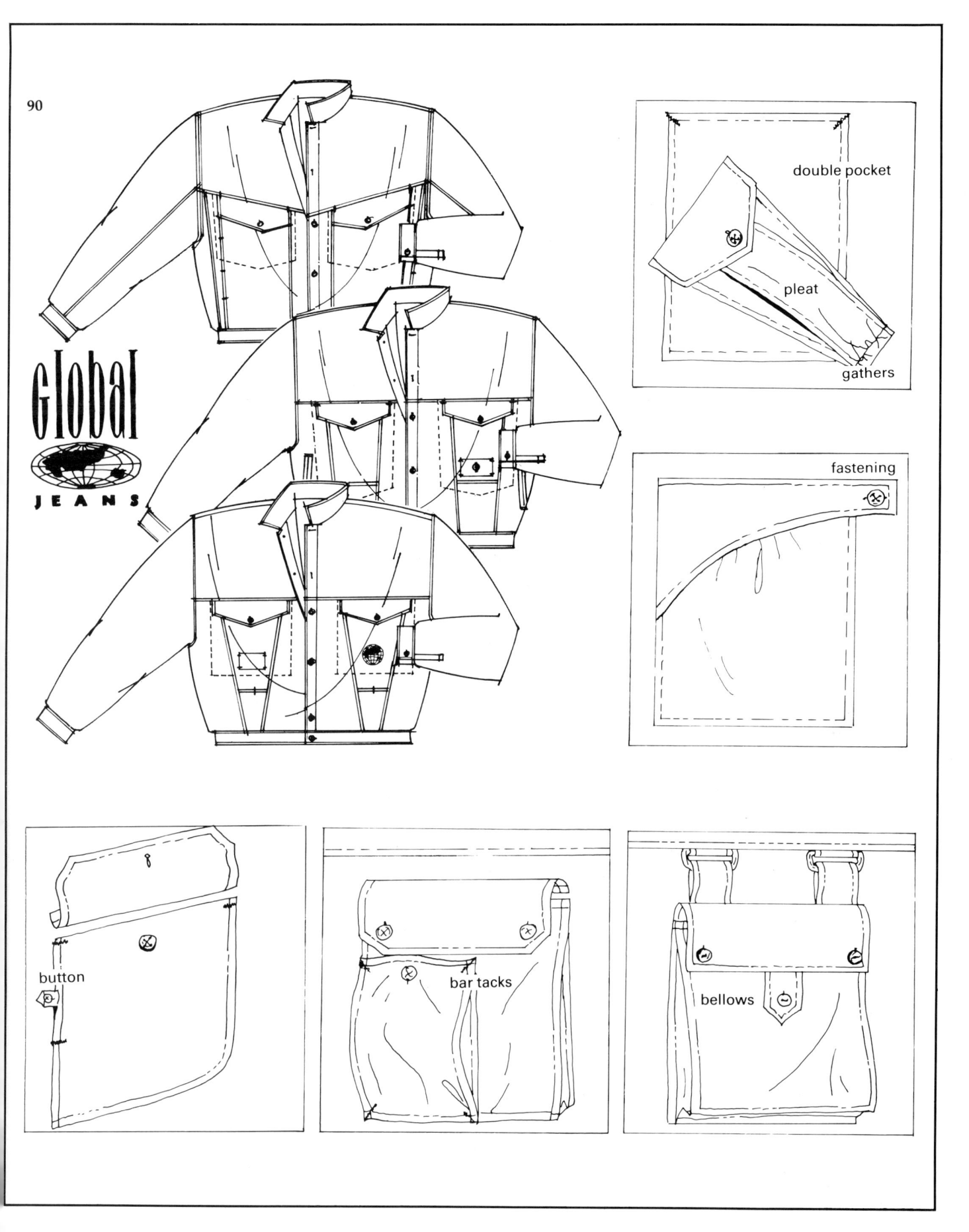

Global
JEANS

double pocket

pleat

gathers

fastening

button

bar tacks

bellows

STYLE 4

SIX-GORED A-LINE SKIRT – direct measurements

This classical skirt shape can be cut in a variety of fabrics, which will completely alter its appearance and mood. By simply adjusting its length and silhouette it can easily be brought up to date.

What to look for

First neatly press the skirt. Examine it, count the gores and make a sketch (Figure 91). This is the most simple of skirts to copy, as it will probably be found that all the gores are exactly the same shape. If they are the same, all that needs to be done is to trace off a pattern from one section and (in this case) use it six times.

Method to choose

This skirt is best copied by direct measurements, which means measuring each gore with a tape measure and then applying these measurements to paper to make a pattern.

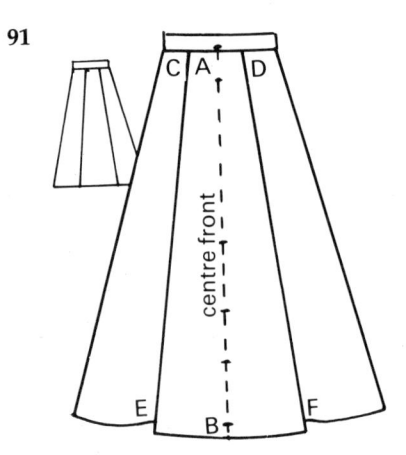

Equipment needed

Paper, tape measure, ruler, set square, pencils etc.

Locating the key points

Place a pin into the centre of the front panel, at the waist and at the hem.

The gore pattern

Draw a line on a clean sheet of paper. Measure A–B on the skirt (Figure 91) and apply this measurement as A–B on the paper (Figure 92). Measure C–D and place half this measurement either side of A on the paper. Measure E–F and place half this measurement either side of B on the paper.

Note If the skirt is tight at the waist, simply increase C to D. If desired, increase the hemline distance E–F.

Connect E to C and F to D to complete the basic gore (Figure 92).

Now curve the hemline as in Figure 93. G from C, H from D, J from E and K from F are all 1 cm.

Add seam allowances around the outline and cut the paper pattern out

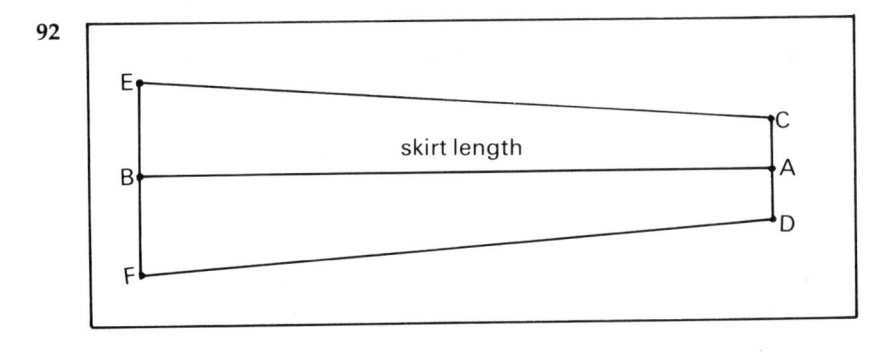

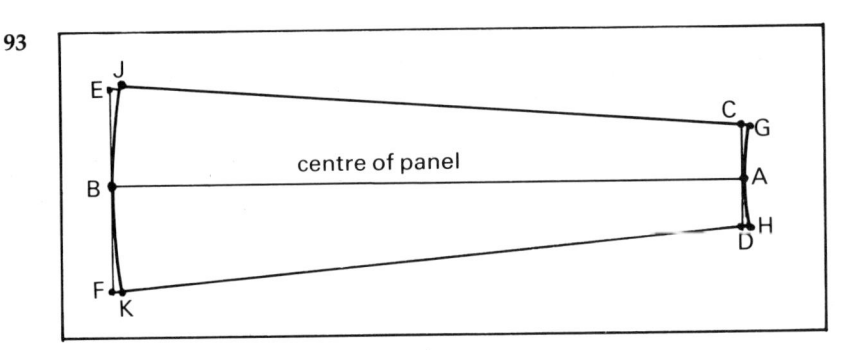

94

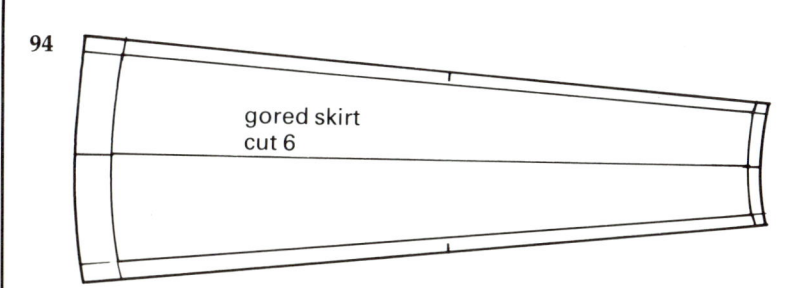

gored skirt
cut 6

(Figure 94). Six of these gores will make up into a skirt.

For the waistband see Figure 48 for the dirndl skirt.

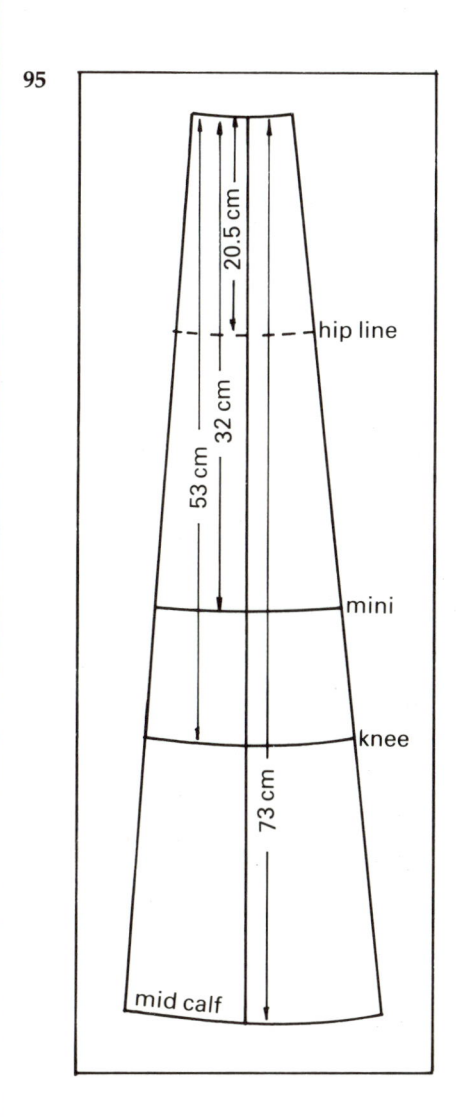

Alterations

Apart from simple adjustments to the length, interesting alterations can be made to the silhouette which will produce various effects.

Length adjustments

Figure 95 shows the standard lengths for a size 12 from the waist downwards.

Fluted skirt: plain, chevrons and godets

The convenience of the basic gored skirt pattern is that alterations need only be made to one pattern piece.

For the fluted skirt shown in Figure 96, copy half of the original pattern and position it on a clean sheet of

96

95

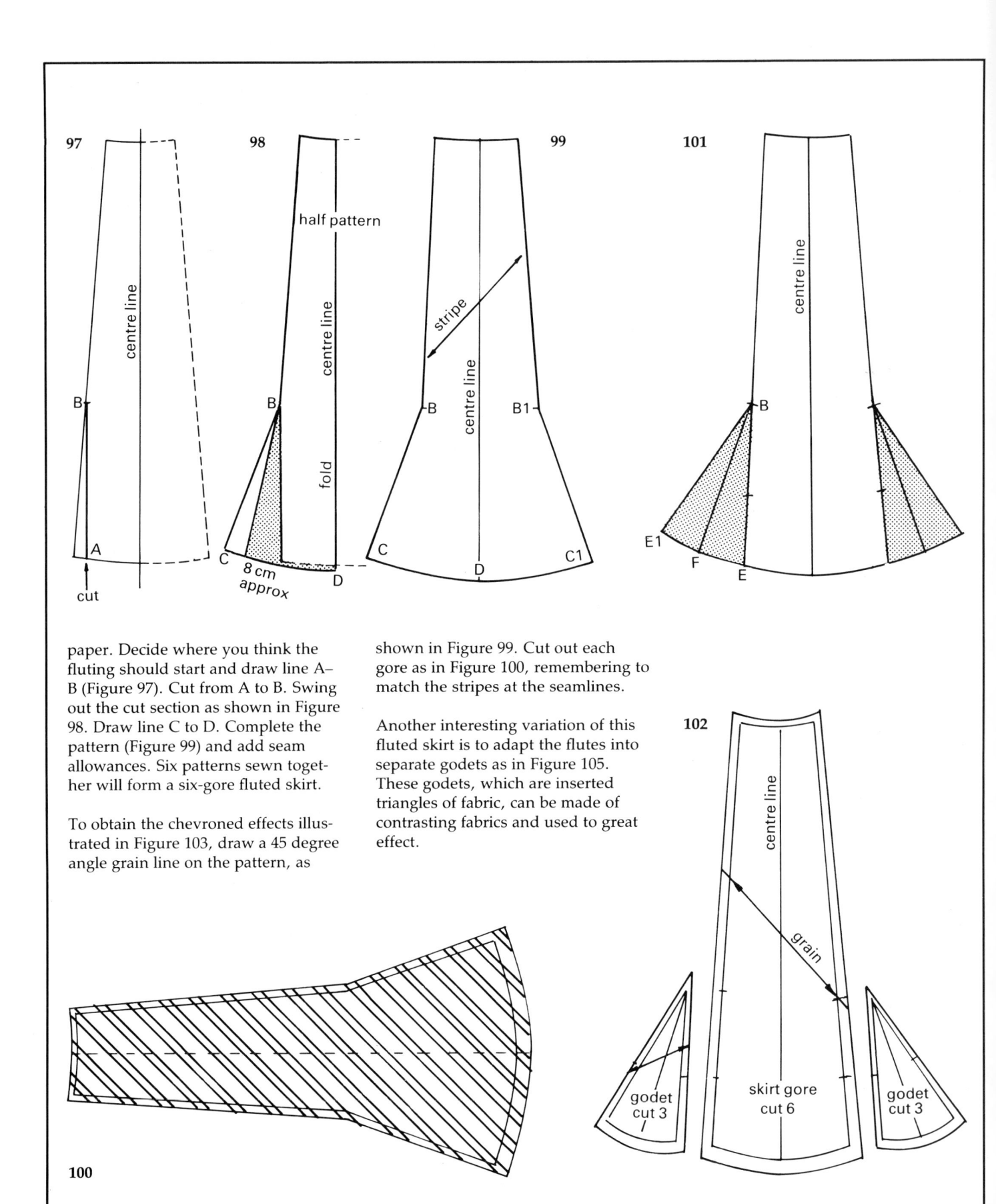

paper. Decide where you think the fluting should start and draw line A–B (Figure 97). Cut from A to B. Swing out the cut section as shown in Figure 98. Draw line C to D. Complete the pattern (Figure 99) and add seam allowances. Six patterns sewn together will form a six-gore fluted skirt.

To obtain the chevroned effects illustrated in Figure 103, draw a 45 degree angle grain line on the pattern, as shown in Figure 99. Cut out each gore as in Figure 100, remembering to match the stripes at the seamlines.

Another interesting variation of this fluted skirt is to adapt the flutes into separate godets as in Figure 105. These godets, which are inserted triangles of fabric, can be made of contrasting fabrics and used to great effect.

103

104

105

To form the godets, draw around the fluted pattern (Figure 99). Continue the main gore line from B to point E at the hem (Figure 101). Trace off B–E–F on separate paper, cut out the shape and lay it along B–F as B–F–E1. The diamond-shaped godet is then separated out (B–E–E1). Add seam allowances and grain lines to give the complete pattern (Figure 102).

Pointed and flared skirts

Figure 104 illustrates a skirt with a pointed hem. This unusual variation has a bound hem line, and each gore has an extra flare added to its full length. This style is a very simple adaptation of the original pattern.

To form the pointed flared gore, lay the original gore (Figure 93) on a sheet of paper and draw around it.

49

106

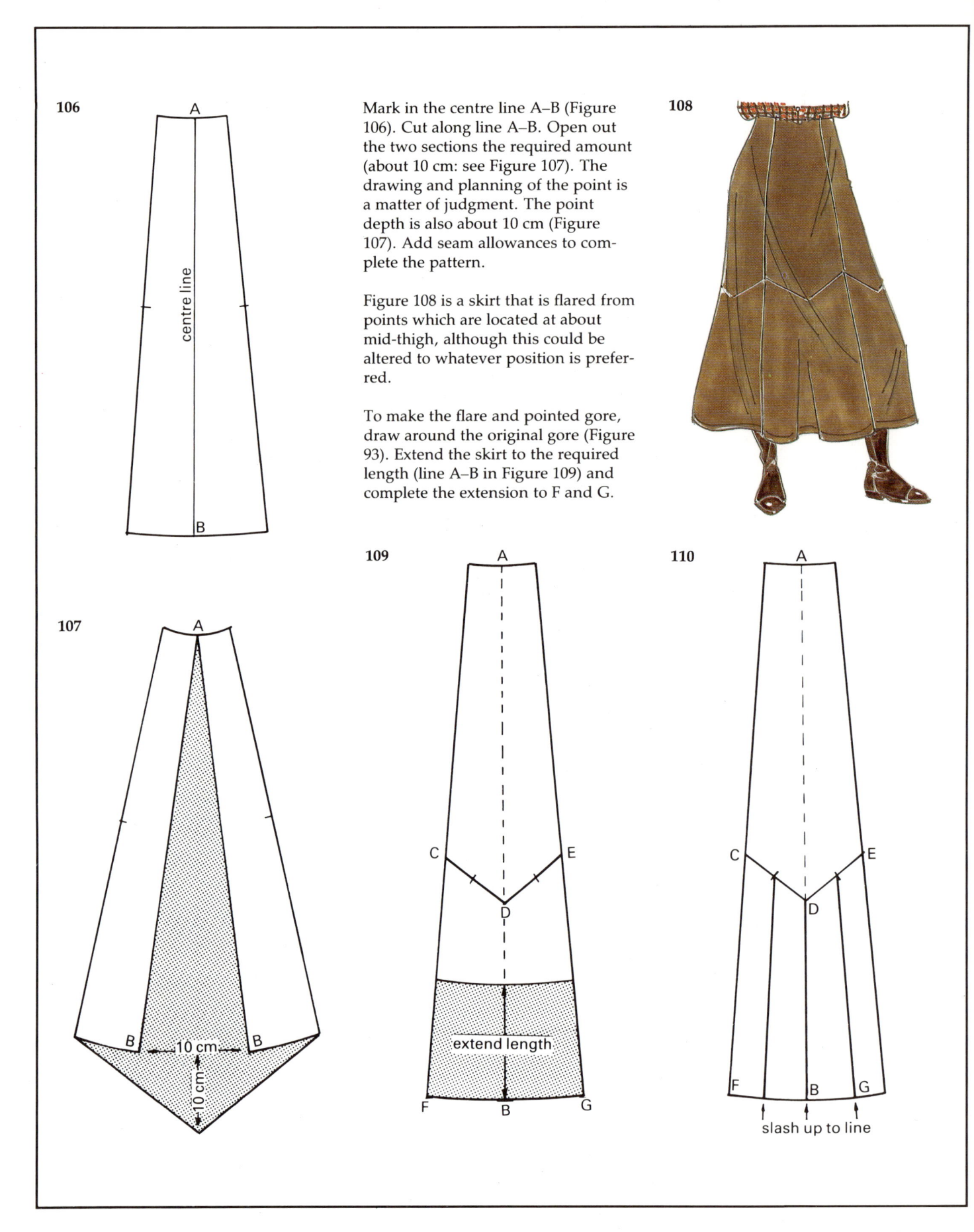

Mark in the centre line A–B (Figure 106). Cut along line A–B. Open out the two sections the required amount (about 10 cm: see Figure 107). The drawing and planning of the point is a matter of judgment. The point depth is also about 10 cm (Figure 107). Add seam allowances to complete the pattern.

Figure 108 is a skirt that is flared from points which are located at about mid-thigh, although this could be altered to whatever position is preferred.

To make the flare and pointed gore, draw around the original gore (Figure 93). Extend the skirt to the required length (line A–B in Figure 109) and complete the extension to F and G.

107

108

109

110

50

111

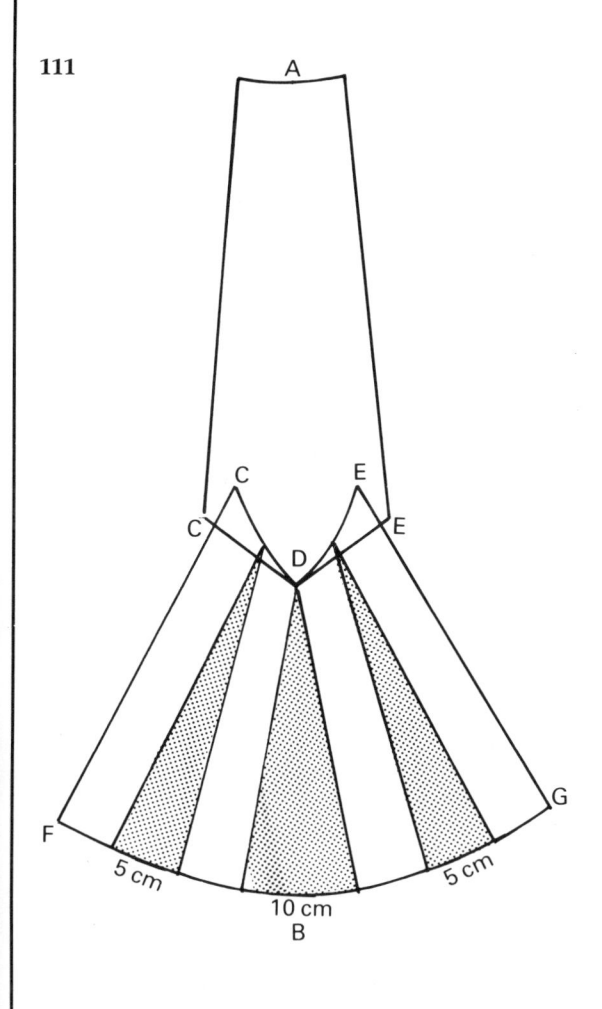

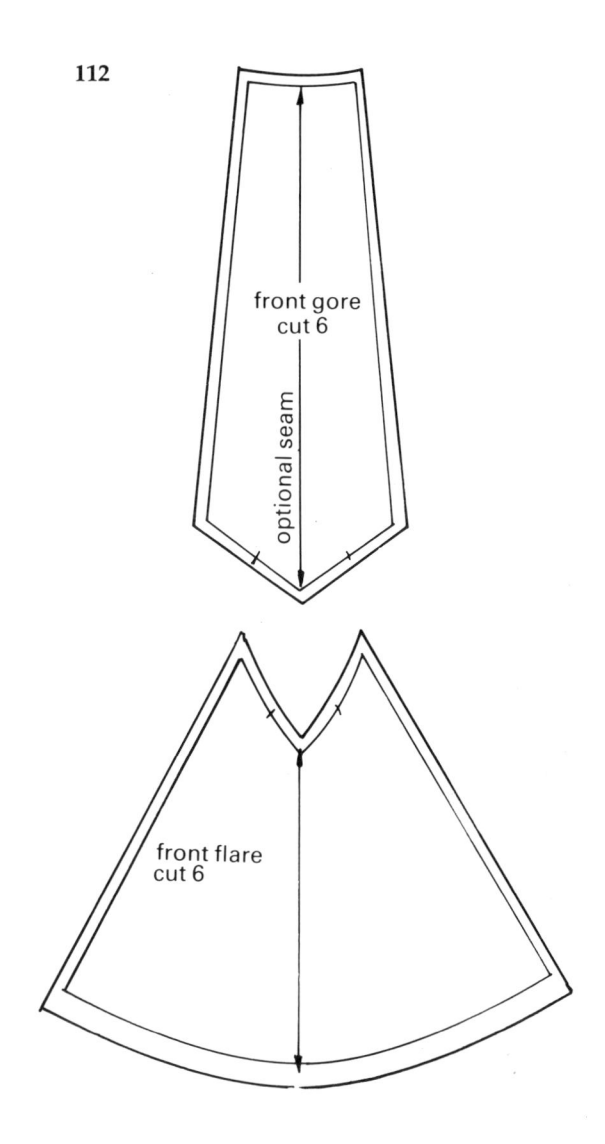

112

Decide where to position the pointed seam and draw it as C–D–E. Draw slash lines evenly as in Figure 110. Trace off section C–D–E–G–B–F.

Cut up the slash lines and open out about 5 cm into each section. Pin the cut pieces on the draft (Figure 111).

Trace off each section and add seam allowances to give the complete pattern (Figure 112). To make this skirt even more interesting, divide the gore along the centre line to make a twelve-gore skirt (see Figure 112).

STYLE 5

DENIM JEANS – fold and spike method

Choose a pair of jeans that fit really well. You will be surprised to find that jeans can easily be reproduced and adapted to various lengths and silhouettes.

What to look for

First neatly press the jeans. Examine the jeans very carefully and draw a simple sketch of them, indicating seamlines and pockets (Figure 113).

Method to choose

The fold and spike method can be effectively used to produce a pattern from this garment.

Equipment needed

Paper, fine spike, tracing wheel, tape measure, set square, pencils, weights etc.

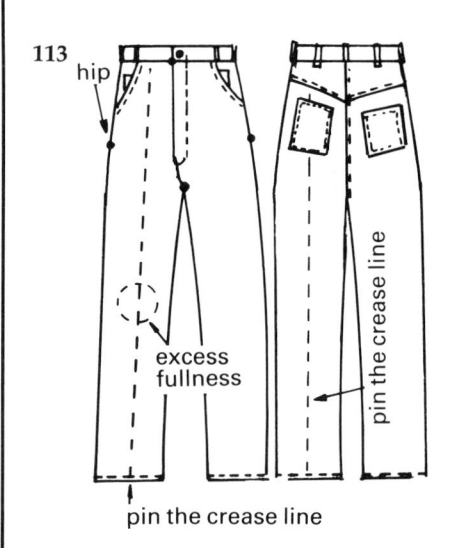

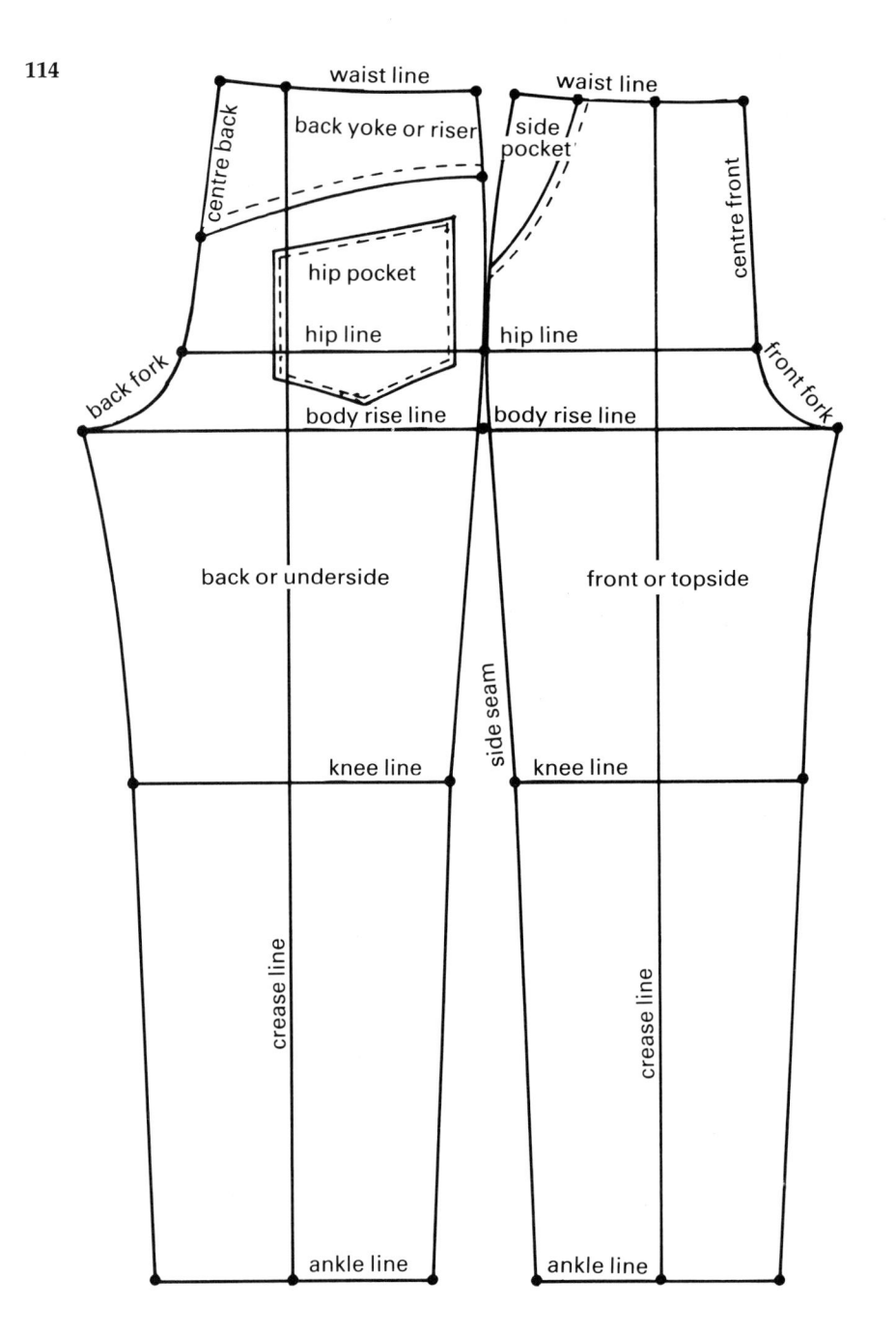

114

113

Locating the key points

The key points on any legged garment are illustrated in Figure 114. This diagram also shows the names and locations of the basic trouser construction lines.

The front trouser

Flatten the jeans out on the seamlines. Pin the crease line. *It is only necessary to work on one of the legs.*

Make sure that any stretching caused by the wearer's knees does not distort the leg outline.

Draw a long line on a sheet of paper.

Lay the trouser front uppermost so that the crease line is directly on the straight line (Figure 115). Arrange any bagginess at the knee into a circle shape by smoothing inwards.

Draw around the leg from A to B to C and to D.

Using a tracing wheel, wheel through from D to E. Spike through points F and G for the pocket.

Wheel through from E to A, accurately and carefully following the curve.

Remove the trouser and connect up all the points (Figure 116).

The side pocket

Figure 117 shows the front trouser on which the pocket is drawn. The pocket consists of two pieces plus the trouser leg. D–H–J is cut in denim and sewn on the pocket bag lining.

Measure the inside pocket bag lining and apply this measurement to the front leg draft to establish points H, K, L and M. Trace off from the draft the shape D–K–L–M. Fold the paper along line K–L and trace wheel F–G. Unfold the paper to produce the pattern.

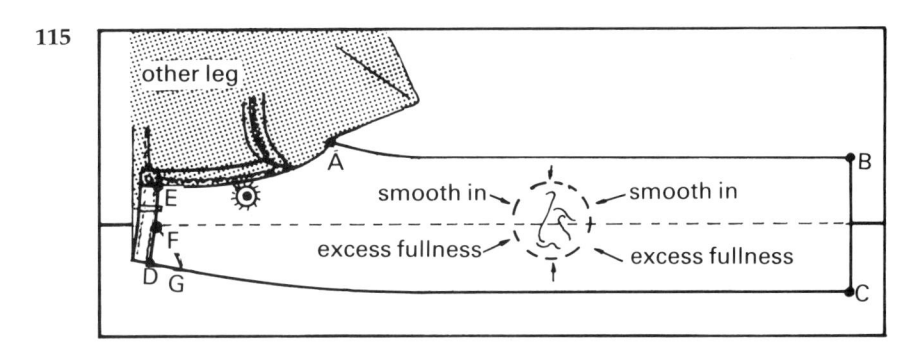

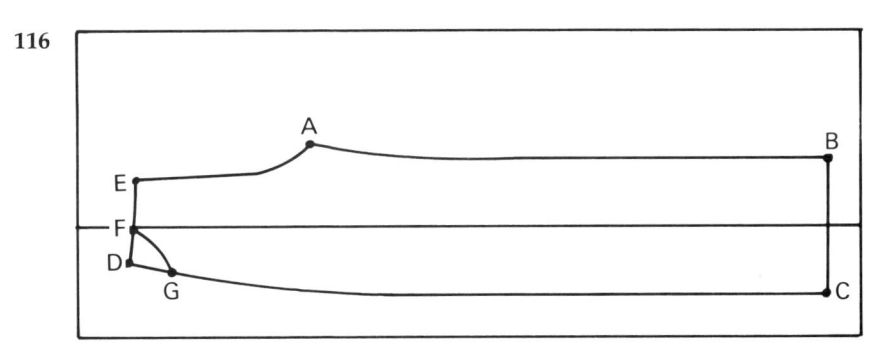

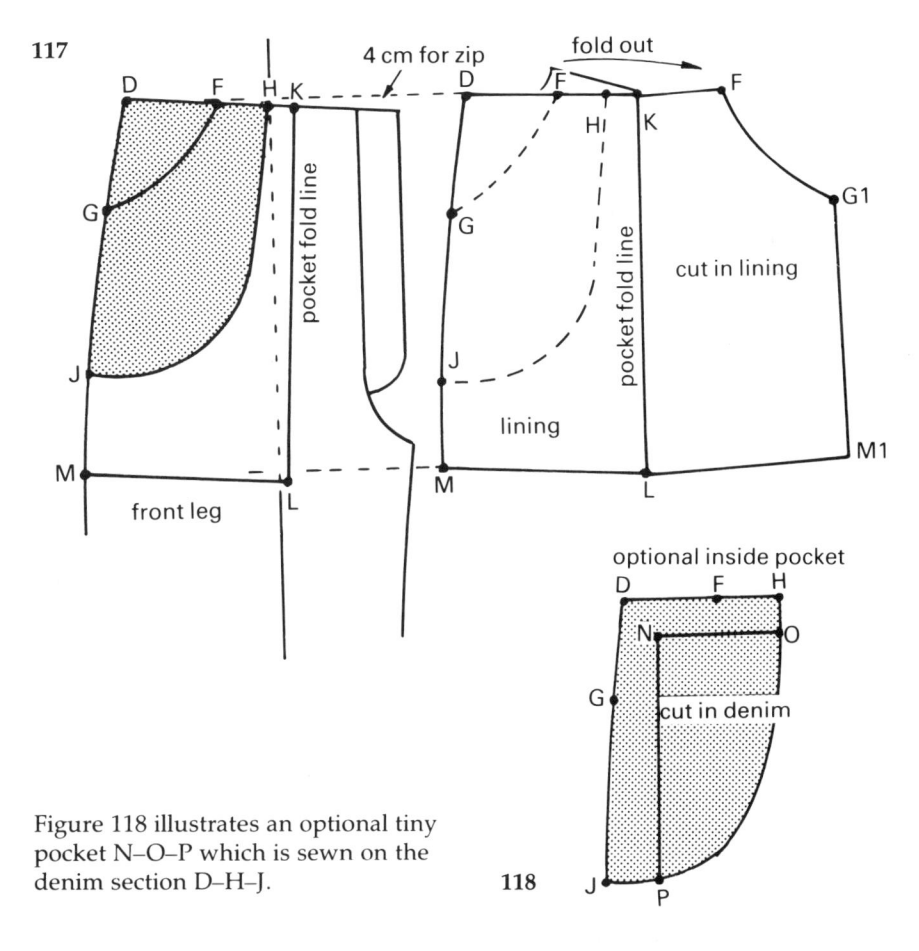

Figure 118 illustrates an optional tiny pocket N–O–P which is sewn on the denim section D–H–J.

53

The fly front opening

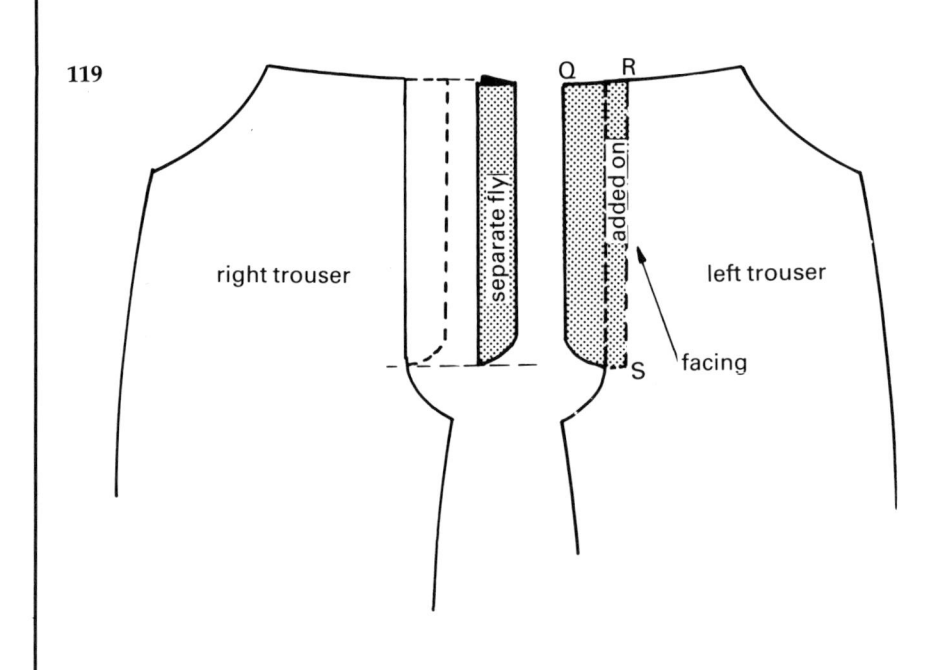

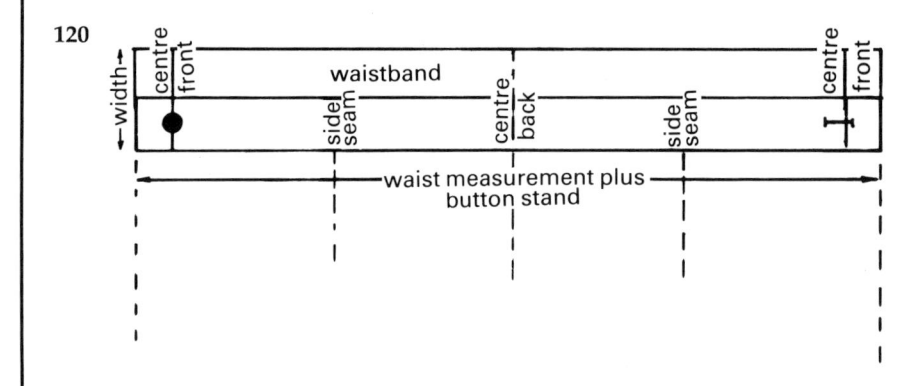

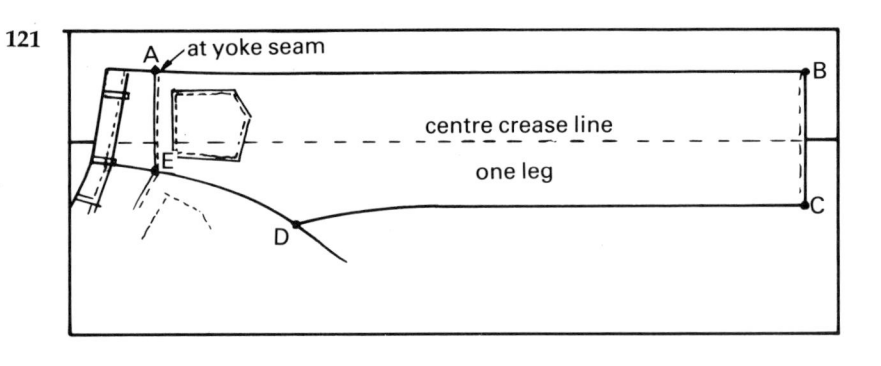

The fly front opening will consist of four separate pieces: the right trouser and a separate fly piece, and the left trouser with a grown-on fly piece and a separate facing.

Figure 119 shows the fly arrangements. Lay the front zip opening on a sheet of paper and draw around it to give the basic pattern for fly pieces and facing. Construction details for zip openings are illustrated in Figures 150–154.

The waistband and belt loops

Measure the waistband and construct a rectangle (Figure 120). Add seam allowances.

The back leg

Draw a straight line down the centre of a large sheet of paper.

Lay the centre crease line of the back trouser on the line (Figure 121). Flatten out the trouser leg so that the seams are on the trouser edges. Draw around the outside edge from A at the yoke seam to B–C and around to D. Mark point E at the yoke, which is at the centre back.

Fold the back trouser legs together so that the back seat seam shape is clearly visible (Figure 122). Lay point E on the trouser to E on the paper and D on the trouser to D on the paper. Mark the seamline from E to D.

Remove the trouser and connect up all the points (Figure 123).

The back yoke

Draw a straight line on a sheet of paper.

Open up the trouser and lay the single thickness of fabric on the line (Figure 124). Spike through points E, A, F and G.

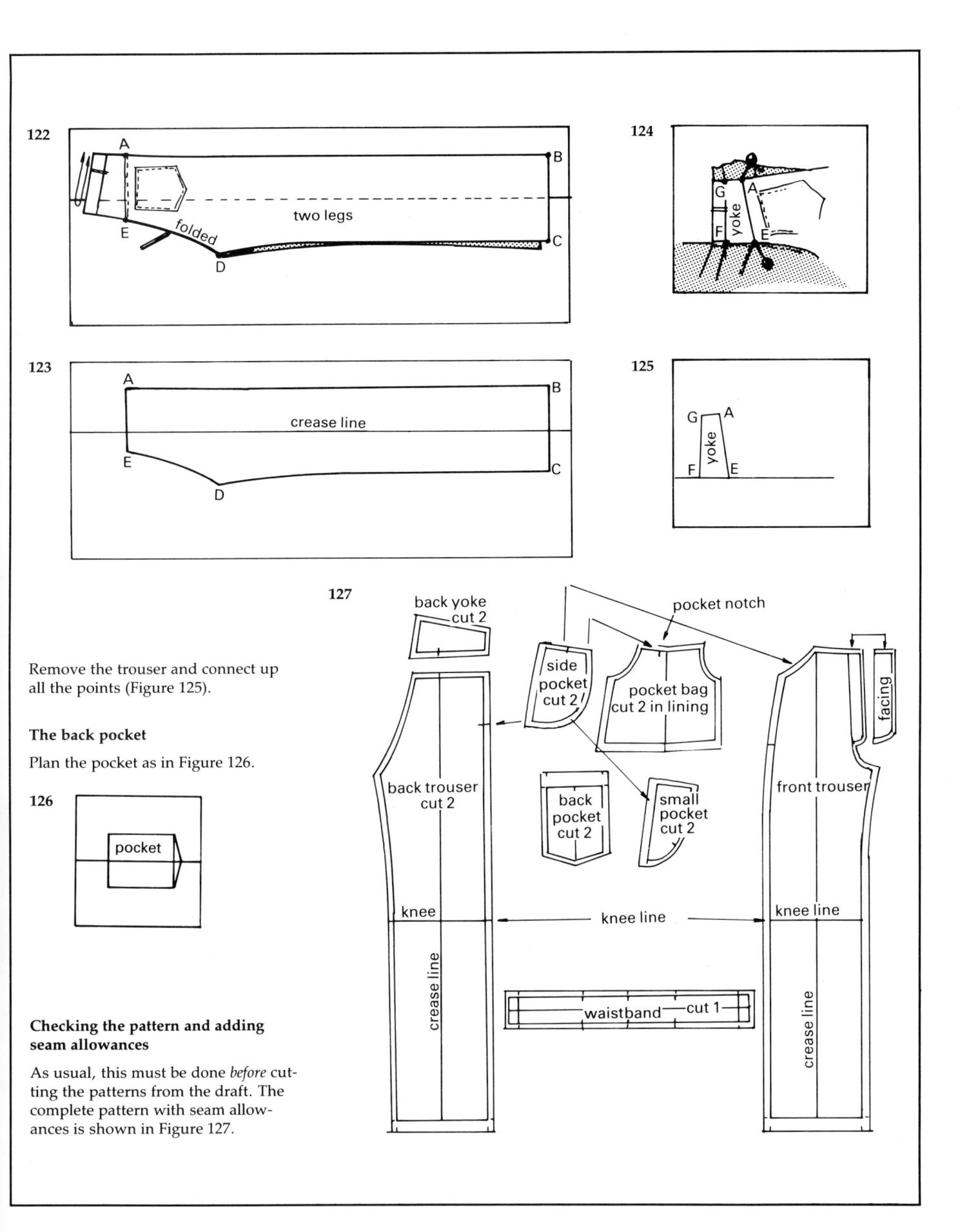

Remove the trouser and connect up all the points (Figure 125).

The back pocket

Plan the pocket as in Figure 126.

Checking the pattern and adding seam allowances

As usual, this must be done *before* cutting the patterns from the draft. The complete pattern with seam allowances is shown in Figure 127.

Pin the back yoke pattern to the back trouser pattern. Pin the front pocket pattern to the front trouser pattern. Now check that the overall lengths of the back and front side seams are the same. They *must* match.

Pin the front pocket patterns together and make sure that they fit. Also pin the pocket pieces on the front leg pattern and check the fit.

Check the waistband for size, and place notches at all the important points.

Mark the knee line (refer to Figure 114).

Add seam allowances to all seamlines.

Cut belt loops on the cross or bias grain.

Fabric layout

Figure 128 illustrates a standard fabric layout. The fabric has been folded and pinned at the selvedge. The patterns have been laid on the fabric with the grain lines placed parallel to the warp.

Either pin the pattern on the fabric or chalk around the pattern outline before cutting out.

Mark the crossway for the belt loops as in the top left corner of the diagram.

Note that the most economical width of fabric will depend on the size of the trousers. Fortunately, denim can be purchased in various widths. Before buying the fabric, plan the layout as in Figure 128 to see how much fabric will be needed.

The pocket lining will be cut separately.

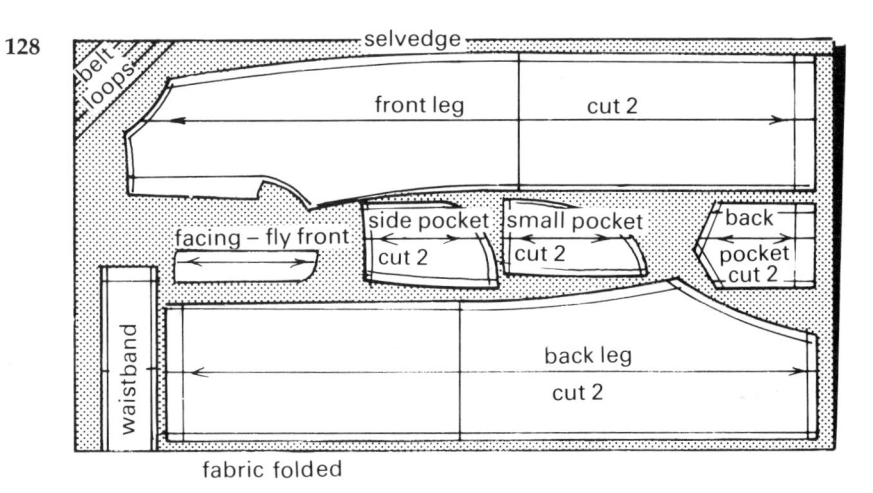

Alterations

A few simple alterations to the length and shape of the pattern, and a change of fabric, can transform the jeans into a variety of exciting garments.

Flared knee-length trousers

These flared denim trousers are shown in Figure 133.

Place the jeans pattern on a large sheet of paper. Draw around the outline, marking the crease line and the knee and body rise lines (Figure 129). Decide on the required length; this example shows knee length. Draw lines from A to B and from C to D, parallel to the crease lines.

Trace off the back trouser, and mark the body rise line and the crease line. Draw a straight line E–F on a fresh sheet of paper. Cut up the pattern crease line and open the pattern out equally either side of line E–F. This will increase the flare in the hem (Figure 130). Mark around the pattern and add seam allowances.

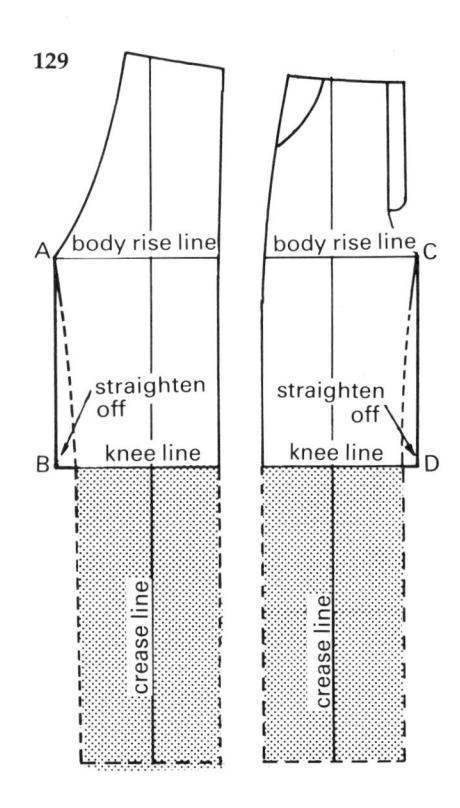

Repeat this process to increase the front trouser (Figure 131). It is important to increase the front leg by the same amount as the back leg, otherwise the trouser will not hang properly.

130

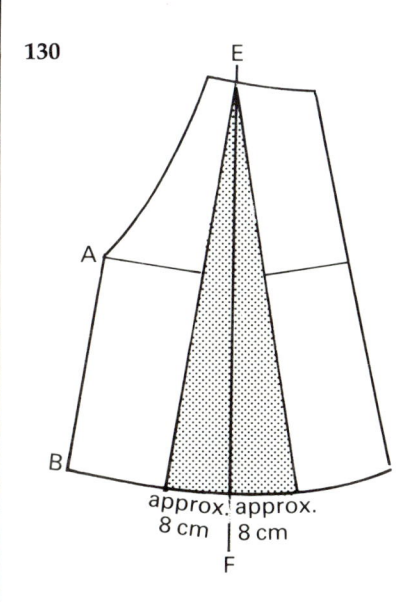

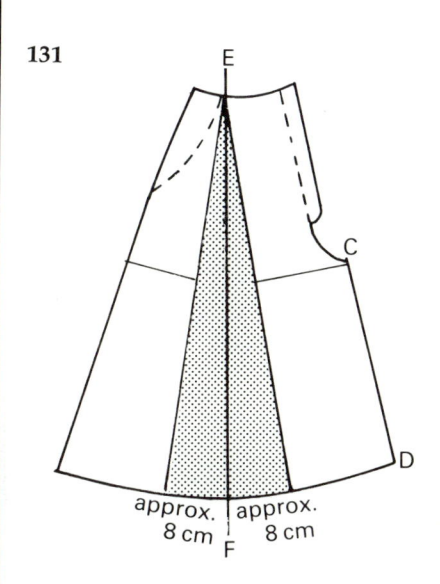

A
B
E
approx. 8 cm | approx. 8 cm
F

131

E
C
D
approx. 8 cm | approx. 8 cm
F

If a pocket is required, remember to increase the original pocket pattern by the amount added to the new pattern at the hip.

Joggers in jersey wool with contrast yoke

These joggers (Figure 132) are loose fitting trousers which can be adapted from the tight fitting jeans pattern. The side seams can be eliminated to make the garment easier to sew.

132

133

Lay the back and front trouser patterns on a clean sheet of paper so that the side seams touch (Figure 134). This seam will be eliminated.

Make the joggers larger as follows. Draw a straight line from B to D through A, parallel to the body rise line. Drop to B to C at 90 degrees to B–D. Drop a straight line from E to F parallel to the crease line. Point F is about 5 cm below the hem on the original jeans pattern. Square across to G and up to H. Trace off the pattern from the draft. Draw parallel lines at the knee and the hem.

Slash up the pattern along the crease lines and the seam line and open out the pattern, adding about 2 cm into each slash (Figure 135). Draw line J–K for the yoke line. Add 5 cm extra height to the line B–D at the waist for elastication.

Trace off the pattern, separating the yoke from the trouser (Figure 136). Add seam allowances.

The waist and the hem can be drawn into the body either by sewing three rows of strong elastication stitches, i.e. threading the bobbin with elastic cotton, or by turning the seam allowances into channels in which to insert a 1 cm elastic.

Shorts with a button front opening

This adaptation can turn your jeans pattern into an interesting popular summer garment (Figure 137).

Lay the jeans pattern on a large sheet of paper. Mark in the centre lines and the body rise lines (Figure 138). Shorten the jeans legs by the required amount by drawing lines A–B and C–D. It may be necessary to reduce the thigh measurement (A–B and C–D) by about 0.5 cm.

Draw the pocket line E–F. Draw the front waistband G–H. Draw J–K, which will be the pocket bag. Mark

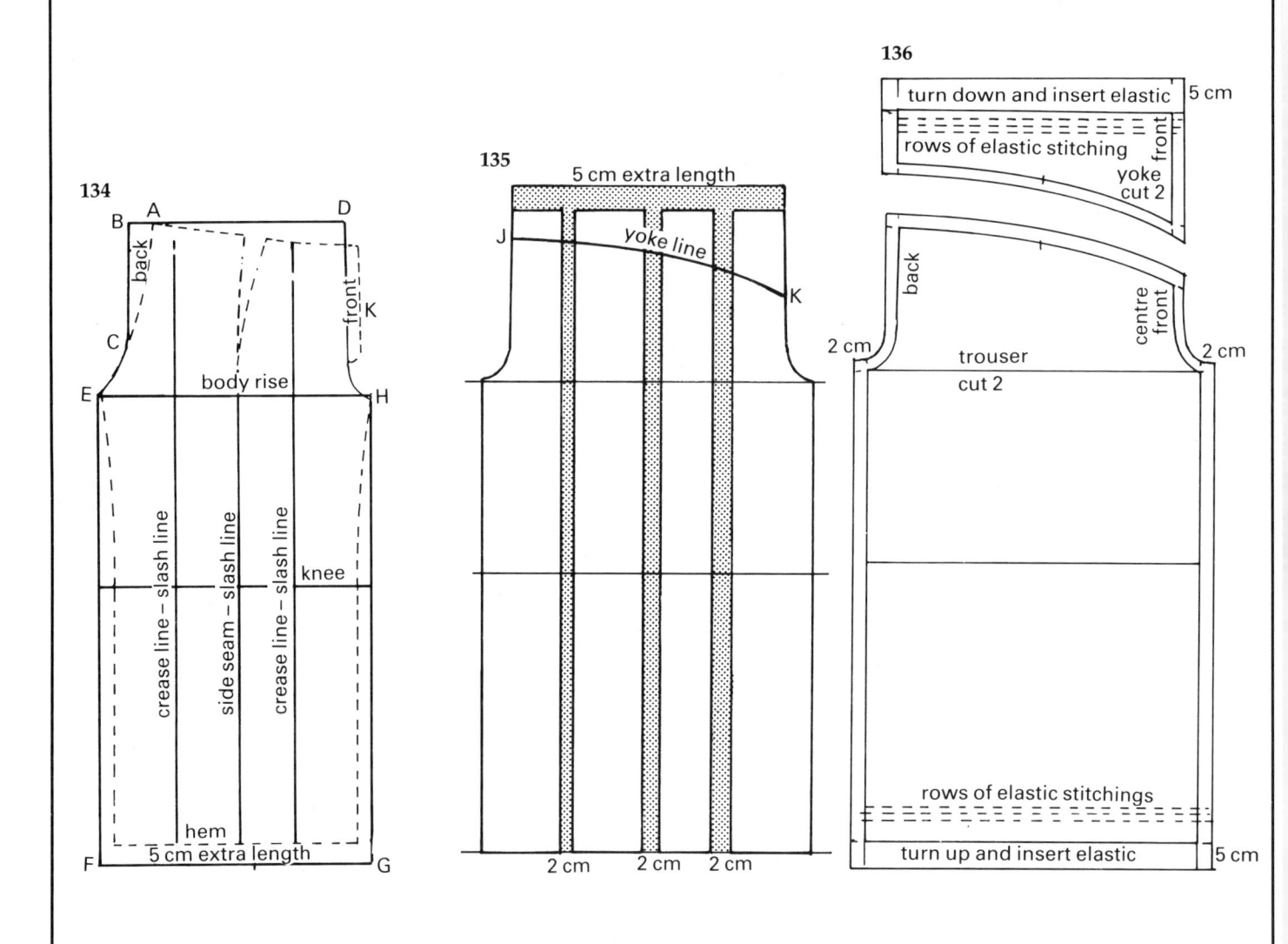

137

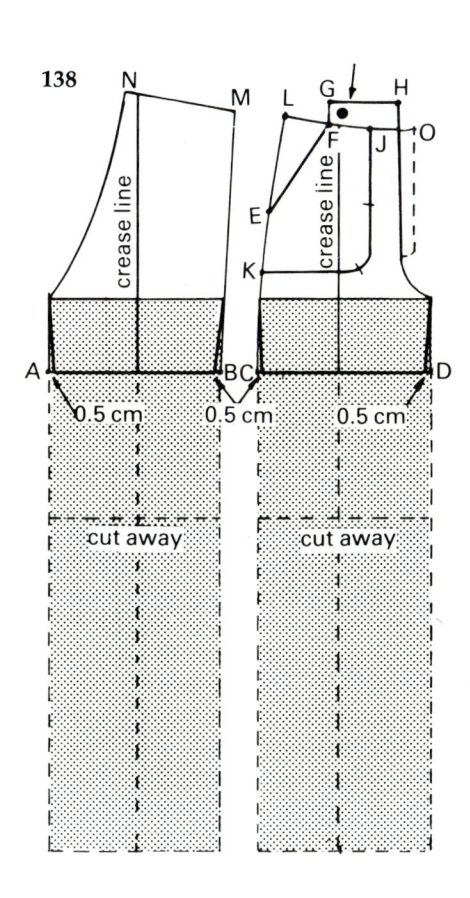

138

points L, M, N and O as in the diagram.

For the front shorts, trace off F–O–D–C–K–E. For the side pocket, trace off L–F–J–K–E. For the pocket facing, trace off F–J–K–E. Similarly, trace off the back shorts and waistband. Add seam allowances to give the complete pattern (Figure 139).

When sewing the shorts together, remember that the front waistband sections G–H–O–F are attached to the shorts and the remaining waistband is sewn to the shorts waist. The button on the small waistband can be unfastened to pull the garment on and off. J–P is left unsewn so that the garment

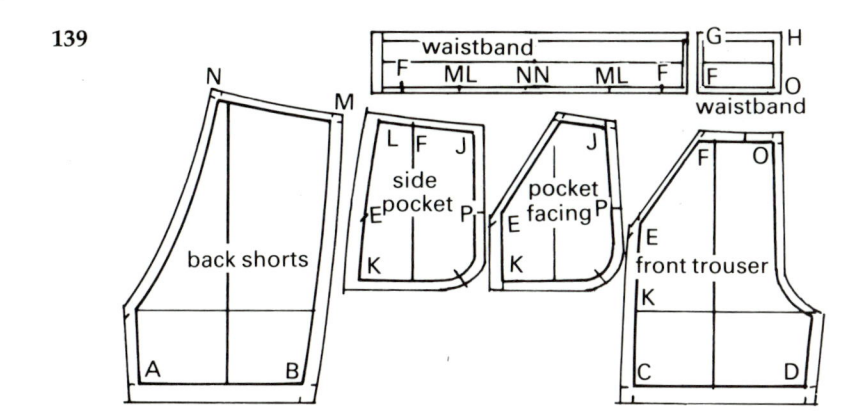

139

can be opened up.

See Figures 155–158 for the buttoned fly manufacturing instructions.

By using fabrics intelligently and daringly, an ordinary pair of trousers can be brought right up to date, as the following examples demonstrate.

59

Joggers with contrasting inset knee bands

These exciting joggers are sketched in Figure 144.

Take the pattern developed in Figure 135. Draw horizontal lines across it (Figure 140). Separate the three sections, and make up the pattern with seam allowances (Figure 141). Cut each section on the grain indicated.

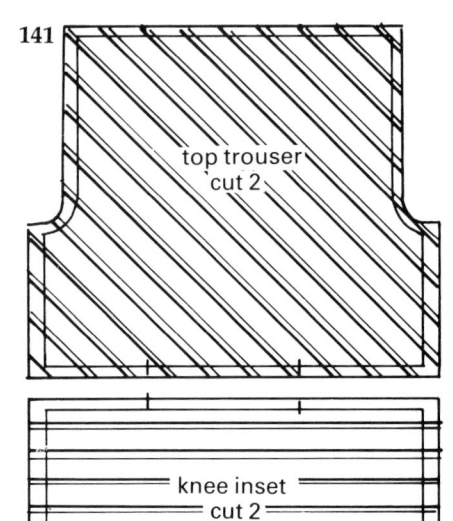

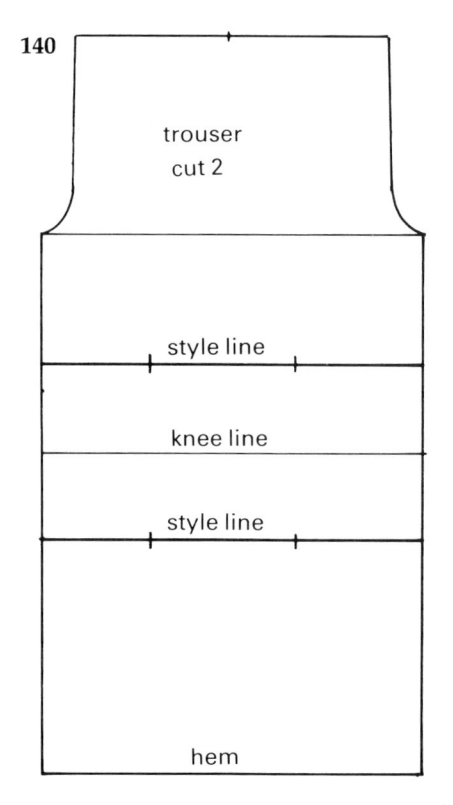

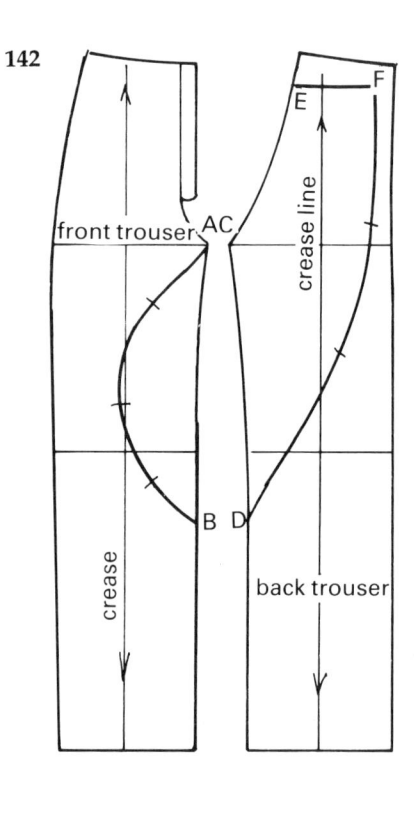

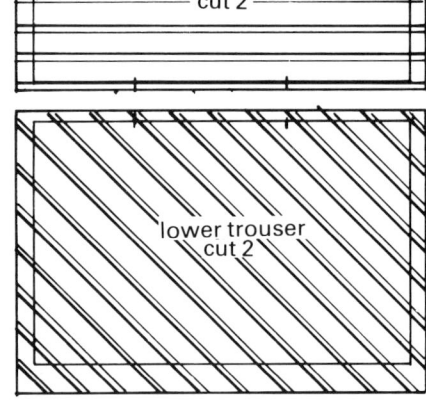

140

trouser cut 2

style line

knee line

style line

hem

141

top trouser cut 2

knee inset cut 2

lower trouser cut 2

142

front trouser
back trouser
crease line
crease

143

front trouser cut 2
back trouser cut 2
back inset cut 2
front

Trousers with curved seamlines

This garment is shown in Figure 145.

Lay the original pattern (Figure 127) on a clean sheet of paper and draw

60

around it. Plan a style line on the back seat and then curve it around so that it creates a curved effect on the front trouser (Figure 142). Be adventurous; try whatever shape appeals.

Separate the patterns and add seam allowances (Figure 143).

The inset section could be cut in a contrast fabric.

Draped trousers from a shaped waistband

These trousers must be made in a very soft cotton or jersey wool to achieve the full effect (Figure 146).

144

145

146

61

Lay the basic jeans pattern (Figure 127) on a large sheet of paper. Join the side seams together and draw around the whole outline (Figure 147). The waistband opens at the side seam, so eliminate the centre front zip stand. Draw the waistband shape. Draw the pocket shapes as in previous styles. Decide on the length of the trouser and draw a band across the leg (shown here as a calf band).

Trace off the separate parts. Slash up the crease lines and the seam line and open out to the required amounts. Remake the pattern and add seam allowances (Figure 148).

Trouser design details

The design details shown in Figure 149 will enable you to add that extra touch to your designs. Tabs, pockets and multiple rows of stitching are always fashionable and will greatly enhance your jeans or trousers, particularly if the top stitching is in a contrasting colour.

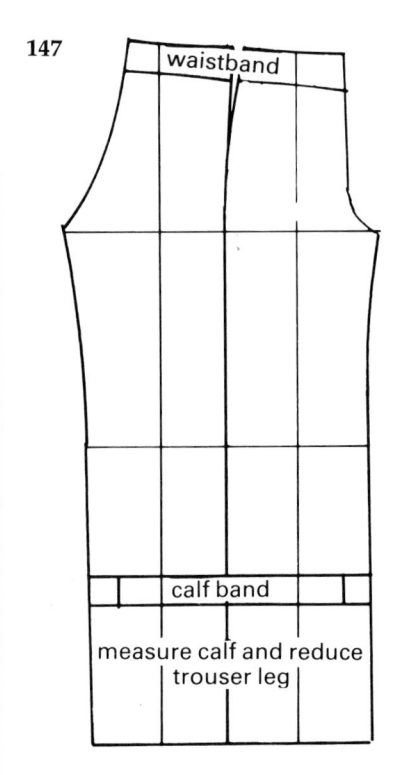

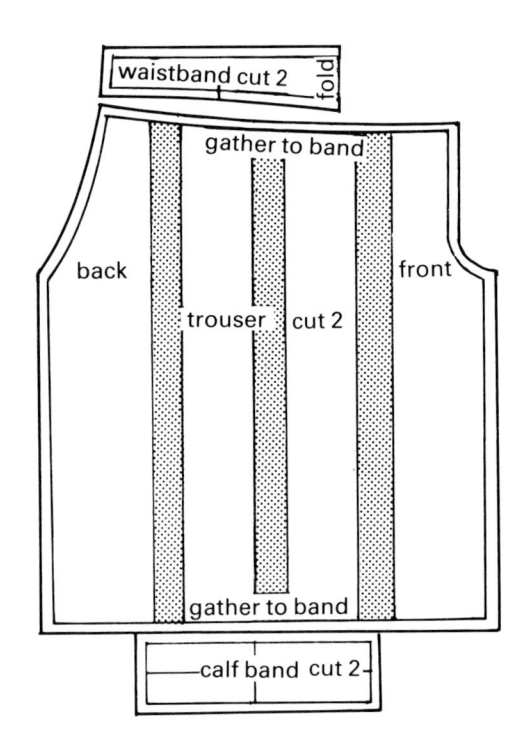

Some of the construction methods may be found in *Pattern Cutting and Making Up* (Martin Shoben and Janet P. Ward; Heinemann, 1987). The following fly insertion methods are taken from this book.

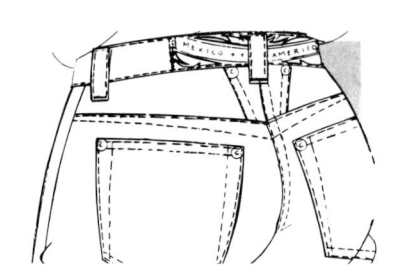

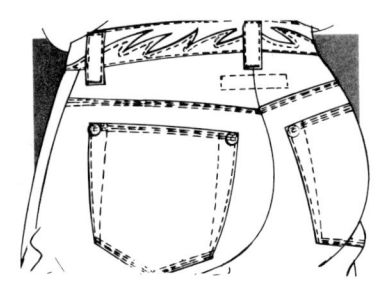

150

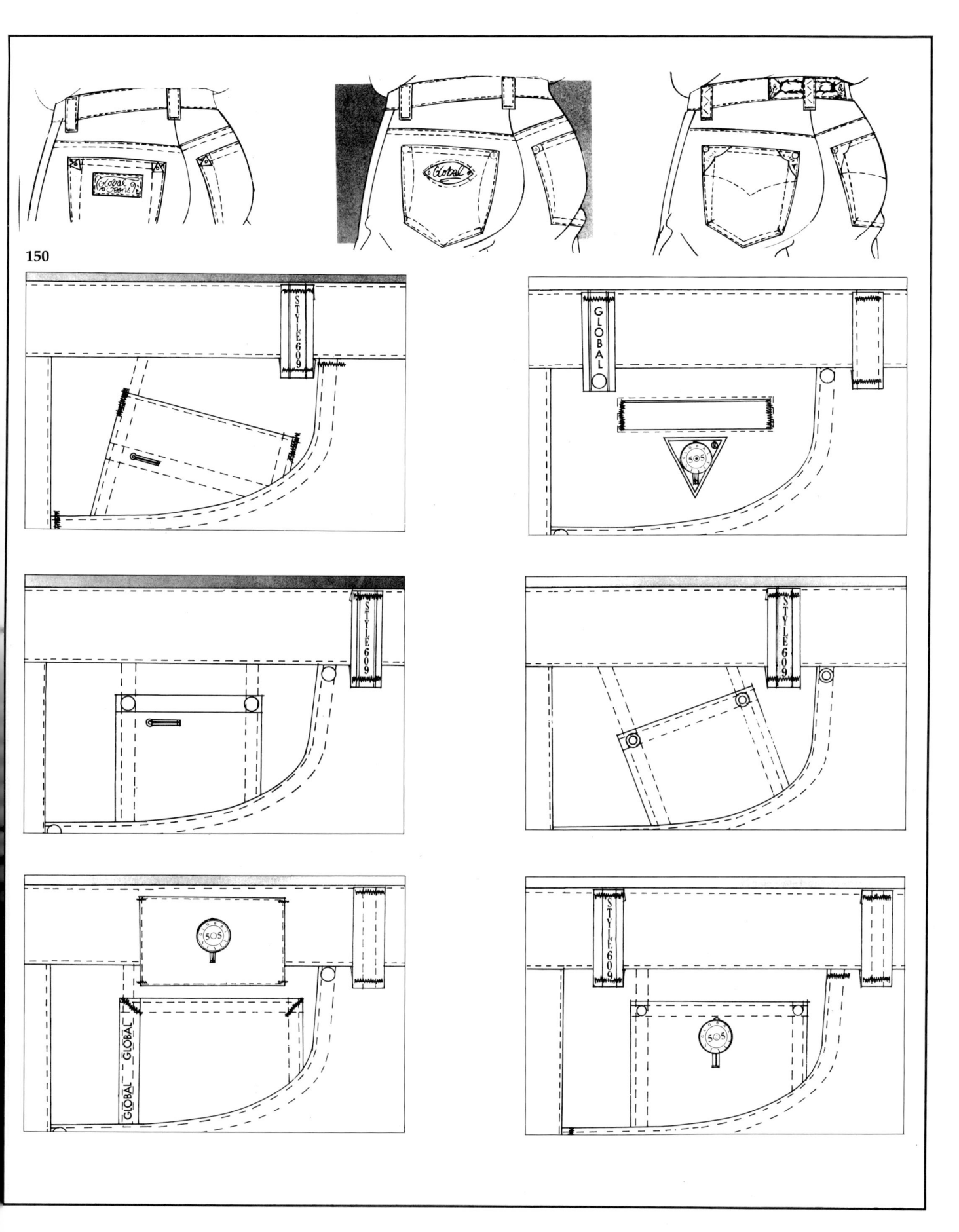

Fly openings

The fly opening in trousers often presents problems. The following section outlines all the stages necessary to accurately insert a zip into a trouser or shorts. A button fly opening is then described.

Zipped fly (separate)

The main advantage of this method is that the zip's position can be determined before the legs are attached to the fly facing.

Place the right side (RS) of the zip to the right side of the right fly with the edge of the zip lined up with the stitching line. Stitch the zip in position as shown in Figure 150.

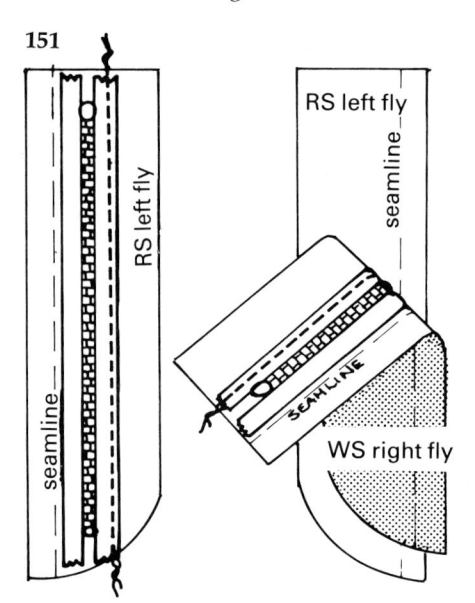

Lay the right fly, with the sewn-on zip, face down on to the right side of the left fly (Figure 151). The edge of the teeth on the unstitched side of the zip should be in line with the stitching line of the left fly. Stitch the zip to the left fly as close to the zip teeth as possible.

Press back, on to the wrong side (WS), the seam allowance of the left trouser at the centre front. With the zip open, lay the pressed edge alongside the zip teeth on the left fly and stitch into position (Figure 152).

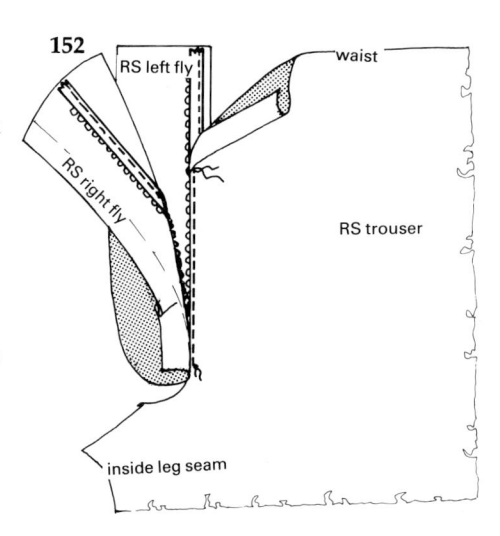

With the right side of the right fly uppermost, lay the right trouser leg face down with the centre front edge against the edge of the fly (Figure 153). Stitch into position.

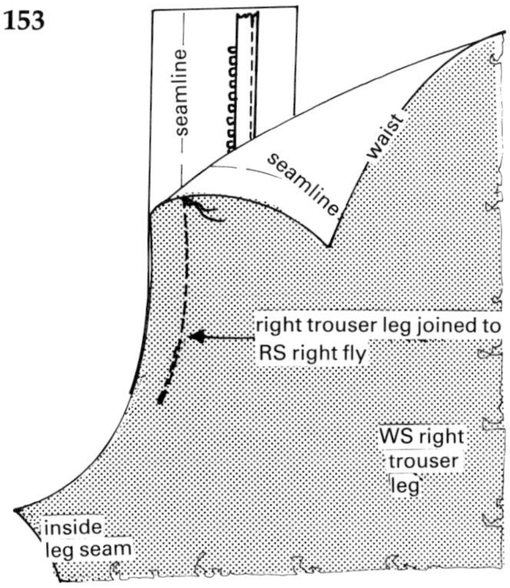

Stitch up crotch seam to base of fly. Top stitch the fly shape, using a template if required (Figure 154). Bar tack the base of the fly zip to reinforce.

The button fly

Sometimes a buttoned fly is preferable to a zip. In this case a double fly piece is required to accommodate the buttonholes.

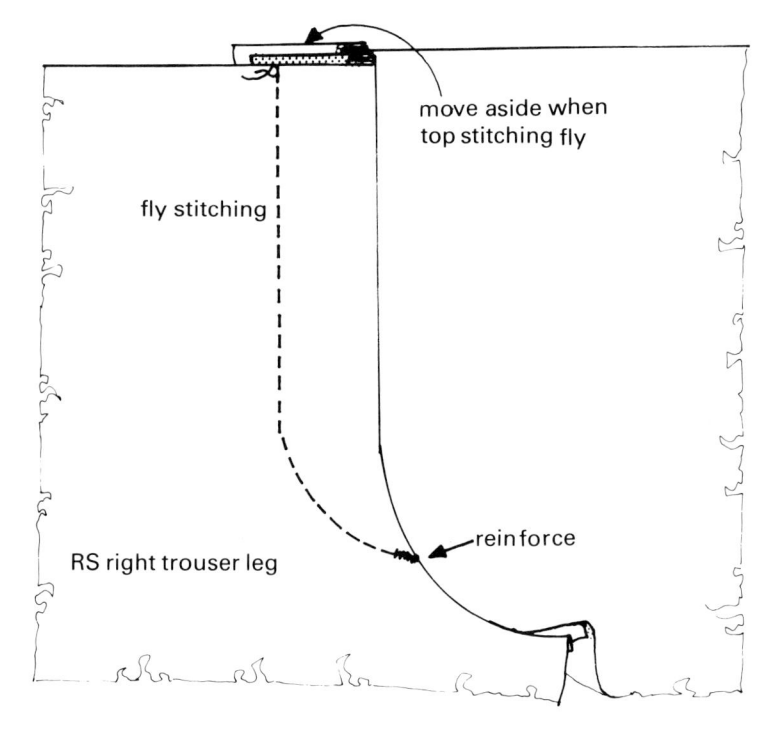

Interline the double fly piece and press in half lengthwise. Work the buttonholes in the folded fly piece (Figure 155).

Attach the fly piece to the right trouser with the grown-on fly pressed.

Bar tack in between the buttonholes (Figure 156).

Top stitch fly stitching on the right leg using a template if necessary. Interline the fly facing. Face the grown-on fly piece on the left side of the trouser (Figure 157). Neaten the loose edge.

Seam the crotch up to the base of the fly opening and then neaten the seam. Bar tack the base of the fly. Finally attach flat buttons to complete (Figure 158).

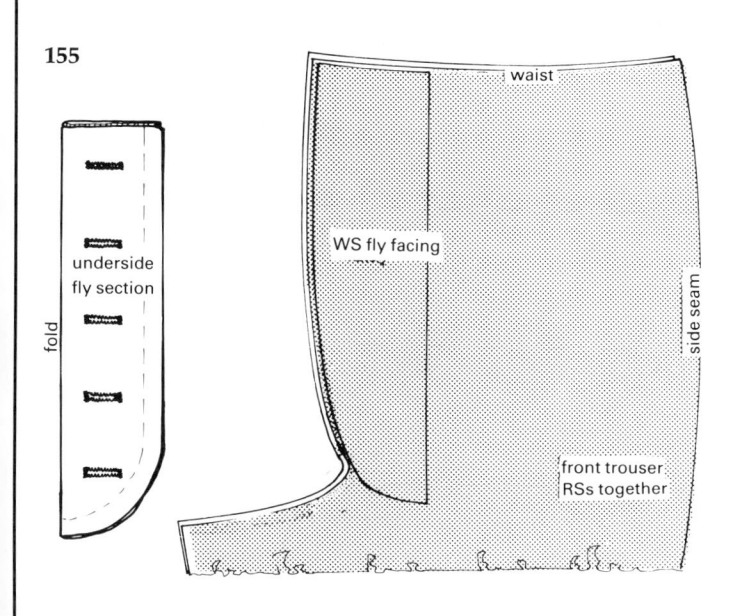

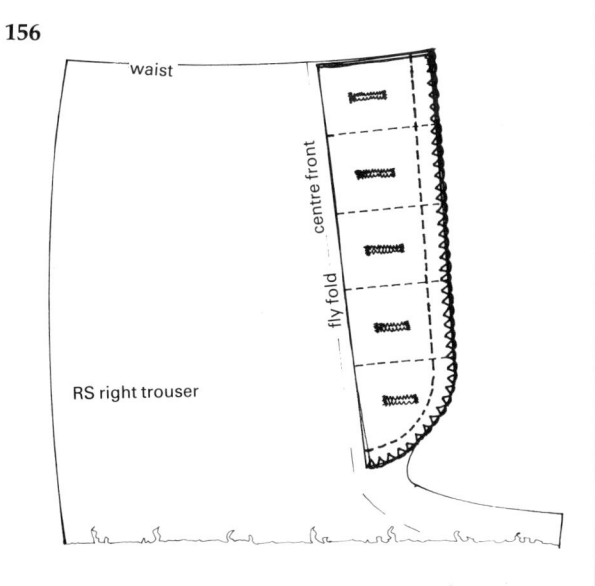

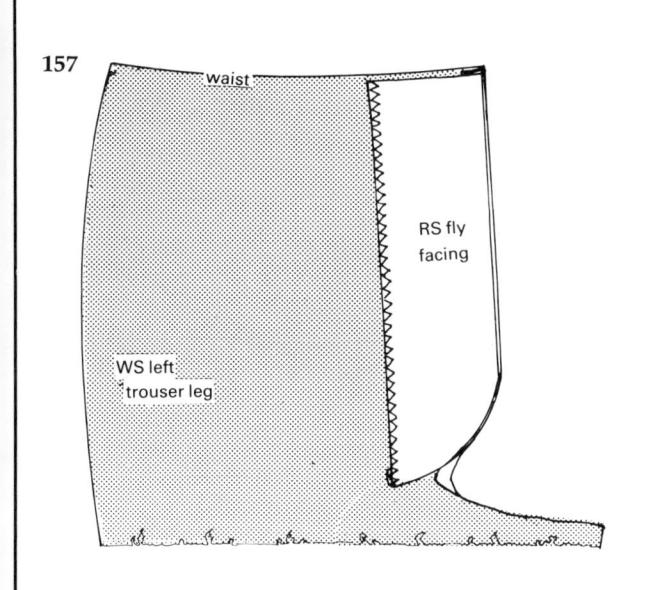

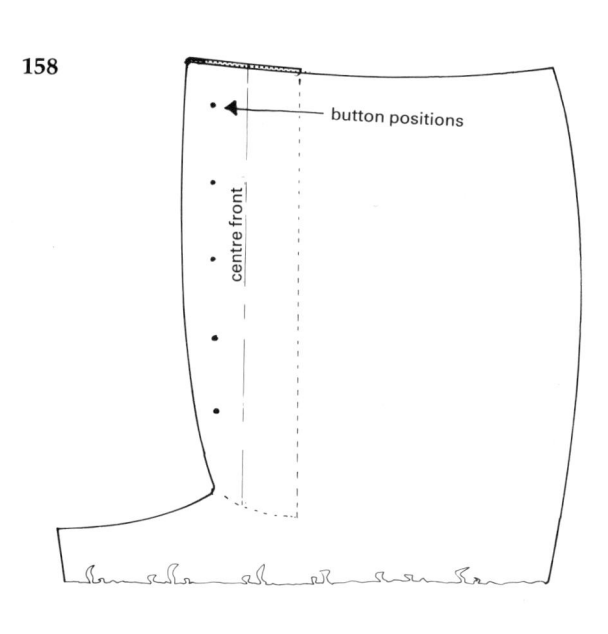

STYLE 6

BLOUSE WITH RAGLAN SLEEVE – overdrape method

This blouse has a beautiful soft shoulder line and will look attractive in almost any soft fabric. The classic style can also be the basis for any number of variations.

Method to choose

The overdrape method is used to reproduce a pattern for this garment. The blouse is placed either on a person or on a dressmaker's stand. A fine fabric or soft tissue paper is then moulded over it, closely following its shape. All the seam positions are marked on the fabric or paper.

Equipment and materials needed

Fine muslin or similar soft fabric or tissue paper for the moulding. Pins, soft pencils etc.

What to look for

Examine the blouse and draw a simple sketch of it, illustrating all the seam positions and key points (Figure 159).

Place pins into the centre front and centre back lines.

Place the blouse on a dress stand or a patient person and fasten up the front buttons (Figure 160). Examine the blouse very carefully and note the grain positions of each section. It is very important to reproduce the grain exactly if the garment is to be recreated.

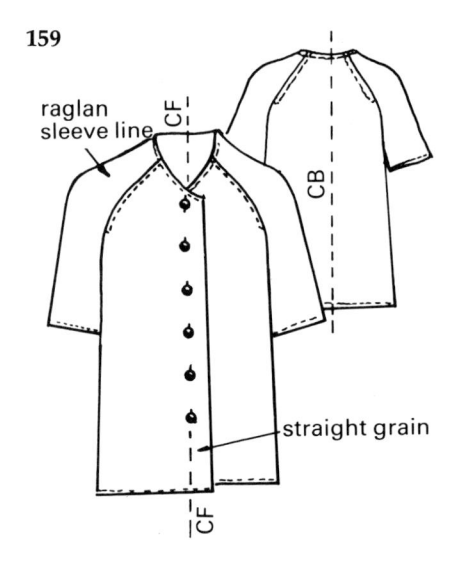

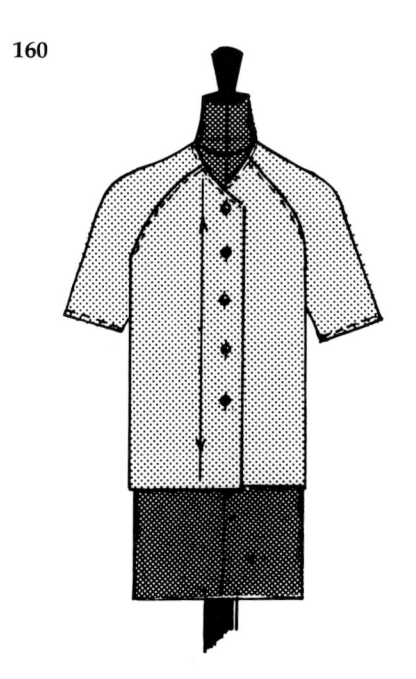

159

160

Front blouse

Cut a square of fabric large enough to cover the front section of the blouse. Using a soft pencil, draw line A–B about 7 cm in from the fabric edge (Figure 161). Draw line C–D at 90 degrees to A–B.

161

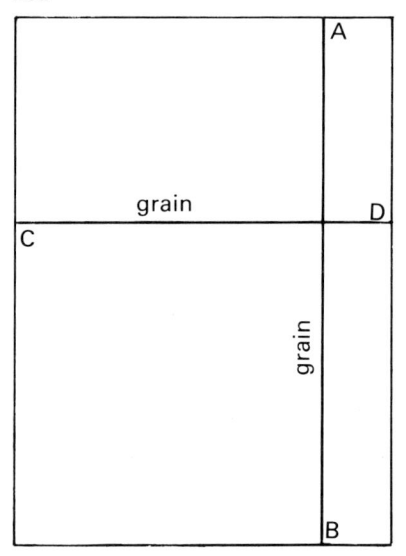

Place the fabric over the blouse and pin line A–B to the centre front of the blouse (Figure 162). Make sure that line C–D is at a 90 degree angle to line A–B. Pin the fabric firmly down on the blouse.

Using a soft pencil, draw over the seam lines from the neckline E to F at the underarm, and then down to G and along to H at the hem.

162

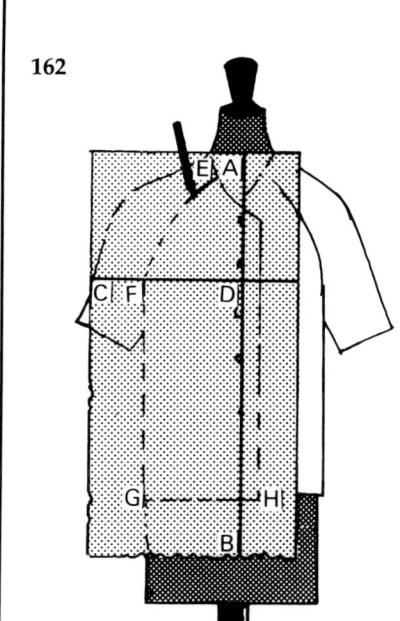

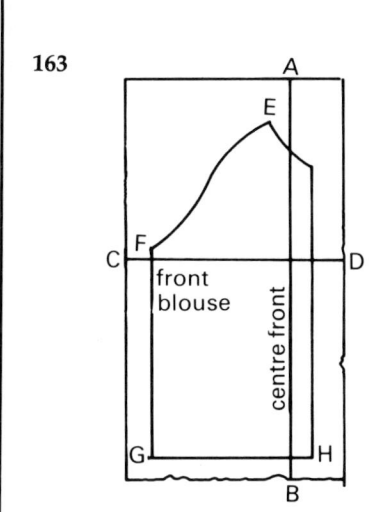

Front sleeve

Cut another square of fabric. Lay line J–K on the shoulder line and pin securely. Using a soft pencil, draw line J–K for the shoulder line (Figure 164).

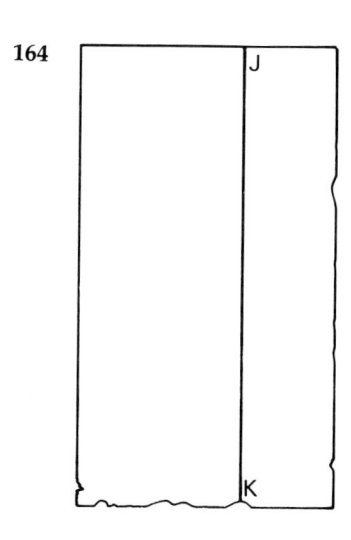

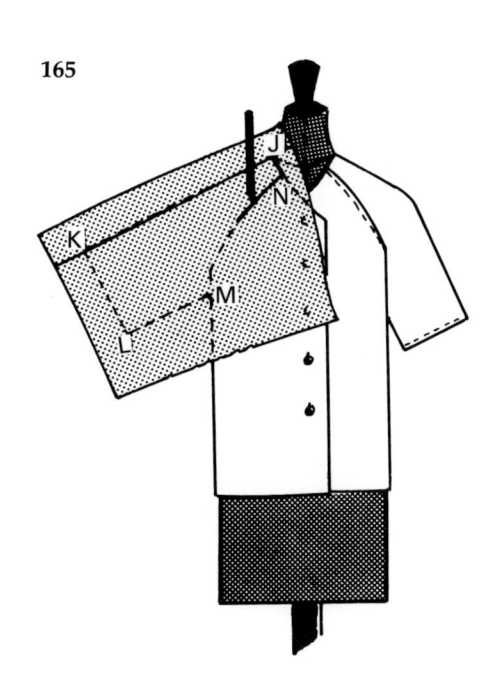

Pin line J–K to the shoulder line on the blouse (Figure 165). Draw K–L for the sleeve end. Draw L–M for the underarm. Draw M–N for the neck.

164

166

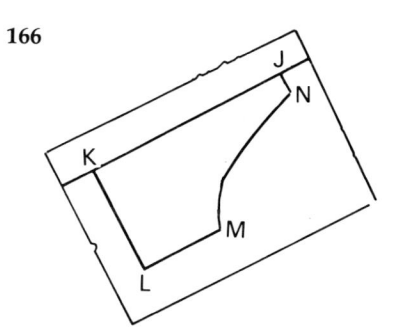

Remove the fabric. Using a set square and curve, redraw over all the lines so that they are clear (Figure 166). Repeat this procedure for the back blouse and the back sleeve. Figure 167 illustrates how the four sections will probably look.

Remove the fabric. Using a set square and a curve, redraw over all the lines so that they are sharp and clear (Figure 163).

163

165

67

Checking the pattern and adding seam allowances

Measure N–M on the front sleeve (Figure 167) and check that it is the same measurement as E–F on the front blouse. Similarly, J–K must equal S–T, and W–V must equal Q–R.

Balance marks must be added to the sleeve as a sewing aid. Y–R should equal Y–V, and X–M should equal X–F. Place a shoulder notch at Z on the sleeve patterns.

Add seam allowances to form the complete pattern (Figure 168).

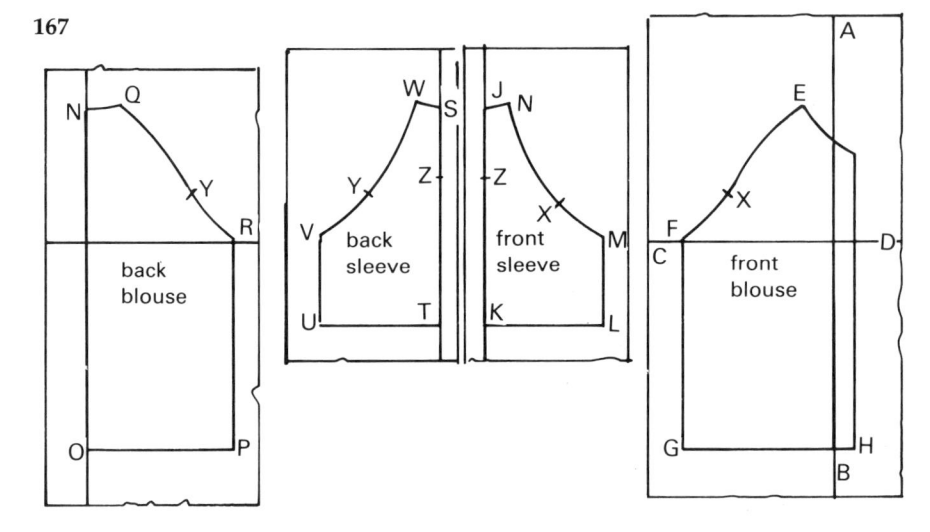

167

168

Facings

Figure 169 illustrates how to cut facings from a raglan sleeve pattern. Lay the patterns together, overlapping the seam allowances to the balance marks. Draw the front and back facings on fresh paper: see the shaded areas in Figure 169.

Alterations

Long tunic dress

Figure 170 shows a long tunic dress adapted from the blouse.

Lay the pattern down on a large sheet of paper (Figure 171). Measure the nape to the required tunic length. Extend line N–O to O1 at the hem. Square to P at the side seam. Connect P to R at the underarm.

Repeat this with the front.

Add a pleat at the centre back of about 3 cm (6 cm when doubled). Don't forget to cut an extended facing.

This fabric layout suggested in Figure 172 is suitable for a fairly wide fabric. Be sure to match the stripes at the side seam.

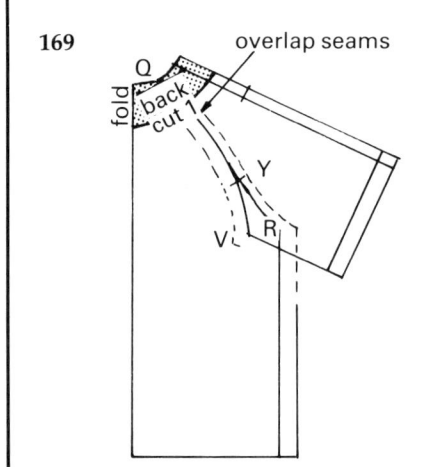

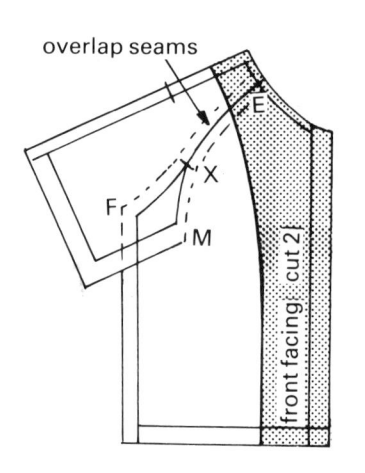

169

170

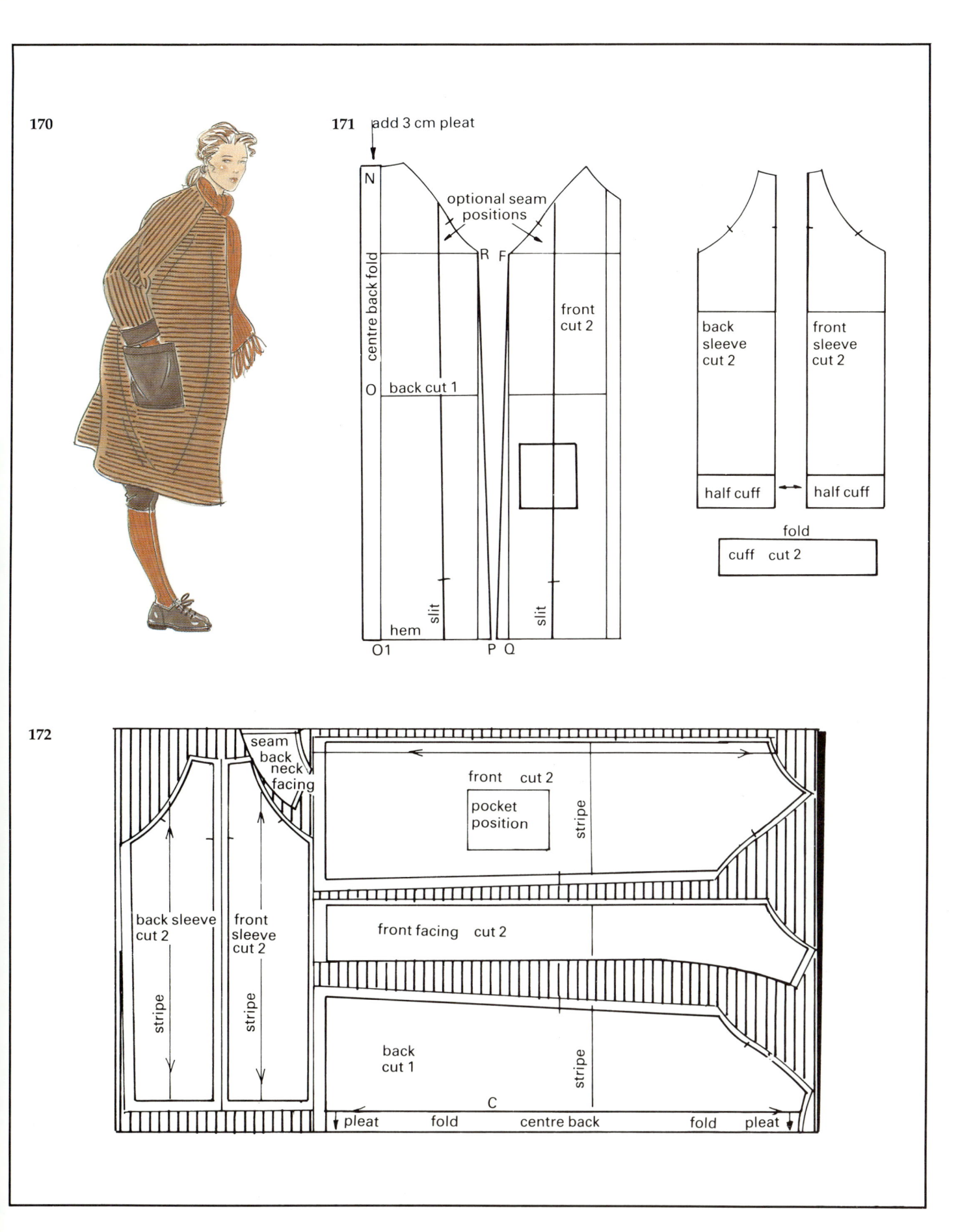

171 add 3 cm pleat

N

centre back fold

optional seam positions

R   F

back cut 1

front cut 2

O

O1   P   Q

hem   slit   slit

back sleeve cut 2

front sleeve cut 2

half cuff   half cuff

fold

cuff   cut 2

172

seam back neck facing

front   cut 2

pocket position

stripe

back sleeve cut 2

front sleeve cut 2

stripe   stripe

front facing   cut 2

back cut 1

stripe

C

pleat   fold   centre back   fold   pleat

173   **174**

Hip-length jacket

This casual unstructured jacket (Figure 174) is suitable for all age groups and can be simply adapted from the original pattern.

On a large sheet of paper, mark around the back and front basic patterns (as used in Figure 167) and join the sleeves together at line S–T and J–K (Figure 175). Extend the centre back line to the required length, i.e. to the hip, and square across to the front. Mark the hip band, which is about 10 cm wide. Draw the front hip band point as on the diagram.

To add extra flare to the jacket, cut out each section of the draft (or trace

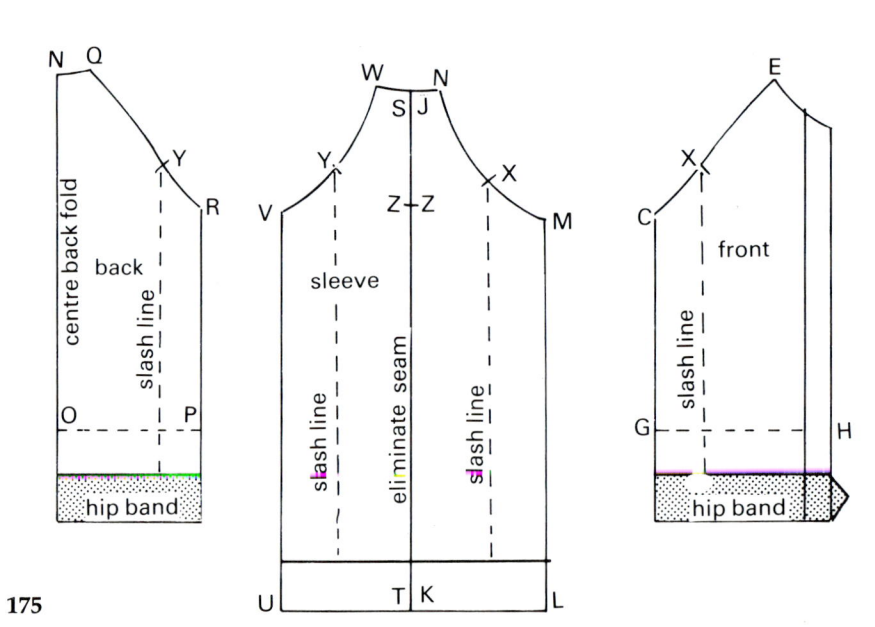

175

70

176

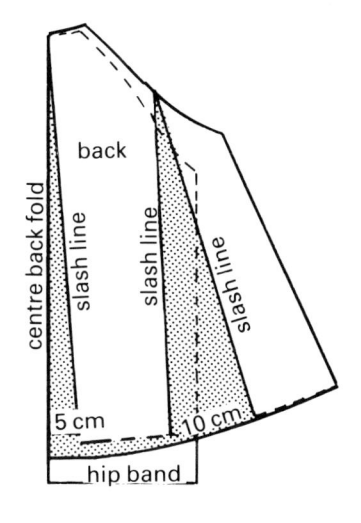

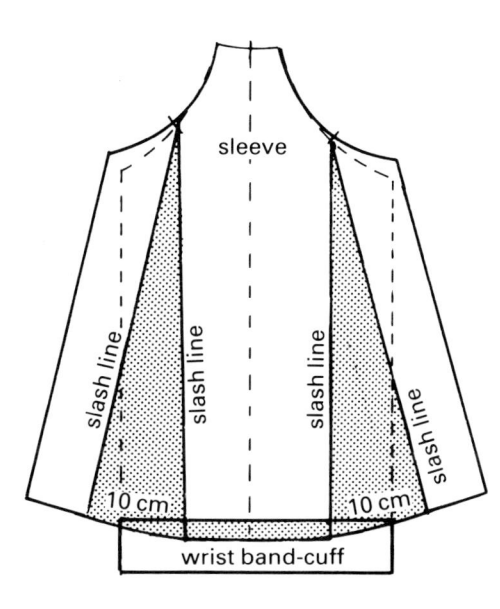

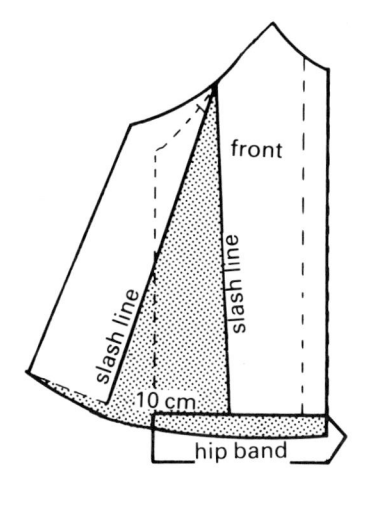

off on another sheet of paper), leaving the hip band (Figure 176). Draw slash lines as in the diagram. Slash up the lines and open out each section about 10 cm. Repeat this with the back blouse and the sleeve.

Complete the pattern and add seam allowances.

Raglan shirt

The blouse pattern can be adapted to a raglan shirt (Figure 173). Although the adaptations are a little more difficult than previous styles, the following diagrams illustrate how the adaptations are accomplished.

Start by enlarging the pattern, as shirts are usually fairly loose and comfortable. Arrange the patterns (Figure 177) on a large sheet of paper. Decide how much larger the pattern needs to be, and add the required amount to lines V–U, R–P, M–L and F–G (Figure 177). Extend the body to the required length.

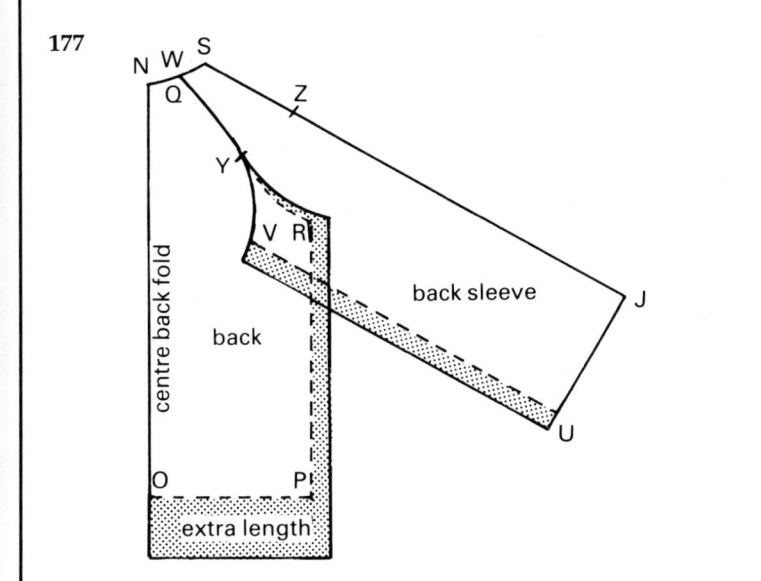

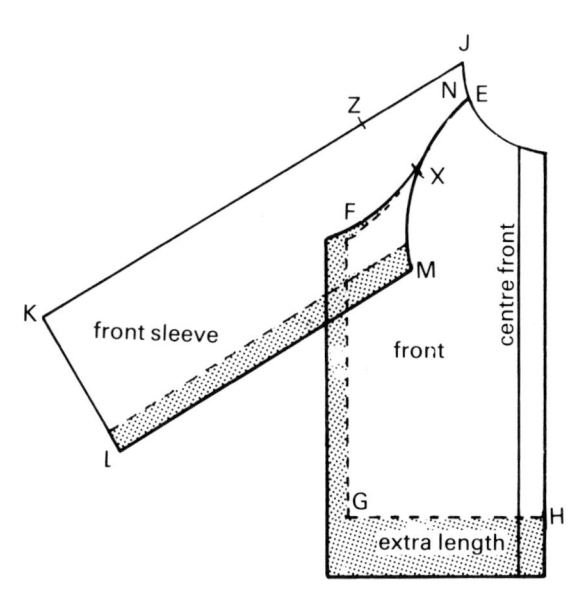

177

This pattern arrangement is referred to as a pattern draft. On it can be superimposed new style lines.

However, the shirt in Figure 173 is more or less the basic pattern (Figure 167) plus a collar and a shaped hem. Figure 178 shows how to plan and cut the pattern for it.

Increase N–O to the required length O1 (Figure 178). Square across to P1 and connect to the side seam. Continue line O1–P1 across to H1 at the centre front. Square down from F to G1. Shape the hem as in the diagram.

The cuff is cut from a simple rectangle, which is based on the wrist measurement and the required cuff width as for earlier styles.

The collar is also based on a simple rectangle. Measure I–J–S–N on the front and back shirts and construct a rectangle of this length. Draw a style point for the collar as shown.

Trace off all the sections from the draft and add seam allowances. The completed pattern should look like Figure 179.

Figure 180 gives a suggested layout for a fabric with a broad stripe.

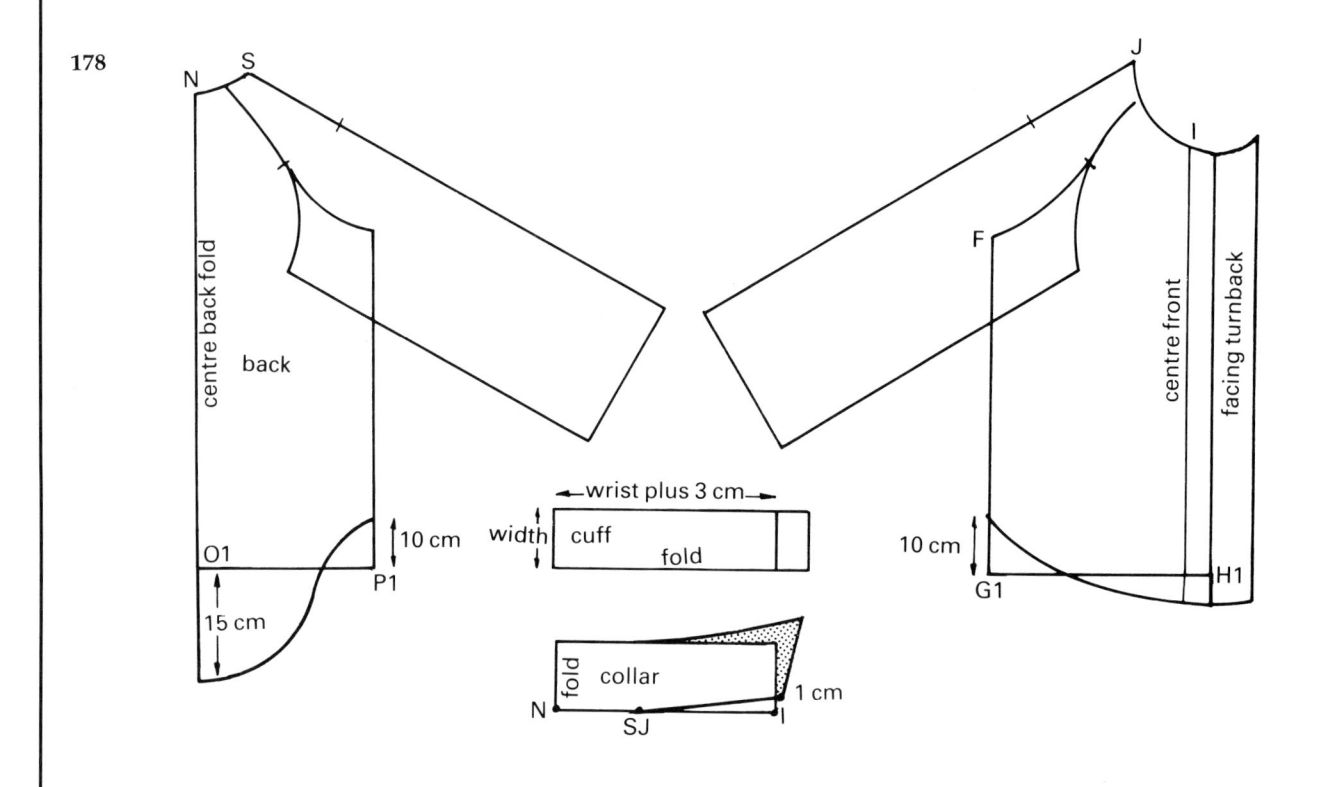

178

179

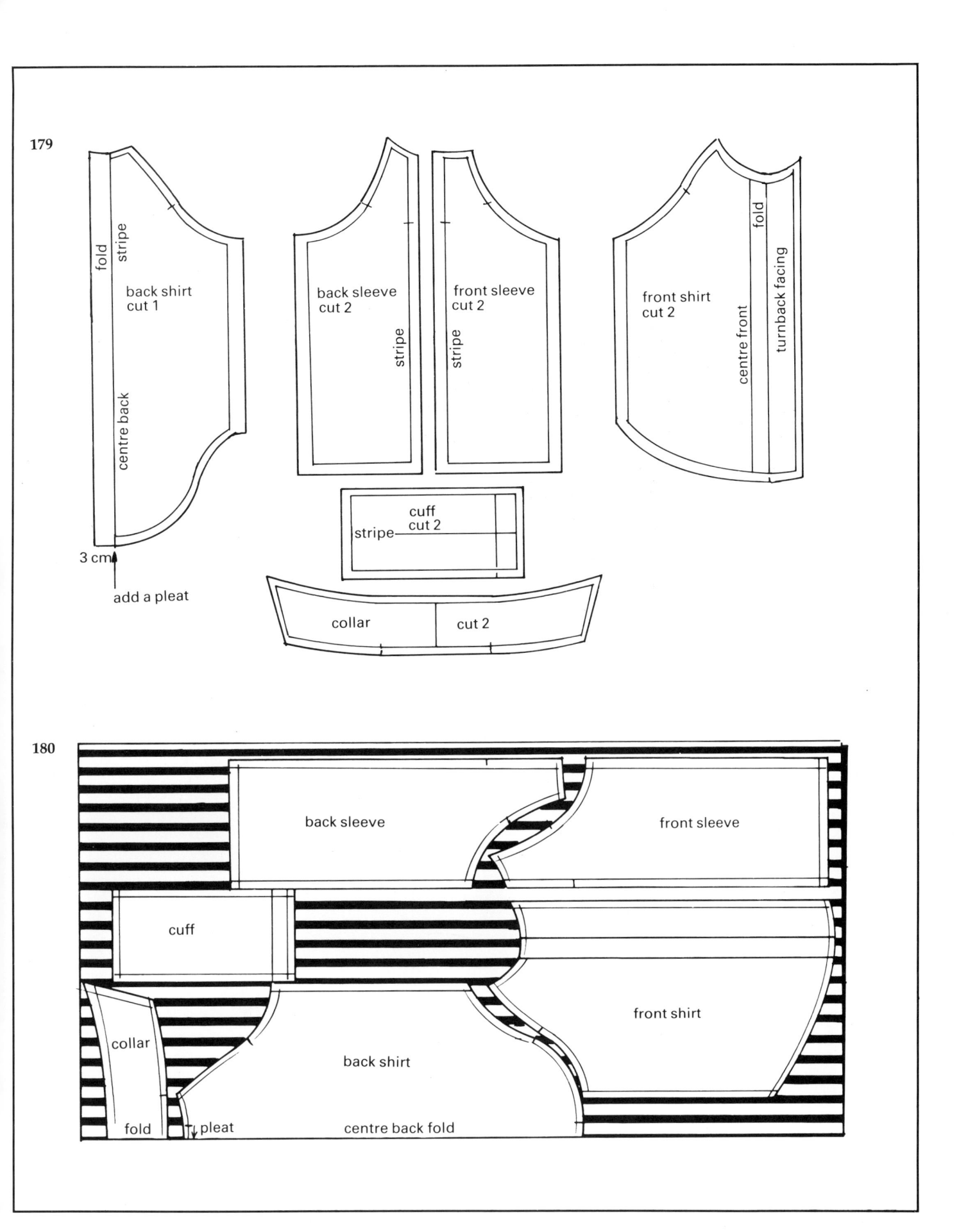

- fold
- stripe
- back shirt cut 1
- centre back
- 3 cm
- add a pleat
- back sleeve cut 2
- stripe
- front sleeve cut 2
- stripe
- front shirt cut 2
- centre front
- fold
- turnback facing
- cuff cut 2
- stripe
- collar cut 2

180

- back sleeve
- front sleeve
- cuff
- front shirt
- collar
- back shirt
- fold
- pleat
- centre back fold

181 182

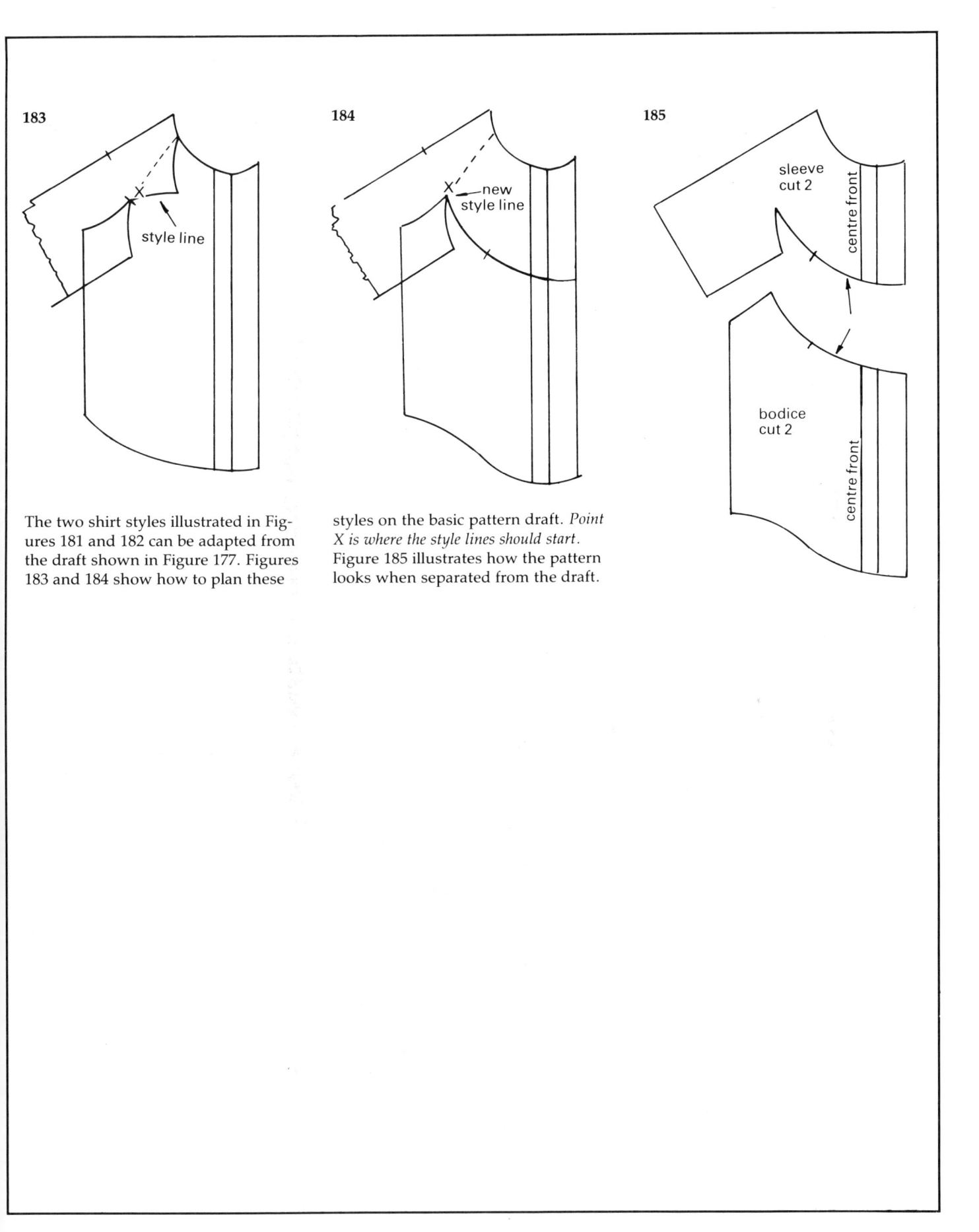

The two shirt styles illustrated in Figures 181 and 182 can be adapted from the draft shown in Figure 177. Figures 183 and 184 show how to plan these styles on the basic pattern draft. *Point X is where the style lines should start.* Figure 185 illustrates how the pattern looks when separated from the draft.

STYLE 7

CLASSIC TAILORED SKIRT – fold and spike method

There will be a smart skirt like this in every woman's wardrobe. A simple remake in linen or cotton and some adjustments to its silhouette will give you a new range of clothes to wear on different occasions.

What to look for

This is a fairly simple skirt to reproduce. Check to see if the front and skirt patterns are the same; if they are, only one pattern is required.

Draw a sketch of the garment, noting the key points (Figure 186).

Equipment needed

Paper, fine spike, metre stick, tape measure, pencils etc.

Front and back skirt

Draw a straight line on a long sheet of paper.

Mark the centre back and centre front of the skirt with a row of pins (see Figure 186).

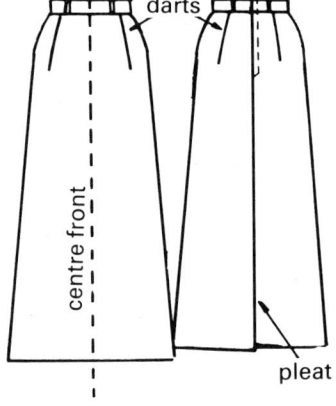

Lay the centre front of the skirt on the straight line (Figure 187). Flatten from A to B at the hem and place a weight to hold the hem firmly down. Draw line B to C.

Using a tracing wheel, wheel through from A to D at the waist. Mark point E at the point of the dart.

Look at line C–D, the side seam. You will probably see that it is not a straight line. Draw along C–D.

Remove the skirt from the paper. Measure from the centre front A to the dart and mark point E (Figure 188). Mark point F at the dart end. Turn the skirt inside out and estab-

186

187

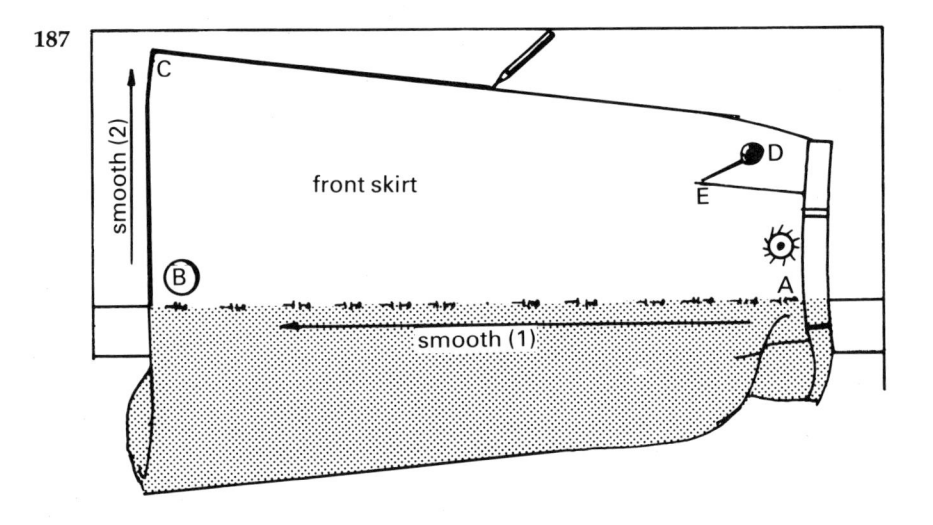

188

76

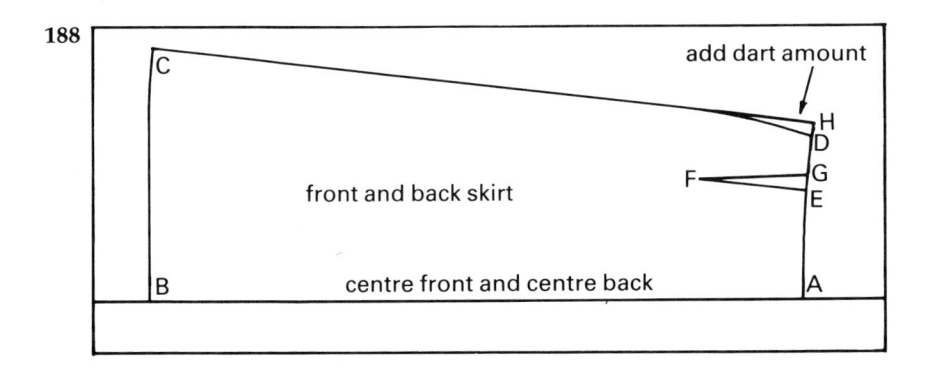

lish the amount sewn into the dart – about 2 cm. E to G equals 2 cm, and H from D equals 2 cm.

The pattern can be used for both the front and the back skirt patterns. However, the back skirt has a kick pleat. Trace off the back pattern from the skirt draft. Add a kick pleat down the centre back of about 7 cm.

Add seam allowances to complete the pattern (Figure 189).

The lining

Cut the lining exactly the same as the skirt pattern (see Figure 189) with the following slight alterations:

1. Shorten the length of the lining so that when the hem is turned up the lining will not show below the skirt.
2. The darts should be pleated instead of sewn.

189

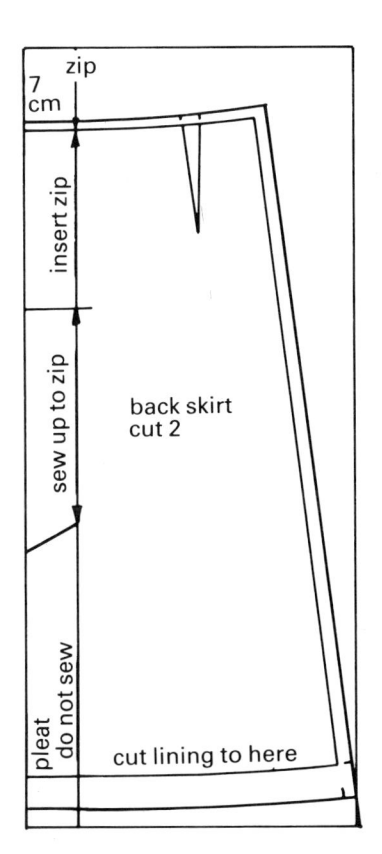

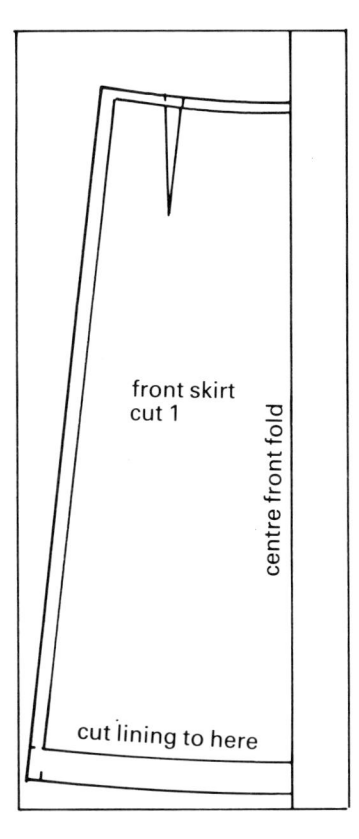

190

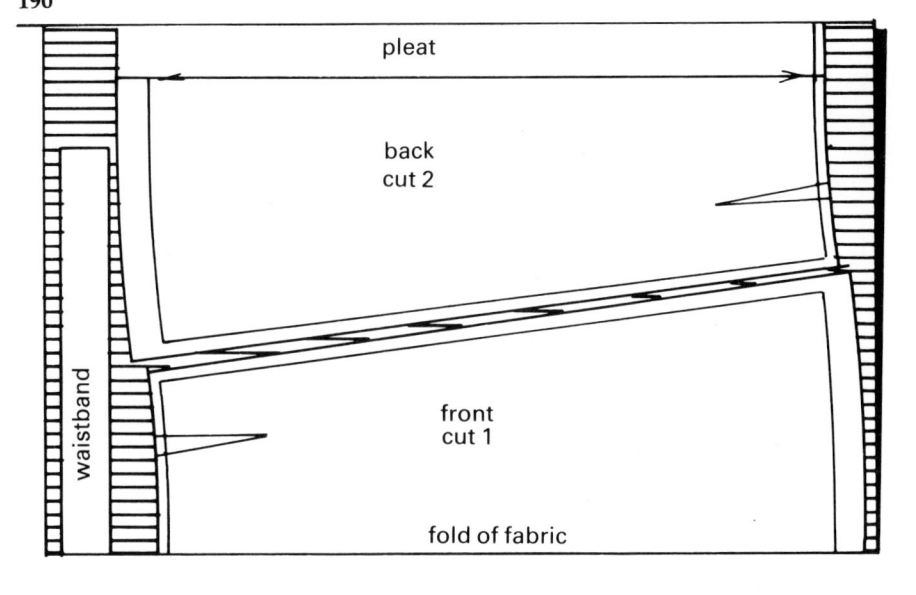

The waistband

Measure and construct the waistband as in previous styles (e.g. Figure 48).

Checking the pattern

Check that the side seams are the same length. Check that the waistband is the correct size for the skirt.

Fabric layout

Figure 190 shows the usual fabric layout. However, be wary; it is only possible to reverse the pattern on a two-way fabric. Also note that the waistband can be laid along the selvedge if the fabric is wide enough.

77

191

192

Alterations

A line skirt cut on the cross grain

Select an evenly printed or woven fabric for this skirt (Figure 192).

The front

Trace off the front pattern from the draft. Draw a line A–B from the dart point to the hem (Figure 193). Slash up to the dart point and close the dart. This will increase the hem (Figure 194).

Pin the pattern on another sheet of paper. Connect B to B1 along the hem. Draw 45 degree grain lines (see Figure 195).

Add seam allowances to complete the pattern. In this case the centre front and centre back will be seamed, not folded. The fabric must be laid open on the table and the skirt sections cut four times (Figure 195). Position the patterns as in the diagram with the 45 degree grain lines placed carefully on the selected stripe.

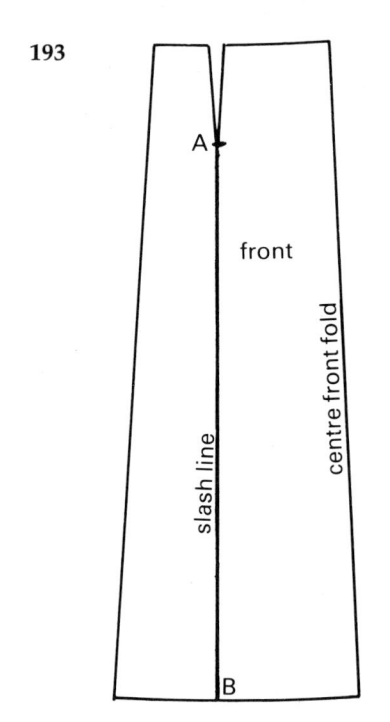

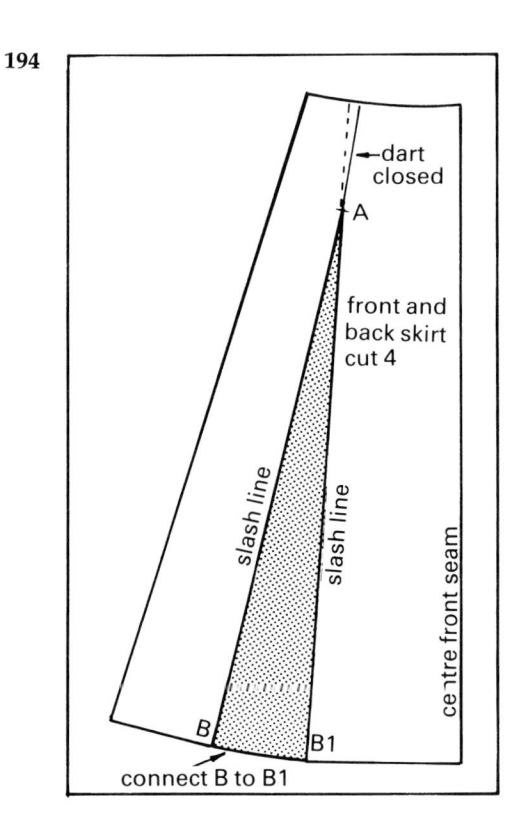

193

slash up to dart point

194

Skirt with a double knife pleat

This skirt adaptation has a double knife pleat at the centre front (Figure 191). This design detail retains the tailored skirt appearance but provides more room for walking.

On a large sheet of paper draw two parallel lines B–B and C–C about 7 cm in from the edge A–A (Figure 196). Crease down the lines as in the diagram, and fold back to leave C–C at the paper edge. Position the front pattern on the folded line C–C and draw around it (Figure 197). Remove the skirt and open out the pattern. Add seam allowances before cutting out (Figure 198). Note that the pleats will be sewn part way down the skirt.

Use the back skirt as in the previous style.

195

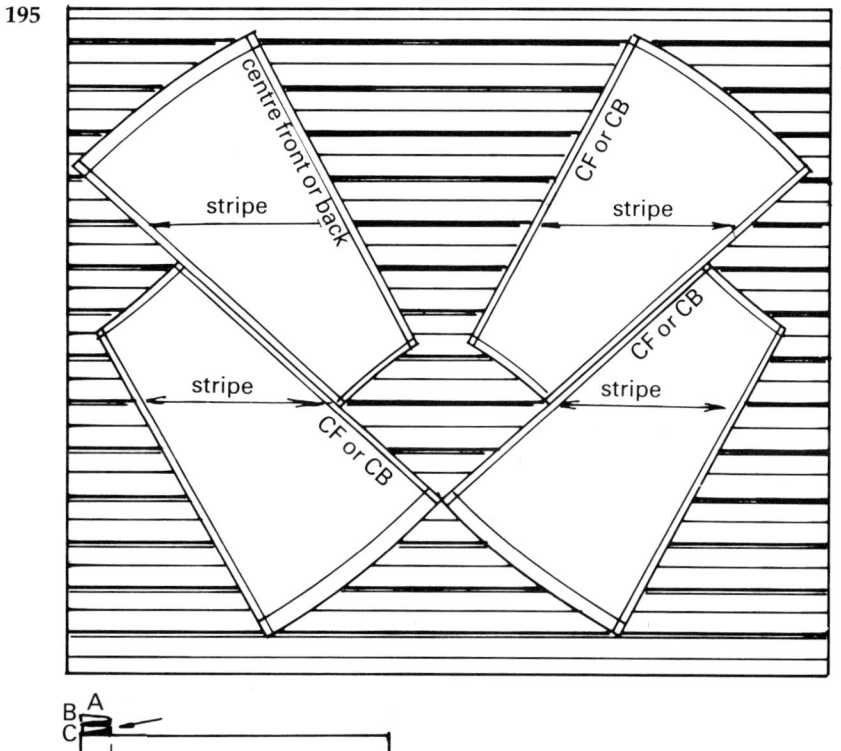

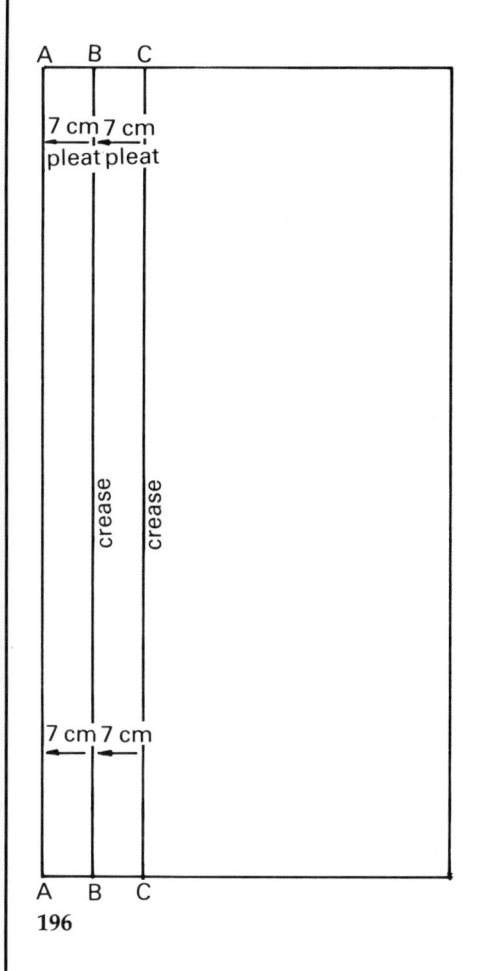

196 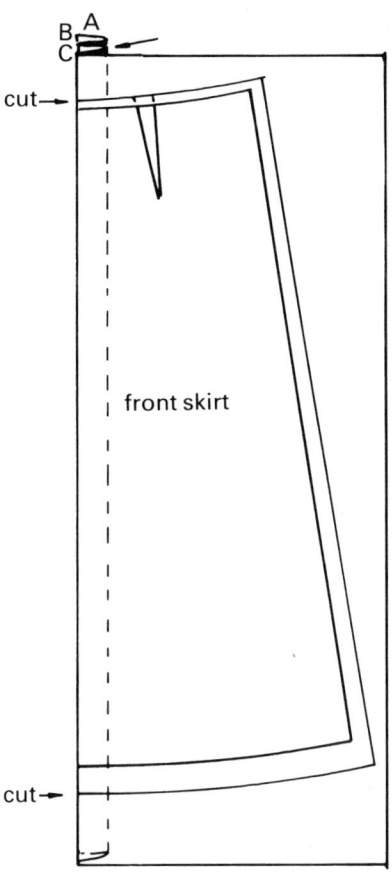　　197 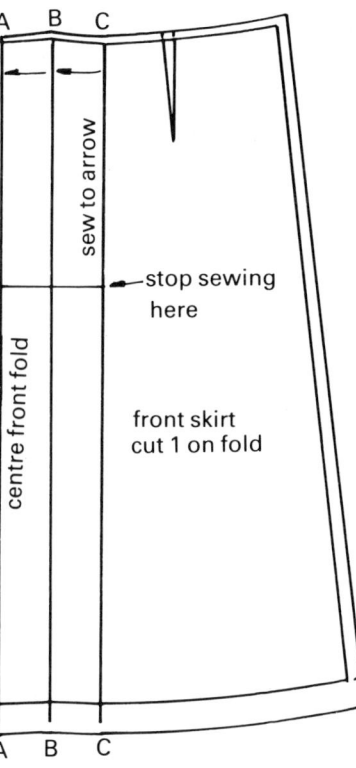　　198

Culottes

Culottes or the divided skirt (Figure 199) is a fairly easy adaptation from your comfortably fitting skirt (Figure 189). They are especially attractive when they have a pleat at the centre front.

Draw line A–B on a clean sheet of paper (Figure 200). Draw the hip line on the skirt patterns and place this line on line A–B (the hip line is at the broadest part of the hip).

Establish the body rise line F–D by measuring down from the waistline of your trouser pattern to the trouser fork (see Figure 114), or apply the size 12 measurement of 31 cm. Mark in F and D.

On the front skirt, G from D equals 1 cm for all sizes. Connect G to C and to L on the hem. H from G and P from L equal 9 cm. Complete L–P–H–C.

On the back skirt, J from F equals 1 cm for all sizes. Continue line E–J to M on the hem. K from J and N from M equal 12.3 cm. Complete M–N–K–E.

Note that the measurements given here are for a standard size 12; adjust the measurements according to requirements.

To prepare the pleated front, draw a line parallel to the edge of a long sheet of paper. Fold a long graduated pleat as deep as required. Make the lower hem end of pleat wider than the waist amount (Figure 201).

Lay the front pattern on the pleated paper so that line C–L, which is the centre front (see Figure 200), lies on the pleat (Figure 201). Draw around the pattern.

Add seam allowances and cut the pattern out as in Figure 202. This figure shows an optional pocket line; see Style 5 for construction methods. There is also an optional yoke seam at the centre back; if this is added, remember to close out the darts at the back waist. The culottes will probably have a side seam opening and an ordinary waistband (see Figure 48). If more flare is required, use the method shown in Figure 193 to increase the hem.

199

81

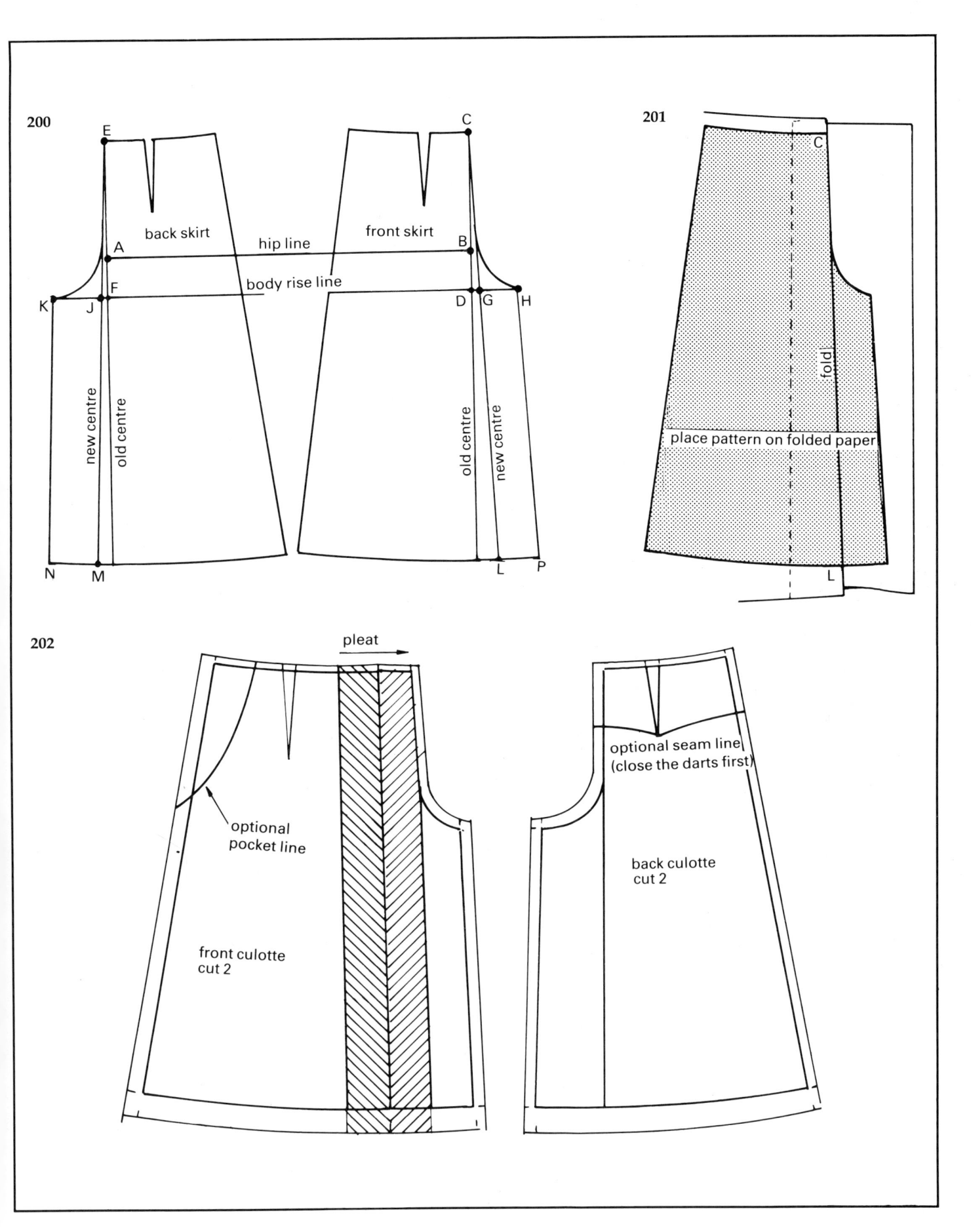

PATTERNS FROM DRAPES AND GATHERS
– overdrape method

This section deals with taking patterns from parts of a garment rather than a whole garment. It develops the overdrape method described in Style 6.

The overdrape method is used to take patterns from complicated garment sections that cannot be laid flat on the table and are therefore not usually suitable for the fold and spike method employed in most of the styles. Some clothes may need a combination of the fold and spike method and the overdrape method to achieve a full pattern. For example, the overdrape method might be used for the draped part and the fold and spike method for a simple skirt.

To overdrape, simply mould a fabric to the contours of the garment and mark around the seamlines. To do this, a knowledge of draping or modelling is very useful but not essential. You will need a dress stand or a patient friend, fabric, paper, pins, soft pencil etc.

The soft cowl

This kind of draped garment feature (Figure 203) is almost always cut with the cross grain applied to the centre front.

Place the dress on the dress stand and carefully arrange the cowl so that it drapes exactly as intended (Figure 204).

203

204

82

It is very important to find out the grain position on the front bodice cowl, as this will affect the way the cowl drapes. Whatever the fabric, the grain position must be reproduced *exactly* to achieve the same effect as the original. The fabric must be of a similar weight and texture to the original if the same effect is required, so choose the fabric with care. Cut a length of fabric large enough to cover the draped front.

205

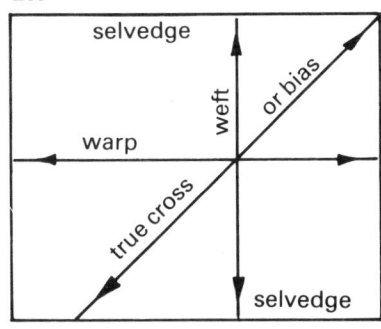

Figure 205 illustrates the names of the grain positions of a woven fabric. Establish the true cross of the fabric by folding the fabric as indicated by Figure 206, line A–B. Open the fabric out again. Make sure that the fabric has not been stretched along the crease line.

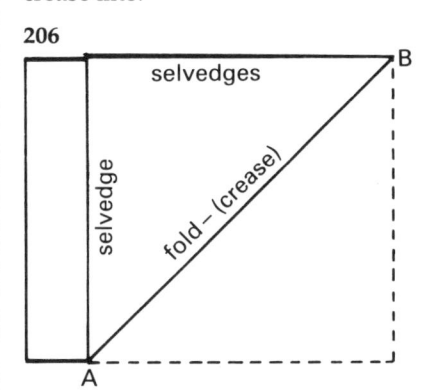

206

Place the garment on the stand (Figure 204). Pull the centre front of the cowl firmly down and measure C–D–E, that is from the neck point to the centre front and back to the other neck point. Apply this measurement to the fabric (see Figure 207).

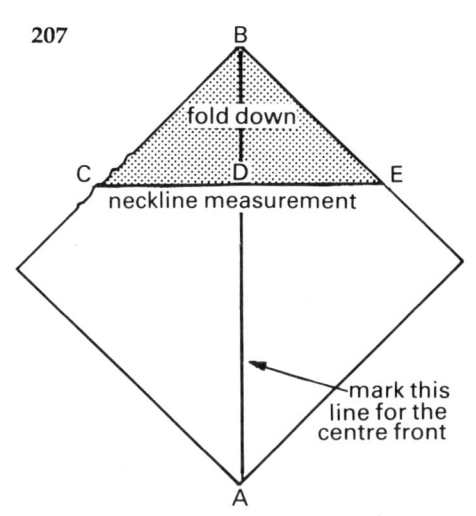

207

Holding the fabric at points C and E, apply points C, D and E to the corresponding points on the garment (on the stand) and pin into position (Figure 208). Then carefully mould the fabric into the drape lines of the cowl. Finally, turn the material at the neck (shaded area B–C–E on Figure 207) underneath the cowl; this will be the facing.

Pin the rest of the fabric on the bodice. Mark the centre front, the waist and the shoulder line (Figure 209). Very carefully cut away all the

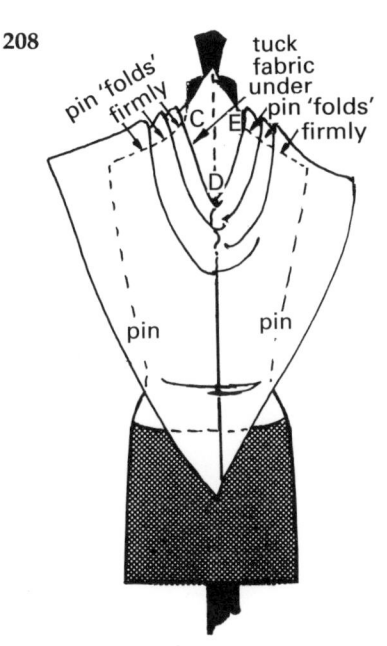

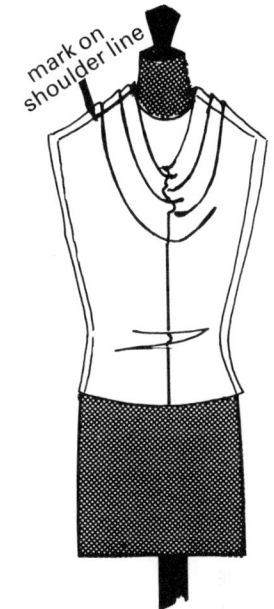

208

209

unwanted fabric, making sure to leave seam allowances around the finished sewing line. Remove the front and lay it flat on to the table. It will look something like Figure 210.

Prepare the rest of the pattern on either paper or fabric. Note that the back bodice will be much narrower because the back of the cowl is usually quite fitted.

Sew a weight to point G on the front (Figure 210) to aid the cowl drape.

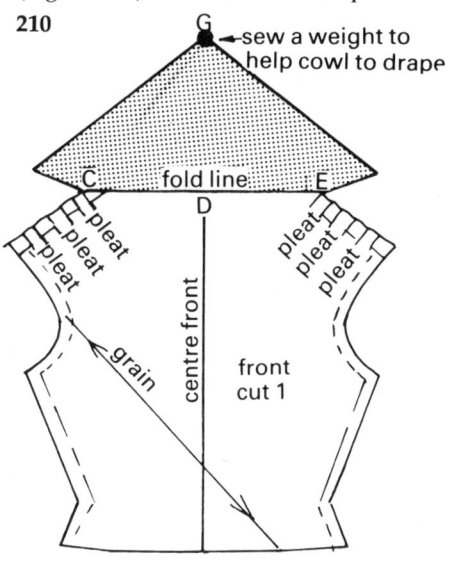

210

83

211

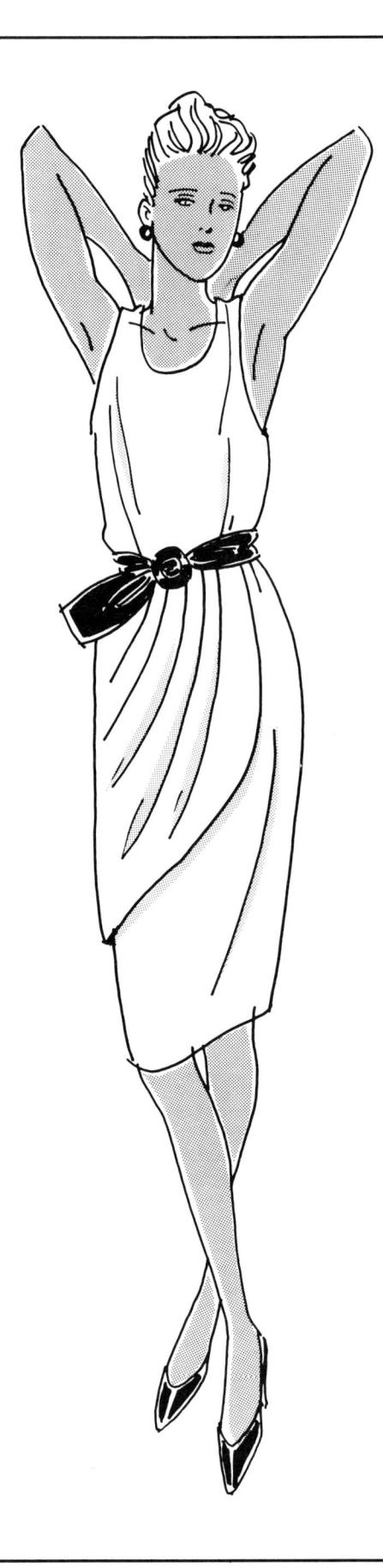

Softly draped front panel over a sheath skirt

This pattern (Figure 211) can be reproduced by using the same technique shown in the previous style.

Place the skirt on the stand and make sure that all drapes are falling properly (Figure 212). Examine the skirt to identify and locate the grain positions. Cut a square of fabric large enough to cover the skirt front.

212

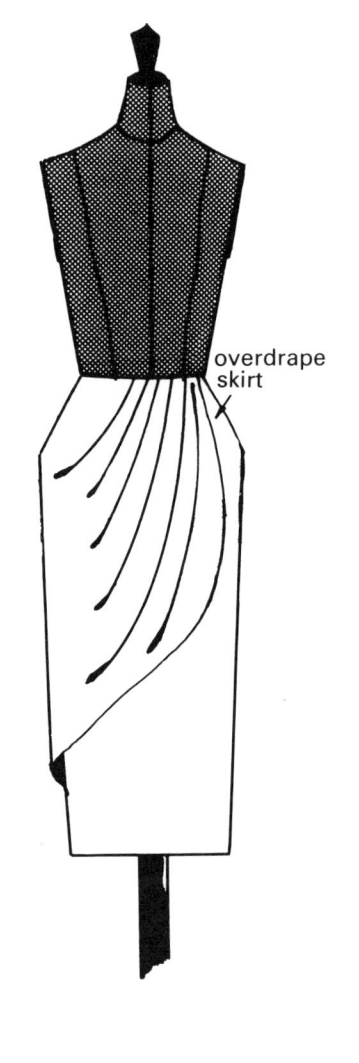

overdrape skirt

84

Mark, fold and open out the fabric as in Figures 213 and 214. Place a pin into the centre front of the skirt line.

213

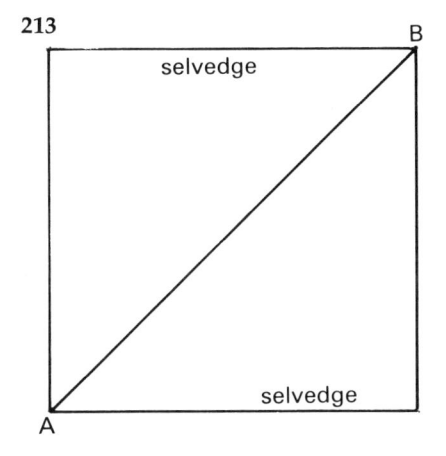

selvedge (B top) / selvedge (bottom) — square with diagonal from A to B

214

selvedge / fold — square with diagonal A to B

215 pin firmly / pin firmly / pin firmly — centre front, A at bottom, B at top

216 mark the waistline / direction of folds / mark side seam

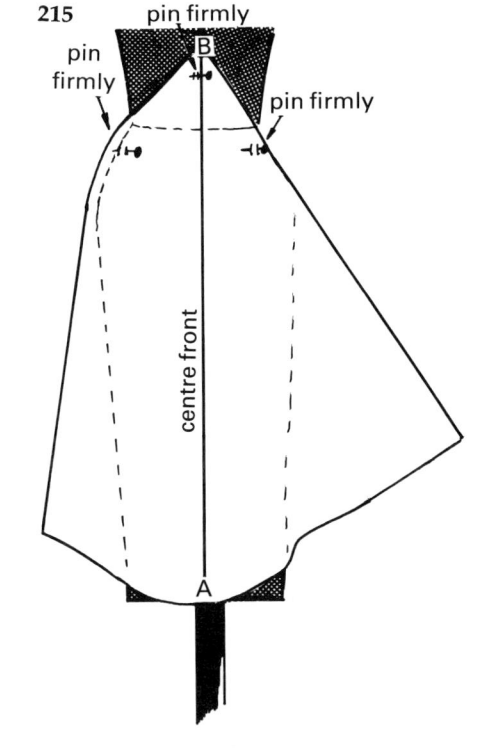

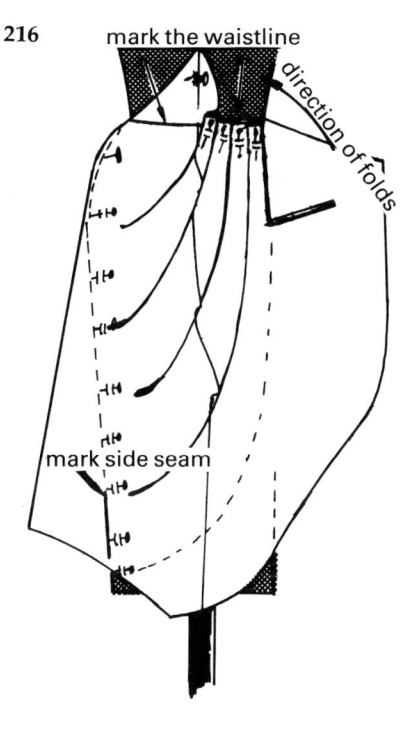

hem and the waistline) can be marked by first pinning the top fabric down and then marking along the skirt seam.

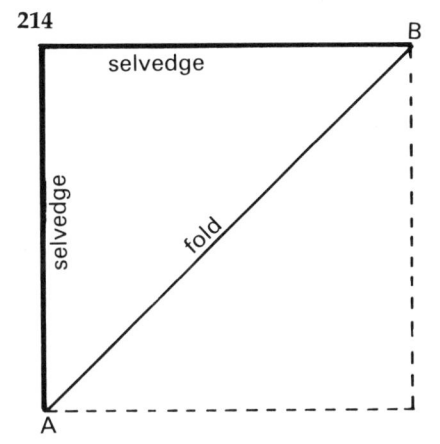

Lay the crease line of the fabric A–B on the centre line of the skirt and pin temporarily into place (Figure 215).

Very carefully mould the fabric over the drapes of the skirt (Figure 216), working in the direction of the folds at the waist (see arrow on Figure 216). When you are satisfied that the fabric drapes follow the skirt drapes, the outline (i.e. around the side seam, the

Remove the fabric from the dress stand, making sure that the drapes are still firmly pinned into position. Mark the required seam allowances and cut away the unwanted section of fabric (Figure 217). The fabric can now be machined at the waist to hold the drapes into position.

Make the pattern for the back skirt by the same overdrape method or by the fold and spike method according to the style.

217 add seam allowances / cut away / cut away

85

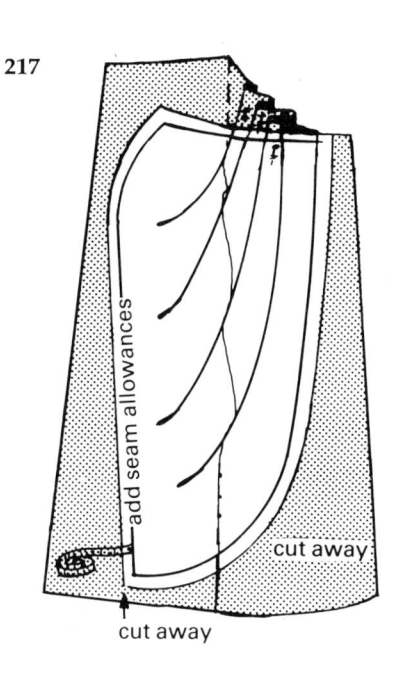

Puff sleeve

This large puffed sleeve (Figure 218) is usually cut on the cross grain.

Position the garment on the stand (Figure 219). Insert some stiff net into the sleeve to form its shape.

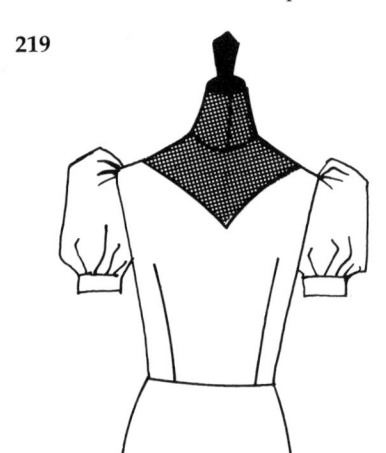

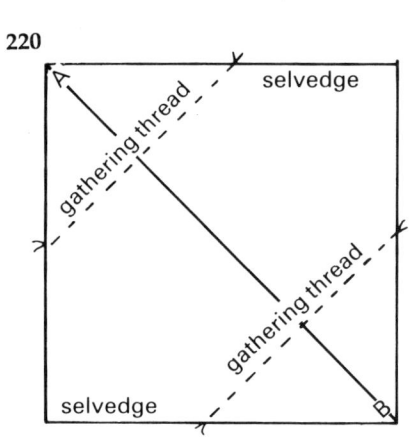

218

219

220

221

Cut a square of fabric and fold it along the cross grain for line A–B (Figure 220). Mould the fabric on the sleeve, closely following its shape (Figure 221). Use pins to hold the moulding to the sleeve. If the sleeve is gathered to the armhole, it might be helpful to place gathering thread into the fabric and gather the fabric before moulding it to the sleeve.

Mark around the seam lines. Remove the fabric from the stand and add seam allowances. Cut away all the unwanted fabric to leave the required piece (Figure 222).

Cut the cuff by direct measurements.

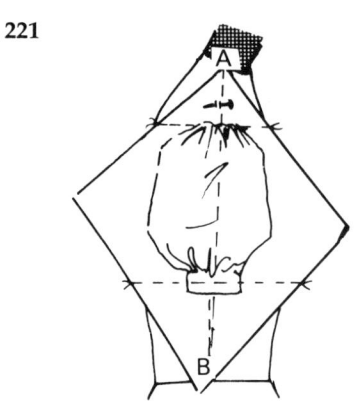

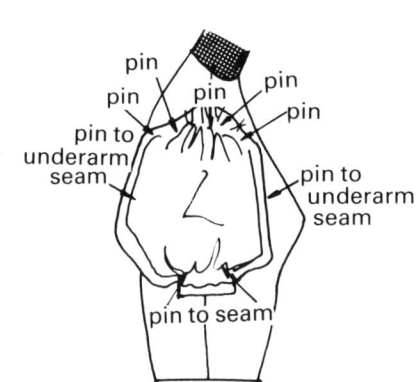

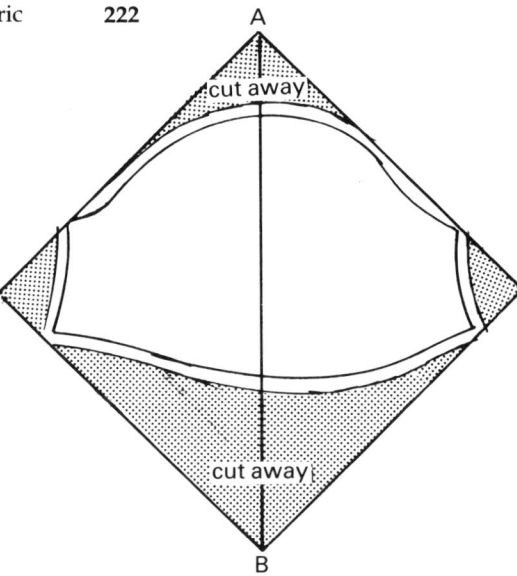

222

REPRODUCING DARTS – spike and pivot method

Many of the fitted or semi-fitted clothes found in your wardrobe will have darts. It is essential to reproduce these darts if the the original fit is required. A classic waistcoat is used here to illustrate the production of darts (Figure 223).

Try to lay the waistcoat flat on the table. You will see that it does not lie completely flat; it is shaped so that it will fit over the bust and close into the waist. This shaping is provided by a small dart at the waist. Establishing the dart is the most difficult part of this exercise. The grain or the stripe will indicate the structure of the darts, as shown in Figure 224.

Draw a simple sketch of the waistcoat (Figure 224).

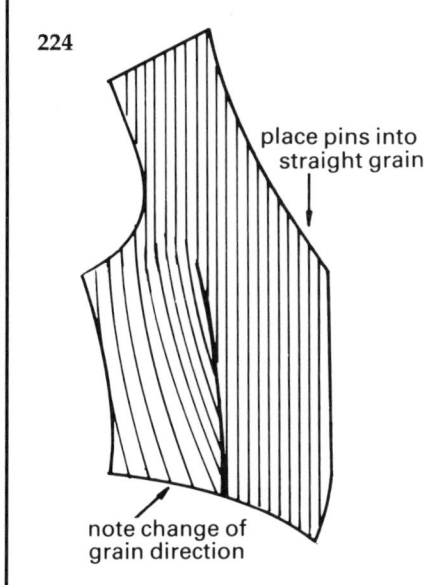

224

place pins into straight grain

note change of grain direction

223

Place pins along the grain or stripe on the breast side of the dart (see Figure 224). Draw a straight line on a sheet of paper and place the pinned line on it. Mark around the waistcoat outline A–B–C–D–E (Figure 225).

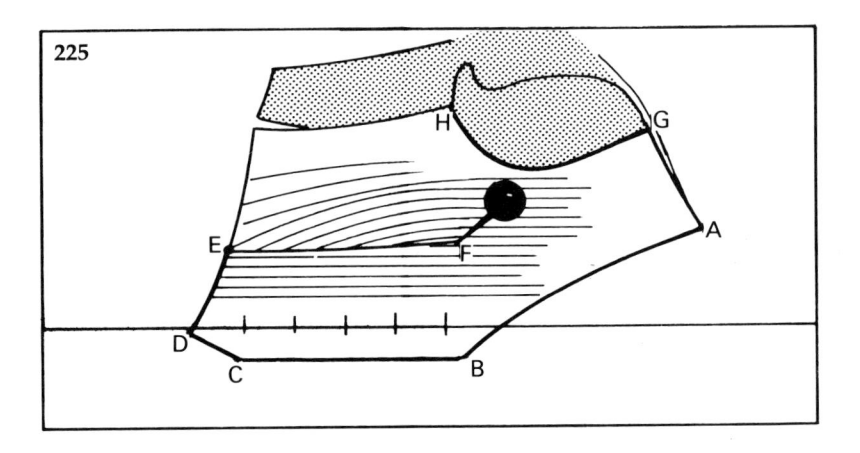

To establish the amount in the dart, carefully spike through the top of the dart (point F). Holding point F firmly down, pivot from F until the grain on the underarm side of the dart is parallel to the original straight line (Figure 226). Mark in from E1 to J.

Remove the waistcoat and connect up all the points (Figure 227). Add seam allowances to complete the patten.

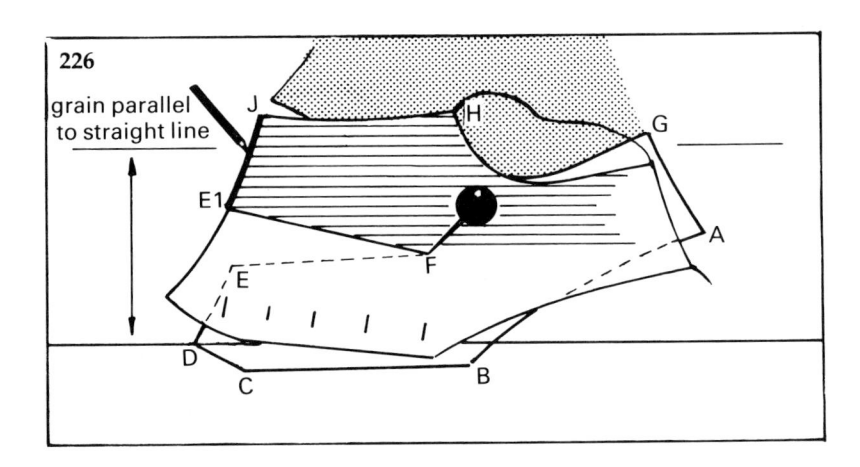

Use this method for all darts wherever they are situated. For further information on the use of darts see *Pattern Cutting and Making Up* (Martin Shoben and Janet P. Ward; Heinemann, 1987).

88

FURTHER READING

Coles, Myra *Sew! Your Complete Guide to Sewing Today* (Heinemann, 1988).
Shoben, Martin *Short Cut to Fashion: Make Your Own Clothes Without Buying Patterns* (Hutchinson, 1985).
Shoben, Martin and Ward, Janet P. *Pattern Cutting and Making Up: The Professional Approach* (Heinemann, 1987).

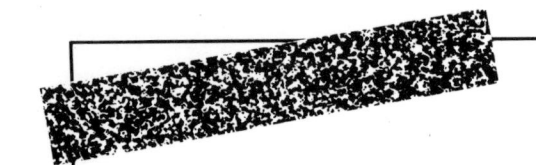

INDEX

Asymmetric draped skirt, 84–5

Balance marks, raglan sleeve, 68
Blouse, with raglan sleeve, 66–8
Border prints, 21, 28

Casual shirt, 6
Coat, long loose, 38
Collar, 9, 35
Collars and cuffs, 22, 23, 24
Cowl neck, 82–3
Crossway stripes, 17
Culottes, 80–1

Darts, 87–8
Dirndl skirt, 26
Drapes and gathers, 82–3
Draped, skirt, 84–5
Dresses:
   flared, 14
   gathered, 12
   panel, 40
   tunic, 68–9

Equipment, 4

Fabric effects, 16
Facings, 68
Flared dress, 14
Fold and spike method, 6
Front facing, 9

Gathered top or dress, 12

Geometric designs, 20
Gored skirt, 46–7
Grain, 66, 83
Grain lines, 17

Hip length jacket, 70–3

Jackets:
   hip length, 70–3
   safari, 42
   unlined summer, 32
Jeans, 32–56

Key points, 3

Length adjustments, 11

Method to choose, 6

Pattern checking, 9
Panel dress, 40
Pockets,
   ideas, 44, 45
   trouser, 53, 62–3
Pressing, 3
Puff sleeve, 86

Raglan adaptations, 75
Raglan shirt, 71–3
Raglan sleeve blouse, 66–8

Safari jacket, 42
Seam allowances, 10, 37, 68
Shorts, 59

Shirts, 6
   asymmetric drape, 84–5
   classic tailored, 76
   dirndl, 26
   the divided skirt (culottes), 80–1
   draped, 84–5
   fluted, 48
   joined widths, 28
   lining, 76
   pointed hem, 49, 50–1
   six gore A line, 46–7
   two tier gathered, 31
   with double knife pleat, 79
Sleeves, 9
   puff, 86
   setting, 10
   two-piece, 35–6
Stripes, 16
   asymmetrical, 19

Trousers:
   draped, 61–2
   flared, 57
   gathered, 58
   joggers, 57–60
   key points, 52
   openings zip and fly front, 54, 64–5
   pockets, 62–3
   with curved seamlines, 60
Tunic dress

Waistband, 27

Yokes, 8, 24, 25